The House at Anzac Parade

ALSO BY VICTOR KLINE

Fiction

Rough Justice
The Golden Dagger Mysteries (Contributor)

Non-Fiction

The Federal Court Reports (Editor and Contributor)
The Federal Law Reports (Editor and Contributor)
The Macquarie Book of Events (Contributor)

Plays

The Rehabilitation of God
Love.Com
The Legionnaire
The Salsa Lesson
Sex, Death and Chocolates
Doctor Faustus Sings
Hedda Gabler (Translation)
The Fruit Bats of Charters Towers

The House at Anzac Parade

Victor Kline

Frances Allen Pty Limited

ISBN-13: 978-0-947245-01-6

CONTENTS

To Katharine Kline, the love of all my lives.

1. INITIATION

"At night she would come to the door of my bedroom. As she stood there drawing back on her cigarette, the hot red tip would flare and tell me:

'It's time to be loved again'.

It was different every time of course. But the core ritual stayed the same. She would stand for a long time in the doorway, and I would watch the tip glow and recede, glow and recede. Then she would start to make patterns in the air, circles or figures of eight. And in the dark the hot red tip would leave shapes for me to ponder.

Now she would move towards me, and the red tip would describe concentric circles closing in on me, until she was very close. Then she would put the cigarette in her mouth. Sometimes I think she put the cigarette in my mouth. But that doesn't make sense.

No, she put the cigarette in her mouth to free both her hands, so she could peel back the bedclothes and pull down my pyjama pants and unbutton my pyjama top.

Then she would take the cigarette from her mouth and whilst holding me firmly in place with the other hand, she would run the cigarette tip up and down my legs not more than an inch from the skin, and then across my belly and chest, and down the inside of my arms.

But she would always end with concentric circles getting smaller and smaller around my little penis, my 'tommy' as she called it. She would point out my penis to me, as though I had to be reminded where it was, what it was.

'There's your little tommy,' she would say.

I hated that word. I can't imagine where she got it from. For years I couldn't look at a boy called Tom or Tommy.

Anyway she would close in on my 'tommy' with her red tip, but just at

1

the last minute when it seemed certain she would burn me there, she would pull it away and stub it out in the ashtray which always stayed in my room. Then she would take my 'tommy' in her hands and stroke and caress it and say:

'See how much Mummy loves you.'"

That is a quote from a play I wrote called *The Legionnaire*. The character who is speaking is Jean-Claude Delacroix, a battle hardened 40 something Captain in the French Foreign Legion. It is Casablanca 1956, at the time of the French-Algerian War. Katharine Sullivan, who is the love of his life, has finally got him to speak of what has been tearing at his life, for most of his life.

Jean-Claude and I have a lot in common. We were both sexually, physically and emotionally abused by our mothers. We both tried to suppress that memory by running away and plunging into a life of danger. In the end, after a long struggle with ourselves and the world in general, we both found a way to heal.

Jean-Claude healed because he abandoned the 'courage' of battle in favour of the courage to face the truth about himself. But more importantly he found the ultimate courage, to allow Katharine to love him and to teach him how to love.

The essentials of my own life have not been so different. I even found my own Katharine. So in truth Jean-Claude's story is my story. I hoped to conceal that fact by setting *The Legionnaire* in a different time and a different place with a central character superficially different from myself.

However when it came to the first reading of the play, the actors and crew immediately saw through all that. They wanted to know what had 'really' happened, what had really happened to me. For them, and for the others who have been loving enough to want to know, I am stepping out from behind Jean-Claude.

Here is my story, in all its crazy, comic, sad, beautiful humanity: from the woman with the cigarette tip all the way to the finding of my Katharine, my greatest angel. Along the way I met some other angels too, just as we all do. My first was a gentleman by the name of George William Rudolf Millington.

2. GEORGE WILLIAM RUDOLF MILLINGTON

My mother's father, George William Rudolf Millington, was a gentleman larrikin. With little education, a tough upbringing in the slums, and a hard life as a wharf labourer, he nonetheless aspired to gentlemanliness, and to gentleness. I remember that gentleness, and I remember the larrikin twinkle in his eye.

He was 'Gentleman George'. I think he liked the title his mates on the wharves had given him, even if some used it with a touch of irony. But if the suit and tie he wore to the races and the money he spent for admission into the St Leger wasn't the way of his friends in their casual clothes across the track in the Paddock, that was all right. He would smile and wave to them and get on with the business of being who he was. He was, as they say, comfortable in his skin.

Although I know little of his childhood, I know he did it tough. And yet he found a way, not just to survive, but to respect himself, to respect others (if they deserved respecting), and to give love freely to those he loved, myself included.

When I think of him, I think of a man in balance. He knew who he was, and he knew who others were. If they were weak and vulnerable, like my sister and I, he would nurture and do what he could to redress the balance. He gave me many gifts, not least of which was the model of a strong, consistent, independently minded male figure. I needed that badly. My father was just the opposite, weak, cowardly and very uncomfortable in his own skin. But I think the greatest gift Pamp gave me was the living example that, despite the difficulties of life, it is possible not to lose your sense of right and balance.

He died when I was twelve but he stayed with me long after that. Through my twenties and thirties, when night time was the time of nightmares, in amongst those horrible dreams, my grandfather would

3

regularly emerge, looking relaxed, smiling at me, that well known twinkle in his eye. In my dreams he balanced me, just as he had done when he was alive.

I called him Pamp. I was the eldest grandchild and it seems as a baby I turned 'grandpa' into 'pampa' which became Pamp. The title stuck and all the grandchildren called him that. Gentleman George on the wharves and at the racecourse was Pamp at home with the kids.

He had one daughter Joy (my mother), two sons, Ray and Rex, and eight grandchildren including my younger sister Marilyn and myself. In the late 1920s, when the now inner city suburb of Maroubra was a place so far out it took the tram 20 minutes to get there, Pamp and Nan bought a tiny semi-detached two bedroom house on the main arterial road, Anzac Parade. They paid forty pounds for it and spent the next forty years paying it off.

My mother and father and my sister and I all lived with them. In the fifties and sixties in a country where home ownership exceeded 70%, and my father was an accountant, we lived a sort of third world existence while Dad made endless charitable donations to his bookie and his card playing buddies.

Nan and Pamp shared the 'big' bedroom at the front of the house on Anzac Parade. That got to be noisy as the years went by and the traffic increased. But Pamp didn't mind. He slept the sleep of the just. He was deaf in one ear and a pipe smoker and he snored like a distressed heifer, much to the chagrin of my grandmother.

She was an invalid, a sufferer from osteoarthritis. And she was a poor sleeper. The traffic didn't bother her too much, but her husband's snoring certainly did. It was worst when he was sleeping on his back. But then the challenge for Nan was how to get him on to his side. Most times she would just grab one of her walking sticks, and with much huffing and groaning she would reach across the gap between the beds and jab him in the side with the rubber tip, calling out:

'Georrrrrge! 'And he would grumble and roll on his side and she would get another hour's sleep before he was off again.

My parents' bedroom was on the side of the house abutting the narrow passageway that ran down to the back yard. Theirs was a room into which the sun never dared to shine, and to this day I remember it as the darkest place I have ever known. Admittedly, given who its inhabitants were, there may be a metaphorical component to the darkness I remember. But nonetheless it was tiny and pokey and had, as its only saving grace that it was bigger than the back veranda, off the kitchen, which I shared with my baby sister Marilyn.

When she got a few years older Pamp extended the veranda to make a small bedroom for me, and Marilyn went to dwell in the even smaller closed in porch off my grandparents' room in the front. As a baby she must have been in the room when my mother would come and stand in the doorway to the kitchen with the hot red tip of her cigarette glowing. But I don't remember Marilyn being there. Perhaps the loneliness and the fear I felt precluded any sense of anyone else being present.

Though I'm sure Pamp did not know exactly what was happening to me, he must have known how crazy his own daughter was, and he would have seen how sad I was. And so he came to offer me his antidote each day before the dawn.

Every morning he would rise before anyone else and start to make his breakfast in the kitchen next to where I slept. He would wake me and I would go out and sit with him, watching his amazing morning porridge ritual. He would pour the porridge out on a large dinner plate. Then he would gently spread butter across it and cover it with salt. After that he ate in rhythmic circles, turning the plate as he ate inwards from the perimeter to the centre of the porridge. Even then I thought how disgusting porridge with butter and salt would have to be. But I told myself it must be what real tough labouring men had to have for their breakfasts, to get them ready for a big day on the wharves.

I'm not sure how much we talked or how much we just sat in silence while I watched his ritual. But the whole process made me feel loved. Though I would never have been able to reason it through, the fact that Pamp would give over so much of his time each morning just to me, was what I needed to feel special.

Not so long ago I was surprised and delighted to hear Marilyn talk about when she was very small and she and Pamp would get together each morning for their special porridge time. I told her he and I did that too. Of course we realised we couldn't both have been doing it the same time, and so he must have given us turns, a morning for her and the next for me.

As far as I know my sister was not sexually or physically abused, but for my parents, the fact that she was a girl excluded her from any serious consideration. She therefore suffered the very real and debilitating abuse of total neglect. So she too needed her Pamp time. How wonderful, and how amazing he found a way to give us both what we needed.

After breakfast Pamp and I would sit together in the lounge room listening on the radio to an endless array of long numbers being called out, punctuated by the occasional place name, like Walsh Bay or Pyrmont. Later I understood they were the wharfies' serial numbers. You waited to hear yours, and if you did, it meant you got a shift that day on such and such a wharf.

He was a day labourer. He was poor. He didn't even have job security. He had to share his tiny house with his crazy daughter and her wastrel husband, and his wife was an invalid. Yet he still had the compassion and presence of mind to wake his little grandchildren turn and turn about to make sure they had some real love and some real companionship in their lives.

His love and caring played out for me too in the back yard of our house. It was a sandy strip with a few lonely blades of buffalo grass. In the bottom left hand corner Pamp had planted a frangipani tree, which had to be the toughest breed on the planet to survive in that soil. In the other corner was a lemon tree. Again a mighty survivor, though its fruit was so small and shrivelled it almost didn't warrant the name.

Across the back paling fence grew a choko vine, the bearer of a fruit (or is it a vegetable), the taste of which made the porridge with butter and salt seem appealing. But Pamp adored chokos, and cultivated that vine with love. I seem to remember pots on the stove, filled with chokos, boiling away for hours, and thinking in my own early environmental way, what a waste of energy that was.

It was on the sandy strip of the back yard, with Pamp bowling to me, that I developed my love of cricket. One run for any hit, two into the lemon or frangipani trees, four for the back fence (three only if it stuck in the choko vine), and six and out over the fence into the Podies.

The 'Podies' (pronounced like 'bodies') were recent Italian immigrants, a rare sight in the Maroubra of the day. Their surname was actually Tripodi, but in those days (though it seems impossible to conceive of now) no-one could pronounce it. So it was shortened to Podi. Hence the collective name 'Podies' for the whole family.

Mr Podi was, of course, a bit of a market gardener himself. But to his great distress he could not make anything grow in Maroubra's sandy soil. He looked with envy at Pamp's stunted lemon tree and his choko vine, and would seek his advice from time to time. I never understood what Pamp told him, but I saw his eyes twinkle, and so I suspect it may not all have been straight from The Good Gardener.

From my point of view Mr Podi's worst crime was his refusal to understand cricket or even to acknowledge its validity. He saw no reason why my ball should find its way into his yard so often. He did not like me climbing over to get it, and even less being called out to get it himself. I saw his attitude as an unforgiveable failure to integrate into Australian society.

However, looking back, I have to admit his lack of enthusiasm may have had something to do with my big six that didn't just clear the fence but went right into the pavilion, via Mr Podi's closed kitchen window. Luckily for me, Pamp was very handy, and very forgiving of me.

'Shouldn't have bowled you such a sitter,' he said, smiling his twinkle at me. Then the next day he set about replacing the Podies' kitchen window.

I suppose I learned to love cricket because Pamp loved it, and I loved Pamp. He had been a fine cricketer in his day, a first grader knocking on the door of the State team just prior to World War I, when he was still only 16 or 17. Somewhere I have the ball that was mounted and presented to him for a hat- trick in a first grade match in the summer of 1913-14. There was no representative cricket during the war and by the time it was over, he was married with a baby daughter. A man had to earn a living, and cricket, for all its kudos in Australian society, was an amateur game. So the chance for cricketing glory passed him by.

His own sons had shown no interest or aptitude, one being too unsporty and the other too wild. So I think he was happy to pass on what he knew to me. Under his tutelage I became a wicket keeper/batsman, though my batting skills took some time to develop.

I'm not sure how much time I actually spent with Pamp up to the age of 12, when he died. Throughout my life whenever I felt upbeat and positive, I would look back to a childhood where he and I were inseparable. But at other times, when the waves of fear and anxiety were in the ascendency, it was as though I had not had nearly enough time with him. Such is the nature of perception, slave that it is to the dictates of fear.

However much time I actually did spend with him, I do know the best times, the times of peace, were when I was alone with Pamp. Simple things like sitting with him on a Saturday afternoon listening to the football on the radio, whilst he methodically poured beer from what would now be called a 'longneck', but was then just called a 'bottle of beer', into a small blue patterned tumbler.

My mother and grandmother would regularly claim Pamp had problems with alcohol. But the only evidence they could cite was when he lost his temper because Marilyn, at about age two, got to the beer bottle while he was out of the room, and left him with nothing but the dregs.

From their point of view his 'overreaction' to that was a sign of alcohol dependency. But I remember thinking, even at the age of six, how I would be annoyed too if I'd waited all week for a quiet beer, only to find the baby had got to it first.

I don't know why they wanted to defame him. I guess if you are troubled yourself, and someone else isn't, you may feel the need to project your deficiencies onto them. Anyway I think Marilyn slept for about 30 hours.

Around that time too, I went through my cowboy period. I had the mandatory silver tin gun in a red plastic holster, and I wanted to be the fastest gun in Maroubra. Pamp might be sitting on the lounge and he would challenge me to the draw. He didn't have a gun but was willing to improvise with two extended fingers and a thumb for the trigger.

Now I had my own very clear cowboy etiquette, which I would carefully explain to Pamp.

'See Pamp, what you do is stand up here, and put your gun in your pocket', and I would make sure his fingers were inside his pocket, 'and when I count to three, and say "draw", you draw.'

He would smile, watch me walk back to my position, allow me to count to two, and then *he* would calmly say:

'Draw.' And he would pull out his fingers and shoot me.

'No Pamp!' I would yell, rushing up to him. 'You have to wait till I say "draw".'

'Oh, I see,' he would say, his eyes twinkling like mad. So then he would watch me walk back to my position, begin to count again, and again he would shoot me on the count of two.

This would repeat itself five or six times, and then Pamp would say:

'Not much of a quick draw, are you?' And he would not laugh, but his eyes laughed. Then he would give me a big hug and tell me to go off and practise and we'd have another showdown later.

I remember too, around that time, when I was about six, often going fishing with him down at Rose Bay wharf. I would catch 20 or 30 fish, the only problem being they were all tiny and really should have been thrown back. I'm sure he knew that, but because I begged and pleaded to be able to keep my trophies, the poor miniatures were destined for a sad end as a pile of fish in a plastic bucket.

They were of course too small to cook. Nonetheless I insisted on taking them home to look at and play with. I think by about day two or three, Pamp had to wait till I had gone to bed, to dispose of them before they smelled out the neighbourhood. By the next morning, in my heartless way, I had forgotten all about them. But I hadn't forgotten the fishing trip, and I still have not.

Perhaps the best fun of all was when I got a little older, perhaps 10 or 11, and he took me to the races. Pamp would put on his suit and I would dress up in my best and only pair of long pants. We would go to the St Ledger Stand early and take a position on the upper deck in the corner closest to the winning post.

In those days, at Royal Randwick Racecourse, there were 3 enclosures. The Members Stand was right on the winning post. Inside the centre of the track, directly opposite the Members', and mixed up with the parking lot, was The Paddock. It was the cheapest enclosure but if you were quick you could also get a spot on the winning post, though you couldn't see the horses till the last furlong.

The St Ledger was on the same side as The Members' but further away from the Post. So when it was a photo finish, trying to work out, from that vantage point, which horse had won, could be very difficult. I can't remember exactly how it worked, but think it was something to do with parallax error. When a race was very close and the horse on the rails looked ahead of the one out wider, it was probably the latter which had actually crossed the line first.

Whatever the trick, Pamp had mastered it. He could pick the winner of a close finish every time. The amazing thing was no-one else seemed to get it. I'm not sure if young George spent large parts of his youth practising the art or whether he just had the right combination of sharp eye and steely nerve. But the upshot was Pamp did very little betting with the bookies. His style of 'gambling' was more original, and a lot less risky. It would go something like this:

It's late in the day, maybe race 5 or 6, and all the men have been drinking. We're all up on the corner of the St Ledger and the photo has been called for. It looks like the favourite *Swift as the Wind* has won on the inside. But Pamp knows *Slow Boat to China* has the money. Inevitably one of the men, emboldened by his inebriation, would call out:

'*Swift* has got it! It's a lay down mazaire!' And his prediction would immediately gain the support of all around. Then Pamp would smile, and his eyes would twinkle, and in the same gentle monotone he used when outdrawing me, would say:

'It's *China*!'

'You're mad mate!' the man would scoff. And all would agree.

'No. It's *China*'.

'Ten bob says it's not.'

'Two quid says it is.'

What always amazed me when Pamp upped the ante was how his smile and his gentle voice never changed and his gaze never left the man. And despite *Swift* being the favourite and everyone agreeing she had won, the man would inevitably hesitate, and look about him for support. Two pounds was a lot of money then.

And of course he would get support. Pamp knew he would. Pamp was counting on it.

'Come on mate!'

'The bloke's a drongo!'

'Take the mug's money!'

'He's throwin' the cash at ya!'

And now the man had no way out. To refuse the 'challenge' in front of all his mates and all those people, especially when it *was* a 'lay down mazaire', would be nothing short of allowing his manhood to be impugned. So he would take the bet, and Pamp would be two pounds richer.

Perhaps the best part of the day was when we walked home together down Alison Road to catch the bus at Anzac Parade. We would stop at the little food van and Pamp would buy me a pie and chips. Walking beside the man as we ate our pies, I felt protected and safe. The tension with which I held my young body would flow away, and, for a short time, it was as if time didn't matter. The world was a fun and a loving place. At least for a little while.

3. MOUSEKETEER GRANDPA

My father was born Leof (later Leon) Alexandrovich Kleinerman in Shanghai China, to bourgeois Russian Jewish parents Vera and Alexander Kleinerman, who themselves had fled the Bolshevik Revolution in 1917. They lived in the French Concession where my grandfather owned Kleinerman's *Confiserie*, selling the best chocolates in Shanghai. He also owned a chain of pool halls and some race horses. Unfortunately he gambled everything away. Then he built up his business interests again, almost to where they had been at their height. But he gambled all that away too.

With the first plunge into poverty the family had had to give up all sorts of luxuries, move home, move the boys to cheaper schools. Now this second plunge was too much for my grandmother. She left Alexander and they divorced. Later she re-married Joseph Radovsky, another Russian Jewish émigré.

Behind his back my father and his brother Mark called their step-father 'Boogle'. I'm not sure why they chose that name. They had a private language which they called 'loongay', a mixture of words from the highly cosmopolitan world in which they lived, including elements of Russian, Yiddish, French, and any other language that suited their purpose. I think 'Boogle' may have meant 'bug eyed' in loongay (because Joseph did have protruding eyes), but which of their many source languages inspired it, I don't know.

When Mao's Long March marched into Shanghai and the Europeans had to get out, Boogle, Vera, Leon and Mark came to Sydney. The story goes that the Australian government, being in a 'populate or perish' frame of mind at the time sent a Sydney Jewish solicitor to visit the threatened Jewish community in Shanghai to 'select' the most suitable ones as immigrants.

Apparently he held out his hand and those who could make his palm greasy enough, got to board the boat for Australia. Boogle had enough money to make sure he and Vera and the boys could come. But my grandfather Alexander, of course, did not, so he had to stay. Somehow he did get out later to Rio De Janiero where he met and married another Vera who was of course a Russian Jewish émigré who had come there from Shanghai.

For years my father tried to get Alexander a visa to emigrate to Australia, even going to the lengths of arranging a meeting in Canberra with the then Minister for Immigration Harold Holt. But the problem was my grandfather had been accused by his business rivals in Shanghai of being a communist sympathiser. It was palpable nonsense as he was the archetypal *petit bourgeois*.

But Australia in the fifties, under the Menzies Government, was riding the backwash of America's McCarthyism and even the mere accusation of communist sympathy was enough to keep an immigrant out. By the time Whitlam came to power my grandfather was too old and sick to travel. He died in total poverty in the slums of Sao Paulo.

I thought at the time my father must really have loved him. The effort he made to get him to Australia was extraordinary by anyone's terms. And this was the man who reached the height of his physical and mental exertion when he crawled behind the couch to look for a lost poker chip. Leon would regularly gamble away the cash for the groceries, but every month he would somehow find money to send to his father.

The irony is that after my grandfather died the second Vera got a visa for herself to come to Australia. Thus even though I never met my own grandfather, I did get to meet his aging second wife, who had the same name as my grandmother, and who came bearing a photo of Alexander at my age. She swore we looked alike, but I just couldn't see it. I think she wanted it to be so.

Of course for me Joseph Radovsky was not 'Boogle'. He was 'Grandpa'. I knew I had another grandfather on the other side of the world, but he was just called 'Grandpa in Rio'. My real grandpa lived right here in Sydney, on the leafy North Shore. I think he loved me as much as any person can love another person who is not of their blood, that is to say every bit as much. He was a very real grandfather to me, and he was another of my angels.

He had no children of his own, and I was the eldest of his grandchildren. He spoiled me shamelessly. I remember one Saturday afternoon when I was about five. We didn't have a television at home, so the only time we could watch was Saturday afternoons when we went to Grandpa and Baba's. It was time for the early evening news, and my parents wanted to watch. I ventured a tentative suggestion that maybe the cartoons would be fun.

'You can watch cartoons anytime,' my father said. 'Now it's adult time.'

Grandpa was a quiet shy man, but he was strong and determined. You can't succeed in business unless you are. And when his grandson's wishes were at stake, he was a lion.

'Whatever my boy wants!' he said. We were all going to watch the cartoons. End of story. No debate.

And that was his attitude to everything: 'Whatever my boy wants'.

Looking back, I'm sure he was far too intelligent not to understand the dangers of totally indulging a child. He wasn't just a tough business man, he was a shrewd one too, and that meant he understood people. So I'm guessing he saw my sadness, and knowing my parents, worked out life at home was not so great for me. I think, not having had children of his own, he enjoyed spoiling me and could justify it as nothing more than redressing the balance.

His spoiling was comprehensive though. He would sit for hours playing children's card games, or setting me arithmetic problems when I went through my dorky phase.

But what still amazes me is despite his very limited English, and his radically different upbringing, how open he was to culturally specific things he couldn't possibly have understood.

When the neighbours looked over the back fence they must have found it just slightly amusing to see an old bald Jewish man in full suit and tie coming in to bowl. When you think about it, the round arm cricket bowling action is completely unnatural. And the concept of releasing the ball, in the middle of that action so it goes to the batsman, not at the end so it goes on your own foot, is a concept likely to escape a man raised midst the snows of Samara Russia.

Though his bowling was bad, his batting was worse. I may be unfair to him, but I don't think he ever actually made contact with the ball. Let's face it cricket was not his forte. But I didn't care in the least. What I adored about him was his willingness to give anything a go, especially if it were something I wanted to do.

I loved watching him shave. So of course, if I were staying over, I could always be present at the ritual of lathering and scraping. I remember one tragedy that came about due to his defective English. I couldn't have been more than four.

'I'm going barbers now,' he called out. 'You want come?'

Well, I thought the barbers would be pretty boring, just watching some man cut off the last remnants of Grandpa's grey hair. But of course he came from an era when barbers shaved people, and that was his way of saying he was about to shave. When I discovered what I'd missed I cried my eyes out and he had to go back and shave again for me, I hope with an empty razor this time.

The best example of his indulgence and his willingness to give anything a go, was the Mickey Mouse Club. This was a television show where a bunch of good looking American teenagers called The Mouseketeers (some of whom, like Annette Funicello went on to adult stardom), did a lot of wholesome up beat singing and dancing. They all wore a black cloth cap with the well known Mickey Mouse ears.

This I lusted after, and although I couldn't get the 'real' ears I did manage to extract from my parents a set of plastic ears. (Much later in life my darling Katharine brought me back the real thing from the Disney store in New York). But for the moment the plastic ears were fine.

Now the highlight of the show for me was the beginning when all the Mouseketeers paraded down some steps towards the camera one after the other, and as they got close they announced their names, Bobby, Cubby, Karen, Annette, and so on.

So in my mind I became a Mouseketeer too, and had to be in the opening parade. But of course I needed Grandpa to be in it too. The poor man had to go out and buy his own ears, because even though I was willing to share mine, they didn't quite fit.

We would stand at a pre-arranged spot in the lounge room waiting for the show to start. All was high anticipation. Eventually the intro music would strike up and Bobby, Annette and the others would come down in turn to announce themselves. At that point I too would make my grand entrance. I would cross to another pre-arranged spot near the television, and call out 'Victor' in my best bubbly American accent.

Then it was Grandpa's turn. He would don his large plastic mouse ears, this elderly, bald Jewish man, with his few remaining tufts of grey hair seeming to stick up in competition to the ears, cross the lounge room and state with profound solemnity in a thick Russian accent: 'Grandpa'. It all seemed perfectly natural to me.

The wonderful thing about Grandpa was that he was really two grandpas in one. First of all there was the gentle cricket playing Mouseketeer. And then there was the story teller. Despite his limited English he had a gift for making a story live. They were all real stories from his own amazing life, and most were about the First World War.

This I loved because Pamp would never talk about the War. Most old soldiers won't talk about the past. Some do, but those ones usually go to the other extreme and play up the grandeur. Grandpa, on the other hand, told it just as it was, without any of the phoney glory. I think he could do that because, like Pamp, he was a man in balance who saw life for what it was. If I have found balance in my own life, Grandpa's example contributed to that.

And I think he gave me my love of history. He was able to make things so much more real than any teacher or textbook ever could. When later I would study the First World War, or any war for that matter, the 'reality' of Grandpa's tableaux would superimpose themselves over whatever I was reading or being told, and it made me feel I understood it all so much better.

One of the first stories he ever told me was about the very early days of the war when mounted Cossacks were still part of the Russian army. The Germans must have still had a cavalry too, because the story was about a Cossack and a German riding at one another, brandishing their swords like medieval knights.

'It was quick,' Grandpa said in his matter of fact voice, 'the German take the Cossack head right off,'

I was thrilled and horrified at the same time.

'But it was beautiful,' Grandpa continued, 'because the Cossack he not fall off, and the horse keep going, his body, with no head, straight up in saddle, riding and riding into huge big red sun.'

And I could see it all so clearly, Grandpa there, a young infantryman, his big army boots sunk deep in the mud, hands on hips in amazement, watching the headless torso of the Cossack officer riding off into the setting sun.

The war ended for him when his company surrendered to the Germans. I think up till that point they must have suffered terrible depredations, because, as Grandpa told it:

'Captain say: "Enough this damn war. We surrender now to Germans. Anyone don't like, I shoot them".'

'What did you do?' I asked eagerly, expecting Grandpa to tell me how he and the other men were scandalised by this act of cowardice on the part of their commanding officer, how they refused to just lay down their arms, how they overpowered the captain, and went on fighting the evil Hun. Instead he said, in the simplest and most straightforward tone:

What can we do? We surrender.'

There are many atrocities in war, but for every one we hear about, I suspect there are dozens, hundreds that pass by the closed eyes of humanity. One such now took hold of my grandfather.

After the surrender, apparently the Germans herded the Russian soldiers together with thousands of other prisoners and then sent them all to a prisoner of war camp inside Germany. They went by train, in cattle cars. Unlike the cattle however, who were valuable and therefore allowed to stand on their feet, the Russian prisoners were literally stacked one on top of the other from the floor of the car to the ceiling, one stack beside another, pressed tightly together so no-one could move. Grandpa explained it all without histrionics, without recriminations, as something which, amidst all the vicissitudes of life, just took place.

It was a three day train trip to the camp in Germany. There were no stops, no food or water, no toilet breaks. The prisoners just remained stacked all the way. When they needed to relieve themselves, they had no choice but to do so where they lay, so that the shit and urine from the prisoners higher up in the stack ran down over those below them.

There were perhaps a dozen men in each pile. After three days those who were in the lower layers, if they had not died from asphyxiation or dehydration or starvation, died from the inhalation of the fumes of all the excrement, or were just crushed by the pressure of those above them. When they arrived in Germany, eighty percent of the prisoners were dead. Grandpa's lottery ticket had given him a spot two from the top. He survived.

I don't know what happened inside the camp or how he made his way back to Russia. He didn't tell me, and I was too young to know what questions to ask. Now I have a thousand questions, not least of which is why, after Lenin pulled Russia out of the war with Germany and civil war broke out, the young Joseph chose to enlist to fight with the White Russian Army against the Bolsheviks.

As a Jew in Russia, my Grandfather would have had few, if any, civil rights, and the Communists promised equality for everyone. Maybe my grandfather was smart enough to realise what they promised was unlikely to be what they delivered. Another Jew of the time, Leon Trotsky, might have done better to follow Grandpa's example.

Be that as it may, I know nothing of why he joined, how long he fought, why he decided to get out of Russia, and most importantly, how he did get out. It's a long way from Russia to Shanghai, and transport was not working well in the midst of the civil war.

I have all these question I want to ask, but he is long dead now, and I will have to wait. Boogle, Joseph Radovsky, senior Mouseketeer and one of my greatest angels is long gone. However, like Pamp, his essence and his importance remains.

4. THE MAD WOMAN OF MAROUBRA

If you ask why my own mother was driven to do what she did to me, I'm not sure I can give an adequate answer. The best I can do is hazard a guess. In our family there was the occasional mention, when I was growing up, of a shadowy character called Uncle Walter who had died before I was born. There were grisly stories of him, like the one where he would get himself through a crowd by elbowing the women in the breast.

I seem to remember, when I was quite small, my mother telling me about him coming to her room when her parents were not there. But the accounts were brief, and I was too young to understand. So I filed Uncle Walter away in my unconscious mind and only remembered him after I had ceased to have contact with my mother.

When I look back I think how strange it was she should tell me about it, almost as if she were making a plea in mitigation to the person she felt would one day come to judge her.   But whatever the reason my mother did what she did, the cause had to be significant. I can't believe anyone is born with a desire to sexually abuse their own offspring.

My mother left school at the age of 14 during the height of the Depression to work at WD & HO Wills' Tobacco Factory in Kensington. She was there for nine years, until she met Douglas Stewart, a man she frankly admitted to not loving, but a man she married anyway, to escape the factory. I know nothing of the clinical bases of madness, but I think it blossoms and grows through a series of bad choices.

Marrying Douglas was perhaps my mother's first bad choice. Nonetheless having chosen to marry for reasons other than love, she probably should have stuck with her decision. But she decided Doug was an inadequate 'provider'. My guess is she had already come to think the world owed her a living, a point of view she would later play out on me with awful consequences.

So if Doug wasn't going to 'provide', he could take a hike. It was a bit of a pre-emptory and indeed an unfair decision on her part as he was an enlisted soldier and it was during World War II. Infantrymen had little opportunity to make their fortunes. Nonetheless just before the end of the War, she left him.

That was her second bad choice, because in fact he did make his fortune. Despite his lack of advantages and his working class origins, he later became a millionaire. His second wife was very grateful for my mother's impatience. My mother, on the other hand, as she showed often in life, was not capable of acknowledging any error on her part. She continued to blame Douglas and see him as just another part of a hostile world trying to deprive her of her due.

So then she set about preparing to commit her third big mistake. And this certainly showed a heightened level of creative thinking. She was an anti-Semite, and as part of that she believed Jews had control of most of the World's wealth. She reasoned therefore that Jews were good at making money so she would find and marry a Jew.

You can see this plan involved a step up on her previous thinking. Not only was she planning to marry a man she didn't love but one she actually despised, or rather whom she would despise once she met him. It took her a few years, but eventually she found my father, a man three years younger, a Jewish émigré recently arrived from Shanghai. She decided he would be her passport out of the hostile world.

My father was grateful for the chance to marry a beautiful woman. He had a swag of problems of his own, most of which would be magnified a hundred fold by his choice of a wife. But more of him later.

If it were ironic she should leave Douglas Stewart because he was too poor, just before he became a millionaire, perhaps even more ironic was how my father turned out to be the only Jew in history, as she saw it, who couldn't make any money. Well, he could make some, but what he did make he gambled away.

Hostile world indeed! So what was she to do? With Doug it was easy to walk out. But now she had two children, and she was in her late thirties. If she left Leon too, what chance would she have to find a third husband, to find someone who could support her as she deserved?

She decided to solve her problem with what was available under her own roof, and thus complete her descent into madness via the hot red tip of the cigarette in my bedroom.

By the time I was seven or eight she had stopped coming to my room. It was more about inviting me into her room, or at least her space. When my father was not there, she would call out to me from the bathroom:

'Vic, I forgot the soap. Can you bring Mummy a little cake of soap?'

And I would go into the bathroom and she would be lying half submerged in the bath, but the water would be just to the level where her breasts and her pubic hair were exposed. And I would give her the soap, and she would keep me there talking about something, school or something, and she would appear to be so engrossed with what I said, that she didn't realise she had sat up fully and was soaping her breasts. Then I would have to tell her more riveting irrelevancies whilst she slid down in the bath and raised each leg in turn to be soaped along the inside of the thigh.

Or she would call me into her bedroom when she was in bed at night:

'Vic, could you bring Mummy a little cup of tea?'

And when I got there she would be sitting up in bed with a magazine, and a breast or a thigh or something, would be showing that shouldn't have been showing. Then she would make me lie down next to her, ever so close to the offending breast or thigh, to look at whatever article she was reading, mostly it seemed, about some virile Hollywood star, and how 'endowed' he was.

Of course she would explain to me what 'endowed' meant, she would explain to me how 'tommies', when you got big, got big too, and how important that was for a man...and for his woman. Then she would reluctantly confess that Daddy was not 'endowed' as he should be. But she was very hopeful I would be, when I grew up.

I felt so sad for Daddy, *and* so fearful for me in case I didn't develop as required.

As a card player, a gambler, my father was conveniently almost never there. But, she explained, that was to be expected with a Jew. Gambling and other 'weaknesses', they were in the blood. Like the lack of endowment. Like the dirt and the dribbling, which was the worst Jewish trait of all. Her favourite story, which she told me, I don't know, a hundred times, was the story of the dribbling Jew.

'And the remarkable thing,' she would say, as though I'd never heard the story before, 'is that I did have my warning. On the boat that time, on my one cruise, I was sitting in a deckchair, and I looked across, and there in the deckchair opposite, was an old Jew, and I have to tell you he was disgusting, there's no other word for it. He was dirty and smelly and he had dribble from the corner of his mouth, down his chin and all over the front of his dirty old coat.

'And I thought to myself: I am going to marry a Jew. Oh my goodness. But then I told myself: Joy, don't be silly, Leon is not like that. Leon is young and fit and clean.' Then she would sigh and add: 'But it didn't take long. I should have heeded that warning. It didn't take long for the dribble to appear.'

I'm not sure in those early days to what degree my father actually was dirty and smelly, or whether it was largely her imagination. But her reality soon became my reality, her perception, my perception. And I think it became his reality too. I think he came to play out her expectations. As he got older his dirtiness was undeniable. When I look back I think she despised him so much, and was so sure of his becoming a dribbling Jew, his only hope of acceptance, in a sick sort of way, was to give her what she wanted and what she expected.

Of course as his son, I was half Jewish. By speaking of his disgusting traits as though they were pre-determined, it didn't escape my notice that they might be pre-determined in me too.

My mother however kept my hopes (and my fears) alive with her own brand of inheritability. According to Joy's laws of genetics, a boy who had a Jewish father, but not a Jewish mother, didn't *have* to become Jewish. But it was an all or nothing kind of thing. You either were, or you weren't: a terrifying role of the dice for the anxious pregnant non Jewish mother.

But luckily in my case, her baby boy had not been cursed. He was born non-Jewish. Her other favourite story was how, when she was pregnant, my Jewish grandparents would tell her that her child would be Jewish. 'The Jewish blood is strong,' they would tell her. But she kept quietly confident that they were wrong. And how delighted she was when I was born with a straight nose and fair hair.

The problem was, she would tell me, that when I got older there was no guarantee things wouldn't change. As a child I didn't understand how this could be. But it would not be long before I found out. When I hit puberty my mother's worst fears were realised. I started to change. My hair got darker and curlier and my nose developed a slight dip at the end.

It was then my mother had to 'reluctantly' admit to me that there are actually two stages in the genetic dice game. At birth, on the first role of the dice, I had been lucky, but at puberty, on the second role, things hadn't gone so well.

She didn't say I had become a dribbling Jew. She didn't have to. She just had to point out how interesting it was that I now looked so much like my father.

Then she never touched me, or showed herself to me again.

And I felt disgusting. At the time I could not have explained why, not even to myself. But of course deep down I knew what is now very clear. Years of 'foreplay' were to prepare me to slay the dribbling Jew and take his place. But I had become a dribbling Jew myself, and as such was my mother's last and worst betrayer.

But all was not lost. Even though I had turned out to be as repulsive as my father, that didn't mean I had to be as big a failure. I was bright. I had topped my primary school and now had been accepted into a selective high school.

I could 'make up' for my treachery and perhaps the treachery of her two previous husbands, by dedicating my bright young mind to her future security and comfort. Of course she never said it like that. But by a thousand implications, she let it be known what my 'duty' was.

I was 12 years old. I accepted my duty.

5. A ROLE MODEL HE WASN'T

In sharp contrast to Pamp in our household, stood the sad figure of my father, a man who spent his entire life trying to humiliate himself, trying to prove to the world how impossibly inadequate he was. It was as though he would go out of his way to fail in everything he did, from study to work to sports to personal relationships.

A lot had to do with how much my mother despised him, and how much she needed to prove him disgusting. He was 'required' by my mother to fulfil these expectations. She was a determined woman, and so he gave her what she wanted. But I think she was working with malleable clay. I think he was a long way down the road to self loathing when she got hold of him.

Unfortunately all this lack of self esteem didn't produce a quiet introverted man. Quite the opposite. He paraded his silliness through the world. He was always willing to give me advice, on all manner of things, whether I sought it or not. And he was always wrong. He had to be. He was drawing on his own 'achievements' as the guide.

It is interesting how someone can stick his finger in a power point, get an electric shock, and then go about lauding the benefits of sticking your finger in the socket. That was my father! Somewhere deep down he had to know he was full of idiocy. And maybe that was the point. His only weapon against my mother and the world was passive aggression, and what better way to exercise it.

The trouble is, when you are a small child, you have no point of comparison. Your father is the only father you know. So when he tells you something you just absorb it and believe it to be true. Of course as I got older I realised he was a walking barometer of nonsense. But the early indoctrination is hard to shake, and quite a way into my adult life I still found myself spewing up pieces of poison I had unconsciously swallowed from him.

I think the best example was: 'You can choose your friends but you can't always choose your girlfriends'.

This is sad and silly and speaks volumes about my father, who had few friends of either gender. Apart from the crazy notion that any man can have any other man for a friend, it assumes he doesn't or can't have female friends. Then it's saying it is better to have a sexual relationship with someone you don't like or desire, than to have none at all. Worst of all it implies you can't be friends with your girlfriend.

Let me make the obvious point, that if you are sexually abused by your mother, you are going to find it hard to form good balanced relationships with women. What you don't need on top, is advice like that!

It took me a long time to rid myself of all his 'wisdom'. Because of how irredeemable my mother was, I wanted very much to believe my father had some redeeming features. After all, I told myself, he hadn't actually abused me himself. However as someone pointed out many years later, my father had an obligation to protect me. He must have known what was happening. He chose to go and play bridge instead.

But at the time I wanted to believe my father capable of love. I watched how much he seemed to love his own father. Perhaps he could love me too. But it was wishful thinking.

What's more it may only have been about the fact that Alexander was the unobtainable parent. If Dad had actually succeeded in getting his father to Australia, he may have treated him with the same disdain he showed his mother and Boogle.

Whatever else he was, my father was a coward. And if, as I have suggested, one's madness is the product of one's choices, my father spent his life relentlessly choosing the cowardly option. Why he was so lacking in self esteem, so devoid of courage, I can't even begin to guess.

He talked a lot about how his mother favoured his brother Mark over him, but watching the three of them as adults, it just didn't look to be the case. And even if it were, it seems a slender thread on which to hang all his tragic behaviour. All I can do is recount that behaviour, some of which borders on the comical. I can't really begin to explain why it was the way it was.

Like my mother, Dad had a small stock of stories he told over and over again. One of the more common was how, when he and Mark suffered anti-Semitism at school, Mark foolishly allowed himself to get upset and was always finding himself in fist fights, whereas Dad just ignored it and was so much the better for that. Even as a child I could see him trying to convince himself of the truth of what he as saying.

Ironically when I thought that I was the victim of anti-Semitism at school, he was all about telling me:

'There are times when a man just has to stand up for himself', and rushed to endorse my decision to engage in a physical fight.

He was just profoundly out of touch with what his real emotions were.

Perhaps the saddest story of all from his time in Shanghai was when, after he had finished school and failed in his first year at University because he had been running around with girls and not studying, and his father refused to pay for him to go back, he decided to take charge of his life and do something important and daring.

So he got his merchant marine ticket, joined the merchant navy and got a job on a boat sailing for the USA. On the day of sailing as the ship made its way up the Huangpu River, he began to get more and more panicky. Just before it got to the mouth of the river at the sea, he begged the captain to put him ashore. The captain no doubt had the legal right to make him stay, but whether he felt sorry for the young man who had just humiliated himself in front of the crew, or whether he saw no point in having such a seaman on his ship, he acceded to the request, and delayed the departure of the boat whilst my father was rowed ashore.

Dad told this story many times too, but here there was no attempt at emotional concealment, no self-delusion. He was quite frankly ashamed of his cowardice and his inability to follow through. It was through this story he revealed how part of him knew exactly who he was, and what his problems were, which makes his inability to do anything about them, so much the sadder.

The strange thing is that he told the story differently to my sister. He told her an American Merchant Navy friend helped him stow away, but before the ship left the dock he decided to go ashore because he had a beautiful French girlfriend he didn't want to leave behind. Clearly the version I got was the correct one, as he wouldn't invent something so unflattering to himself.

The question is why did he tell Marilyn a different version? Maybe he was ashamed for his daughter to know his cowardice. But why was he willing for me to know? Was he reaching out to another male who just might be able to forgive him, help him forgive himself? Or was he trying to warn me not to be like him? I just don't know.

I think it does say something about the difference between my parents from my point of view. Although I could never fully comprehend why my mother behaved as she did, over time at least I came to understand her modus operandi. Yet with my father I neither knew what drove him nor what he was really about.

I do know he was terrified of conflict. That's probably one of the key reasons why he was out playing bridge most nights of the week and most of the weekend. If he ever came home he might have to confront my mother over any number of things, including why he was out most nights, why we had no money, and not least of all, why she was doing what she was doing to me.

That was not the only reason he played bridge. I have no doubt he was genuinely addicted to it. And he had a string of girlfriends, mostly associated with bridge playing. I saw some of them, even met and talked to one or two. Most were the living embodiment of his philosophy about how you can't always choose your girlfriends. The most famous was the widow Mrs. Meads, but more of her in a moment.

His fear of conflict was universal. He would complain about how he was being treated at work, but would never do anything about it, could never find the courage to confront the bosses. And this was how he dealt, or rather didn't deal with conflict with friends, his mother, his in-laws and even his son when he grew up.

I remember one afternoon at the Sydney Cricket Ground when for some imagined offence some man gave him a huge kick in the bum. Dad did nothing about that. He was not even willing to politely query why the man felt the need to do what he did. He just smiled his, I want to avoid conflict at all costs smile, and walked on. I was about 12 or 13 at the time. The guy was obviously a psycho, and perhaps on this occasion, doing nothing and saying nothing was the wise choice.

But the telling thing is I blamed myself for not doing anything to protect or revenge my father. It was ludicrous I should feel that way. After all, my father was a grown man like his attacker. I was a skinny boy, and it was not my job to leap to his defence. But it does show how completely he had abrogated the role of father and protector.

It was, I guess, the beginning of the role reversal that he somehow put in place. Over time, more and more, I became the one he turned to when he needed to avoid dealing with anything difficult or conflictual. It was his counterpoint to how my mother saw me. In her mind she had managed to turn her abuse of me into a debt I owed her. In his case he had turned his failure to protect me into proof that he needed me to protect him.

The best example involved the aforementioned Mrs. Meads. It was when I was about 19, and they had been together for six or seven years. Everyone knew she was his girlfriend but he always denied it. Even after she moved to Maroubra not far from us and he spent lots of time at her house, it was always that he was just over there to discuss bridge tactics or some such.

So one night at about 10 pm the phone rings and my mother answers. It's Dad and he has to speak to me. No. No-one else can help. Luckily for him I am at home. I come to the phone and he whispers that he needs me to come to Mrs. Mead's house. He can't explain. He doesn't know what to do.

'And please, don't tell your mother or anyone'.

I'm not sure how I managed to get out of the house without saying where I was going, but ten minutes later I am at Mrs. Mead's house. The front door is wide open, and as I walk down the hall, I can see my father's back. He is standing at the doorway to her bedroom looking in. He hears me walking down the hall and turns and rushes up to me.

'I think she may be dead,' he says. 'But I don't know. How can you tell?'

I look at him quizzically, say nothing and go on down to the bedroom. There is Mrs. Meads sitting up in bed, her face colourless, her eyes staring fixedly forward, not a movement.

'She looks dead to me,' I say.

'But how can we be sure?' By this point his voice is getting really panicky.

'I really don't think there's much doubt,' I say. 'Have you touched her?'

'O God no!' he almost yells. 'I couldn't do that'.

'Would you like me to touch her?' I venture.

'Oh yes please.'

So I go over and touch Mrs. Meads and sure enough she is as cold as marble.

'Cold as marble,' I say.

At this point my father starts to break down, and I'm thinking that's natural enough. He's been with this woman for a long time and no doubt has some affection for her. But he starts carrying on about what is he to do and who is going to deal with this, and I realise he couldn't give a toss about poor dead Mrs. Meads. He's just worried about his own inconvenience, and of course the potential conflict involved in having to deal with her family.

Eventually I calm him down enough to discover Mrs. Meads has a son a couple of years older than me. So I ring him and find myself saying:

'Hi! You don't know me, but I'm Leon Kline's son, and I'm not sure if you know that your mother and my father...

'Yes I know about them', he interrupts, but in a way to help me out of my embarrassment. I remember thinking that he sounded like a nice boy. After that there doesn't seem much point searching for further small talk. 'Look I am really sorry,' I say, 'but I'm afraid your mum has died.' There is a moment's silence before he says:

' Where is she?'

'At home.'

'Are you there?'

'Yes'.

'I'll be right over.'

After that my father sits in the lounge room so he doesn't have to look and I wait on the front porch. When the son arrives, he is indeed a very nice young man. He greets me politely, goes into the bedroom, closes his mother's eyes, and then returns to the hall. His own eyes are full of tears, but he is holding it together well.

'I'll take it from here,' he says, and he shakes my hand and thanks me.

I ask him if there is any more I can do. But he is clearly embarrassed I have had to do anything at all. Again he politely declines any further help, and I leave him to it.

The next morning at breakfast, my father behaves just as he always does. It is as though nothing has happened. I never see any sign of grieving from him and it is never mentioned again.

They say that all bullies are cowards deep down. Well my father was a coward who was a bully deep down. That is, provided he was sure the conflict in question would not lead to his own physical risk, he could be aggressive in the extreme.

The best example of this involved the same Mrs. Meads a few years earlier and made my father's name notorious in the bridge world across Sydney and probably across Australia. He was apparently always someone who would not tolerate errors on the part of his bridge partners, and would yell and carry on when they played the wrong card.

The Mrs. Meads incident was at the Double Bay Bridge Club in Sydney. At that time it was probably Sydney's premier club. I'm not sure how long Dad had been partners with Mrs. Meads, but it was well known she was much less experienced than he (Dad had won the Australian pairs in 1956), and he was training her up. No-one imagined for a moment this was out of the generosity of his heart. They all knew it was because the good players had refused to play with him years before.

The trouble was he was never going to be able to allow for her inexperience. His impatience demanded great play from her right away. Apparently, on the day in question, she let him down badly, as he saw it. I know nothing of bridge, but it seems the card she played was a little inexplicable. Not satisfied with just yelling at her, he walked over to the table where the afternoon tea had been set, picked up a large cream cake, stormed back to the table, and in true Marx Brothers fashion rammed the cream cake into Mrs. Mead's face.

Years later when I was dating my first wife Agatha, and she took me over to meet her parents, her mother looked at me askance when she discovered my surname.

'You're not by any chance related to Leon Kline, are you?'

'Yes I am'. I had struck this before. 'Are you a bridge player?'

'I am,' she said warily.

'Well I don't play bridge,' I said.

She looked somewhat relieved, but not totally. I guess she felt I might play out the violent cream cake genes in other ways.

She was not the only one who worried I might turn into my father. I worried about it too, for a good part of my life. Now, when I look back, it seems about as likely as my turning into Stalin. But we all fear turning into our parents, and in my case there was a lot to fear.

6. THE COUNT OF MONTE CRISTO

In the end all abuse is about the deprivation of love.

In my own case the deprivation of love came in stages, or rather that's how I perceived it. Before puberty my mother's inappropriate touching and psycho-sexual displays were to say the least unhealthy. Nonetheless they were accompanied by the implicit promise of love. She was saying to me over and again in so many ways:

'I have been let down, betrayed by men, especially your own father, a dirty dribbling Jew who won't even earn us a decent living. But you are not like that. You are young and handsome and Anglo-Saxon. So let's keep playing these sexual practice games, and as soon as you are old enough, you will make it all better for me.'

Now it goes without saying there is no real love in that. But for a young abused boy who is desperate for love, however sad and uncomfortable he might feel, he is still able to tell himself, on an unconscious level, that one day he *will* be loved, that one day it *will* be all right.

But when I reached puberty I changed physically. In my mother's eye I became a dribbling Jew myself, and that's when all hope was removed. That's when she 'went cold on me'.

'Going cold on someone' was my mother's favourite control tactic. It's something she told me about many times in relation to others. If someone wouldn't give her what she wanted, she would say:

'I'll just go cold on her till she does'.

And she would. She would remove all warmth and affection from the person until they capitulated. I have seen her do it to my sister many times. And it was a frightening thing to watch. So when she decided to do it to me, I knew what I was in for.

But the really frightening thing, whether or not at the time I fully understood, was that I was in for a very long winter. She was telling me I had to make up for my failure as a man, and the only acceptable way to do that was to provide for her, and provide for her well, unlike her previous husbands.

Given that I was only 12 and had to get through school and University before I could start providing, that meant I was effectively looking at around 10 years of the big chill. And that is exactly what happened. I was denied any warmth, any compassion, and any human dignity from there on in.

Furthermore it became her daily work to keep me psychologically debilitated and miserable, so I would never feel I had the right to question her 'plan' for me. And her determination to keep me out in the cold never wavered, as you will see.

For starters rest and relaxation were unacceptable luxuries. I was bright, and had topped my primary school, but now I was at Sydney High, a selective school, and everyone there was bright. In fact they were very bright. This was a school that had provided more superior court judges than any other in Australia. I was not going to come top here.

Oh yes I was. Right from my first year, whilst I was allowed and encouraged to play sport (because my mother was sporty and I needed to stay fit for the task ahead), all other time was to be given over to study. No debate. If I ever wanted to be loved again, if I ever wanted to escape the ice box, I would study from when I came home to when I went to bed and all weekend.

This I did, and at the half yearly exam I came 13th in the year. That is out of 180 of the brightest boys in the city. Not bad, you would think. But no, I had to work harder. So I did. I stayed up that little bit later every night. At the final exam I improved to 12th.

Clearly that was the best I could do. You would think my mother would be happy. After all, to do that well at Sydney High was always going to guarantee a good career and plenty of money to provide for her. But she was not satisfied. She had now reached a point where the purpose of her obsession had been subsumed in the obsession itself. I had become a mere function of that warped obsession, and the function was going to come top.

The problem was how? There weren't any more hours in the day for study - or so I thought. In my second year I found myself not only studying till late, but getting up at between 4-5 am to study before school. By the time the half yearly exam came round I was running on empty. Life was unbearable and I had regular thoughts of suicide.

Nonetheless I did top the year. Unfortunately I hit a time in Australian educational theory which was all about encouraging the battlers. No-one was to be discouraged by rankings. There would be no rankings. So although everyone knew I had come first, there was to be strictly no acknowledgment, no prizes, no announcements at assembly, nothing on the report card. My history teacher apologised to me, but he was sure I would understand it was for the greater good.

I was a 13 year old prisoner of my mother's insanity. I had been told by her I had only one value, only one thing I need live for. I had achieved that. It had been taken away from me. Unfortunately, to my history teacher's surprise, I didn't understand.

On my way home that day my main concern was how to deal with my mother's disappointment, especially since I had decided I couldn't go on with the study regime and the lack of sleep. There really didn't seem much point, if I couldn't give her what she wanted anyway. But I knew she wouldn't see it that way. A part of me knew it wasn't really about needing me to come first. It was about her being able to see me locked away all day, every day, studying in my room. Then, and only then, would she feel her future was secure.

I came home and tried to explain to my mother how exhausted and disappointed I was. I said that if I went on getting up at 5 am and driving myself as I had, I might really break down, or worse. My mother looked at me with the disappointment I expected. Clearly I didn't love her. She burst into floods of tears.

Did I feel angry with her? Probably, deep inside. But my conscious emotion was disgust at myself for my failure, for letting her down.

If it seems remarkable that my mother could keep such an iron grip on me, it should be said her modus operandi was two pronged. She didn't just drive me to study. She also made sure I felt worthless and disgusting, something she could easily achieve thanks to having fertilised the ground by her early abuse.

She knew a person with no self esteem never rebels.

She took a reasonably good looking young boy and convinced him puberty had distorted him into something akin to a medieval caricature of a Jewish money lender.

'What a shame your nose has that *sleepy* end', she would say, 'and that beautiful soft hair is all *wirey*.' Then she would add gratuitously, 'but don't worry. Looks aren't as important for boys as girls. Women are more interested in personality.' Then she would sigh as though that were the last thing she really believed.

She had a hundred such 're-assurances', that she would circulate like empty faced wooden horses on a never ending carousel, playing tinny, out of tune music. It was a carousel I must continue to ride, and from which I would never be allowed to step down.

But undoubtedly her most creative form of humiliation (and therefore control) was when she turned something quite natural, and something I should have been proud of, into a running sore of self loathing.

Soon after puberty I began to grow a moustache. Now for most boys that is a rite of passage. The family congratulates him on his first sign of manhood, and his father shows him how to shave.

But for my mother it was as though this were the final straw, the final stamp of Jewishness. As though Anglo-Saxons didn't grow beards.

'See it's because you're dark now,' she would say, holding me by the chin and twisting my face up to the light so she could see the moustache better. 'But what are we to do? What are we to do?' And she imbued her voice with a sadness normally reserved for conjoined twins or patients with third degree burns.

And I walked about touching it and examining it in the mirror, wondering what I could do to rid myself of this blight. It was then, after letting me agonise for a several days, that Mum came up with the 'Final Solution'.

She would bleach it for me!

And she did, with a ritualistic solemnity that would be repeated again and again. But of course it looked ridiculous. A boy with olive skin and a snow white moustache. And that was only the beginning, because young men's moustaches don't just sprout a few hairs and stop. They get luxuriant. But Mum was not to be deterred. Every few days, she came at me with the bottle of peroxide and the cotton ball, dabbing away at the ever increasing hair, until I had a thick white moustache the little man from Monopoly would have been proud of.

Where was my father, you might ask? Why didn't he intervene and stop this, take me off and show me how to shave? Don't worry. He wasn't totally uninvolved. Over breakfast he would laugh at it and call me the Count of Monte Cristo.

This went on for something like six months. Every day I would go off to school in a state of total shame, wondering how I could hide it. But of course there was no solution other than to parade that shame before the whole school.

At that time in my life, when my mother was 'having her way with me', naturally I couldn't possibly face what was happening, and transferred my pain onto all sorts of other innocent objects. For example I convinced myself that my misery was totally caused by the horrible school I went to and the mean careless boys who inhabited it.

But in the entire six months I suffered under the persona of the Count, not one boy made fun of me. And given that adolescent boys make fun of one another over every little thing, you have to say that showed remarkable restraint and maturity on their part.

The worst that ever happened was that one or two older boys came up to me and suggested confidentially:

'Why don't you have a shave, mate?'

I did take their suggestions to my mother. But that was out of the question. She told me it was crazy to start shaving too soon. Shaving would only make it grow quicker. If I took that 'risk' next thing I knew I'd be shaving every day.

Daaah!! That's what men do. Where was my father? Why didn't he point that out?

Around this time too, I engaged in one of my great acts of transference. I had a friend named Les Dunn. He was a tough kid, and not without his faults. But he knew how to have fun, and he was a natural leader. Well one day my mother came to volunteer at the school canteen. It was the only time she had, and I was excited. It seemed like everyone else's mothers did, and now mine had too.

I rushed up to Les and said: 'Hey Les, guess what, my Mum's doing canteen duty!'

I can't remember what he said exactly, but it was something along the lines of how uncool it was to get excited about your Mum being at the canteen. It was an innocuous enough thing to say, and besides he was right. It was uncool. Anyone else would have forgotten his remarks in moments.

But I think it touched off something inside me that was the culmination of all the abuse I had suffered up to that point. I took it as an impugning of my relationship with my mother. And that couldn't be allowed to happen. Otherwise I might have to face what was being done to me, how hopeless and imprisoned I was.

So instead I blamed Les, and accused him in my mind of insulting my mother. I even managed to convince myself that his remark was racially motivated. Of course it had to be. I was a disgusting Jew. What else could be the reason? I know it is insane. But the tortured mind is capable of all sorts of unbelievable twists and inventions.

I went home that night and announced that the anti-Semite Les Dunn had insulted Mum and I was going to challenge him to a fight to defend her honour. Neither my mother nor my father questioned this. My mother just preened a little and my father, despite having told me a hundred times how he had always chosen the pacifist route at school, encouraged me to stand up and be a man.

When Pamp came home he was confronted with the job of having to teach me how to box. He was confused and seemed pretty doubtful, but saw I was determined, and my parents were determined. I think he felt there was no way he was going to prevent it, so he had better make sure I didn't get murdered. Les was from a tough working class family in La Perouse, and would certainly know how to fight.

So Pamp spent that evening teaching me the fundamentals of stance and guard, how to throw a left jab and a right hook. The palm of his hand must have been sore from the number of times I punched it. But I was

THE HOUSE AT ANZAC PARADE

quite naturally athletic and by the end of the evening Pamp declared I might stand a chance.

'One last thing,' he told me. 'When you walk out to fight him, look him straight in the eye. Never look away and especially never smile'.

The next day Les Dunn was astonished to receive a challenge from me. Of course he couldn't possibly work out what my problem might be. But in a boys' school the code didn't allow you to ask too much, for fear of looking weak, looking like you were trying to find a way out. So he said very little, accepted the challenge, and we agreed to meet in Moore Park next to the school when lessons were over.

I felt sick in the stomach most of the day. I had never fought before, and it was scary. But I buoyed myself by recalling the righteousness of my crusade. Nonetheless when we met in the playground at the end of the day, I was pretty scared. I forgot Pamp's advice and smiled out of fear. I also looked away. I realised that I needed to go to the toilet.

'I'm just going to the loo first,' I said.

'Why,' he asked quite seriously, 'are you going to change into shorts?'

'No,' I confessed, 'I just want a piss.' And I tried to imbue that remark with a tough sound.

'OK I'll see you in the park.'

When I went out into Moore Park, he was waiting for me. A lot of other boys had crowded around. A fist fight was always worth a look. They were all very quiet. I think they saw this as a serious matter.

We stood facing one another and I remember seeing a look in his eyes that said:

'What the hell are we doing here? We're friends, aren't we?'

For a moment I too thought how silly it all was. But of course I had to drive that thought from me. So we set too. I forgot everything Pamp had told me and began swinging away wildly. Les wasn't much better. The only difference was he had the sense to keep his head tucked down so it wasn't as big a target as mine.

I don't know how long we slugged away, but I know I got very tired. Eventually Les held up his hand and said:

'Are you finished yet?' It wasn't a capitulation by any means. His voice told me he was willing to continue. But it also implied my silliness really ought to have satisfied itself by now.

'Yes,' I said. 'I'm finished.'

I looked at him and it was clear I hadn't put a mark on him. I felt he hadn't got me either. But at home I discovered he'd landed one good blow on my forehead because a big red egg shape had emerged.

However for the moment he held out his hand, which I shook, and we went our separate ways home. I don't quite know how because we normally caught the same bus. Perhaps one let the other go first and took a later bus.

Anyway, after that we always showed one another mutual respect but we were never friends again.

Next morning, before I went to school, my mother put ladies' make up on the swollen redness of my forehead. Clearly that was another shame that needed covering.

Soon after that Pamp was diagnosed with bowel cancer. It must have been a late diagnosis because the tumour was too advanced to operate and he was soon in a nursing home. I went to Waverly by bus every day after school to visit him, and then caught a cross town bus home. It meant I got home late and that impacted on my study routine. But Mum only mentioned once or twice that I might consider visiting less.

One afternoon, as I sat by his bed, he said:

'You know I've never seen you bat. I would really like that.'

'So would I.' I knew if it didn't happen soon, it wouldn't happen.

Somehow we managed to arrange it. On the next Saturday morning the 13As were to play Sydney Grammar School at their home field in Elizabeth Bay. It wasn't far from the nursing home. Dad and I came for him in the car, and the nursing home gave us a fold up wheelchair. By now he couldn't walk at all.

The problem was that when we arrived at the ground the pedestrian access was too narrow for the wheelchair to get through. However there were big double gates to the ground that were opened to admit the rollers and mowers. So I went up to the coach of the Grammar team, explained that my grandfather was dying and that he would really like to see me bat. I asked if he could arrange to open the big gates so the wheelchair could get in.

He just looked at me as if I were an extra terrestrial and said:

'Absolutely not!'

I thought he must have misunderstood.

'But see he's dying, and he taught me cricket and if he doesn't get in today, he may never see me bat'.

He said nothing. Just kind of sneered at me and walked away.

Since I've healed, I have looked back on that moment and tried to see how I may have misinterpreted it. After all, as the Les Dunn incident showed, I had a tendency then to twist reality. But try as I might, I can't see how that could be the case here.

Over the years I have met a number of students and old boys from Sydney Grammar School and, with apologies to the no doubt thousands of wonderful men it produced, I do seem to have met an inordinate number of hard assed bastards from that school. Maybe the coach of the 13As was just one of those.

The next week Pamp was dead. He never did see me bat. One afternoon after school I went out to the nursing home and into the room he was sharing with some other men, and he was gone. My mind of course wouldn't accept, and I went rushing for the nurse to find out where he was. I remember her as a tall woman. She looked down at me with a big smile and said in a breezy voice:

'Oh it's all right. He's dead now.'

I think maybe she had been trained to keep the relatives in check. But how she managed the big smile and how she mustered that offhand way of delivering the verdict on his life, I can't imagine. Maybe I should have introduced her to the coach of the Grammar cricket team. They seemed well suited to me at the time.

Be that as it may, Pamp had died in his mid sixties, and my greatest angel had left me just when I needed him the most. I went home but I couldn't cry.

About a month after that Baba contracted lung cancer. The scenario was different from Pamp's. With my grandmother it seemed to go on much longer. There was a lot of talk about how she might have tuberculosis or some other curable illness. But she lay in her bedroom crying and moaning whilst Grandpa would pace about the living room saying over and over again, like some sort of sad mantra:

'Poor Baba. Poor, poor Baba.'

Then she was gone and I don't even remember saying goodbye. But I couldn't cry.

Grandpa was so attached to her he quite literally went mad. He lost all perspective on life, became wildly paranoid and began accusing everyone, especially his solicitor, of trying to rob him.

'Become a solicitor', he told me. 'They rob you, and even when they not rob you they rob you!'

And he would quote all sorts of facts and fees at me I couldn't possibly understand. Even at the time I found the basis of his career suggestion a little weird. Amazingly it didn't stop my mother quoting it years later, as one of the reasons I should decide to become a lawyer.

Soon after, Grandpa was admitted to a lunatic asylum. I think it was Callan Park. But wherever it was I remember having to take several buses to get there.

Mental health care was still primitive then. When I look back I can't believe just how primitive it was. It seemed to have much more in common with the eighteenth century than with now, just a few decades on.

When the nurse took me to see Grandpa I was sickened to find he was being kept in a big open air cage with lots of other people who walked funny, made strange noises and poked at one another. I had to pick my way through them. It was very frightening for a 12 year old boy. The warders actually cleaned the inmates by hosing them down. I saw them doing it to a group. But the group in question had been quite rowdy, and even then I suspected the hose was used as much for discipline as for cleanliness.

But Grandpa wasn't noisy. He sat silently on a chair staring straight ahead of him. He did not know me at all. At that age I couldn't see how that could be, and thought there must have been some mistake or problem I could overcome by force of will. So I spent a long time there desperately trying to reason with him, to make him see that it was me. But there was no hope.

A few weeks later I understood his madness was at least partially if not wholly physiologically based, because I was told he had died of brain cancer.

So now I was not quite 13 years old, and my Baba and my two great angels were dead. Still I couldn't cry.

Nan was still alive and even at that age I saw how ironic it was for a woman suffering from debilitating rheumatoid arthritis, not to mention a whole range of other ailments, to outlive my other three grandparents, all of whom a few months before had been perfectly healthy and totally alive.

But Nan's grief was all consuming. I can imagine how she felt. Apart from losing the love of her life, as an invalid she was trapped with and dependent upon Leon and Joy. It was a bleak prospect.

As some sort of attempt to console herself, she would take me aside from time to time and say:

'You're my little Pamp now'.

But it broke me up every time and in the end I had to say:

'Nan, please don't call me little Pamp. I can never be a Pamp.'

It was something that came straight from the gut. I didn't know exactly what I meant then, and maybe I still don't. But Nan understood and didn't call me that again. She just retreated into her own quietness where she lived for another 10 years.

I was numb and hollowed out. I was the Count of Monte Cristo without his sword. I had lost all the loves from my life, and I was disgusting.

I hadn't cried when any of my grandparents died. But a few weeks after Grandpa's death, at the breakfast table, when my father started in again on the Count of Monte Cristo, I completely lost it and started sobbing uncontrollably.

'What? What? What?' my father demanded in amazement.

The mixture of grief and loss and self loathing was beyond my ability to understand let alone express. In the end it all just focussed in on the moustache:

'It's so ugly!' I gasped between sobs.

'What?'

'The moustache!'

'Then shave it off,' he said, as if I had kept it because I thought it looked dashing.

And he got his electric razor and plonked it down on the kitchen table in front of me and went to work shaking his head.

I looked at my mother.

'If you really want to,' she said.

I did want to. I had no idea how to use an electric razor, but I turned it on and attacked my face with it. The moustache came away like an old scab just waiting to be flicked. I looked at my face in my father's shaving mirror. It was pure and bright. Yes, I thought, I am human underneath.

The joy was momentary however. I needed to get back to my studies. I needed to come top. I needed to have the glory stolen from me, and my mother condemn me in floods of tears for not having the guts to go the distance.

The day that happened was a turning point in the life of an abused boy. To begin with I learned a lesson I would relearn again and again throughout life, a lesson I am still learning. It is that if you push too hard for something, as I had done for the top place in the year, if you drive yourself for the wrong reasons, even if you achieve what you are seeking, the Universe will find a way to steal it from you.

But I also learned that may not be a tragedy. Indeed it may be a blessing. What if I had been acknowledged as top of the class? Maybe I would have tried to go on as before? And maybe I would have found another way, a more permanent way, to escape?

So our saving moments sometimes come, not brought by our angels, or even by a wonderful event. Sometimes they are wrapped up in what appears to be just the opposite. As I stood there watching my mother cry, even though I felt I was the most useless, most disgusting son on the planet, a part of me knew I was not going back to that inhuman study regime.

My decision that day was small scale. I would still work hard at school. I just wouldn't try to appease a mad woman anymore with my own mad attempts at the impossible. This small first step was just that, a first step. The rest of the journey would take another 40 years. But the first step had been taken.

7. A MIRACLE OF MODERN MEDICINE

So I had taken my first step of defiance, my first stumble towards healing. But apart from refusing to live on five hours sleep a night, I was otherwise compliant. In due course I got myself into Sydney University Law School.

The law can be fascinating if taught the right way. Regretfully in those days Sydney's only law school, made everything as dry as two hundred year old parchment. My only escape was sex. I remember I would sit in baffling commercial law lectures thinking: 'If only I could get hold of a girl and jump into bed with her, I wouldn't have to stay around for this boring nonsense'.

That may not make a lot of sense, till I explain that at this time my mother developed a growing fascination with my sex life. She was particularly interested in my 'hunting' techniques.

As she cross-examined me on the details I came to realise she was fine with me taking time off study for the hunt. Relationships which threatened to be ongoing were almost of no interest to her. It was the hunt that was going to get me out of commercial law.

It never occurred to me I could just choose not be in the lecture, indeed that I could choose not to be at Law School at all. Sport had been all that could get me out of study in High School. Now it was the sport of the chase.

Obviously this latest 'delight' was unlikely to foster healthy relationships with women. It was equally obviously going to morph into sex addiction. My 'relationships' with women would not just become a way to escape work, but also a way not to look at myself and my life.

It was not my only addiction. I was already heavily addicted to tobacco. My mother had introduced me to cigarettes when I was 13. She said they would help me relax and help me study more effectively. By 18 I was a pack a day man.

There was a part of me which already understood, on some level, the uselessness of the one night stands. Deep down I knew my mother's encouragement of my sluttyness was nothing more than the latest weapon of my gaoler and torturer. I sensed a long term relationship was not just the answer to the addiction, but was also a way of real escape from my mother and the sick existence she wallowed in, and would have me wallow in too.

I had always been a loving child, and despite my mother's perversion of the concept, miraculously I had never lost an understanding of what real love ought to be like. After all I had known real love with my angels.

Growing up my mother had often accused me of being 'too loving'. I know it sounds absurd, but those were her words.

'You're such a sucker,' she would say. 'Some woman is going to come along, and work out you're way too loving, and she'll get her claws into you.'

Of course it was a real fear for Joy, that her golden goose would have all his golden eggs stolen by some other wily female. But I think I understood this, and a part of me wanted to plunge headlong into a real relationship, as a way to stop the addiction, and more importantly as a way to realise Joy's worst fear and thus escape her.

I was still only 21 when I met Agatha to whom I would soon be married. How unfair it was of me. Though I told myself I was in love, there is little doubt I was marrying for fundamentally the wrong reason. And I was offering a very defective product, both psychologically and, as it soon turned out, physically too.

I finished law school and was offered a job at the Commonwealth Crown Solicitor's Office, in the prosecutions department. At Law School criminal law had interested me. In fact it was the only subject which did. But Sydney University Law School was extremely conservative and criminal law was given little emphasis. That and family law were then described scornfully by its alumni as 'people law'.

In other words real lawyers worked in equity/commercial or tax law and had as little to do with 'people' as possible. Crime on the other hand was irretrievably interwoven with grubby people, their grubby lives and their irrational demands for justice.

I however was a misfit and thought law ought to be about people. I was very happy to be posted to the prosecutions department with the other 'people lawyers'. I remember one of the senior men there telling me:

'Criminal lawyers are the only real lawyers. All the rest are just used car salesmen.' When I heard that I knew I was in the right place.

There were nine other prosecutors in the section and we worked most often out of what was then called the 'Special Federal Court'. I was to be admitted to the bar a month after joining the Crown, but with the permission of the resident magistrate in the Special Federal Court, the head of prosecutions, Lou Jarman, threw me straight into court work.

At first these were only pleas of guilty, but Lou had me down to do a trial in Dubbo soon after I was admitted. The night he assigned that case to me Agatha and I were going to meet friends for a drink in Coogee. I had a motor bike then, a Honda 250, and Agatha was on the back. On one of Coogee's incredibly steep hills a car braked suddenly in front of us and we had to stop. The hand break was not enough to hold the bike on a hill like that, so I did what all bikers do and put my feet down to take the weight.

Suddenly I felt a searing pain in my testicle and groin. It was very painful trying to hold the bike in place. I had been noticing for some time how my left testicle had been getting more and more swollen, and was giving me discomfort on ejaculation. I hadn't been too concerned. I was young and the young worry less about their physicality. Besides I was pre-occupied with my new job. But now I thought I should have it checked out. So I went to the aging Doctor Thomas in the practice I had been going to since I was a small child.

Doctor Thomas was an old world gentleman and a very caring man. He examined my testicle, which was by now probably twice the size it should be. He announced that I had fluid retention.

'Give it a month,' he said, 'and if it hasn't gone down, we'll put a needle in it and draw off the fluid.'

The idea didn't fill me with delight. But events were soon to make that thought obsolete. My appointment with Doctor Thomas had been on a Tuesday, but on Thursday morning he called me at home and asked me to come in urgently.

In the surgery he explained he had been playing Wednesday afternoon golf at the Royal Sydney Golf Club with a surgeon friend and had mentioned my swollen testicle. I was astonished at how dedicated he must have been, worrying about patients on his afternoon off. It was later suggested to me he may have been joking about the size of my testicle.

Either way the surgeon didn't think it was funny. He told Doctor Thomas he had had a patient of my age with identical symptoms only the week before. He had performed an urgent orchidectomy (removal of the testicle) after it was discovered the boy was suffering from a rare and aggressive form of teratoma or cancer of the testicle. Doctor Thomas's surgeon friend feared I might be suffering from the same.

The next day I was in surgeon Swain's Macquarie Street rooms. After examining me, he said he thought I was suffering the same disease as the other boy.

'I will admit you to War Memorial Hospital on Sunday and we'll operate on Monday morning,' he told me.

'But I'm being admitted to the bar on Monday,' I said.

'This thing moves quickly. If we don't get it all with surgery, there is no other treatment. We can't afford to leave it.'

It has been said before that such an experience borders on the surreal. It is very hard to accommodate the thought that a medical specialist is telling you he needs to operate very quickly because you have an aggressive and deadly disease.

'I did four years at law school,' I said weakly, almost irrelevantly.

Swain looked at me with the understanding of someone who has worked hard at a professional university course. He thought for a moment before saying: 'What time are you being admitted?'

'Around eleven.'

'We'll get you into War Memorial straight after that and operate in the afternoon.'

Of course it still hadn't sunk in.

'But I've got my first real case next week. I have to go to Dubbo.'

'You have to go to hospital,' he said, and there was such urgency and such determination in his voice, I knew I had no choice.

Agatha's father Mike was a doctor, a good man, but a plain speaking one. He told her and he told my parents:

'I'm afraid he's a dead man.'

He didn't tell me, but Agatha reported back. Apparently my particular form of testicular cancer was one that invariably attacked young men in their early 20s. It was rare. Contracting it was a 100,000 to 1 shot, but if you got it there was almost 100% chance you would die from it. Surgery was the only option, but it was rarely successful. They would almost never get it all and so it would metastasize, or spread to other areas of the body. In my own case the tumour had taken over 2/3 of the testicle already, so things weren't looking good.

Monday morning came but not surprisingly my mind was elsewhere. I had completely forgotten to arrange a wig and gown. In those days the only way you could get a wig was to order one from London. Obviously that took months, so new barristers often didn't have their own in time for admission and had to borrow one from someone else. The only one Lou Jarman could get on short notice must have belonged to someone with a huge head because it was very very loose.

We gathered outside the old Supreme Court Building, the prospective new barristers and their friends and family. My parents both worked in an office about two hundred metres from the Court but by the time we all started to shuffle in they still hadn't arrived. They did finally get there but not till about 12.30 when it was all over and people were on their way home. They made no apologies or excuses. I think it was their rather unsubtle way of letting me know the value they placed on a golden goose gone to the abattoirs.

It was a cruel message, but one that did not impact on me till later. Right now I was sitting in the upper gallery of the old Banco Court with its 160 year history, crowded around by all the other candidates. I was in awe of the surroundings and of the moment and of course I was still trying to free myself from the all encompassing fog of my diagnosis.

On the floor of the Court stood a group of senior lawyers, ready to move the admissions of their young colleagues. All the lawyers from the prosecutions department were in other courts but Lou Jarman had arranged for someone from another department to move my admission. I didn't know what he looked like, and I just hoped he had made it.

So obviously it was an anxious moment for me. Admission to the Bar, absent parents, the possibility of no-one actually being there to move my admission, and the very real possibility I was about to die.

But despite all these not insignificant concerns, the thing that worried me most was the wig. It was hard enough to keep on even now. I had to sit very still. And how uncool would it be if it were to fall off during my admission? My anxiety grew exponentially when the proceedings began. Up till then I hadn't really known what the process would be. Lou had said it was simple and I would pick it up. We were in alphabetical order so there would be plenty of time to work it.

And that was true. I had it worked out by the early 'A's - to my horror. This was February 1974 and the Chief Justice was Sir John Kerr, the man who would very soon be appointed Governor General and who would be responsible for the sacking of the Whitlam Government. He sat on the bench flanked by two puisne judges. But it was not Kerr per se who worried me. It was what his august office required of candidates for admission. Here lay the seeds of my potential humiliation.

After the Court tipstaff called the name of the candidate, the sponsor would say to the Court: 'Your Honours, I move that Alan Albert Adams being admitted as a barrister of this Honourable Court.'

Then Kerr would say out into the void (because of course he had no idea which one was Adams): 'Mr Adams, do you move?'

I remember thinking, amidst all my anxieties, what a ridiculous phrase that was. Was he asking the candidates about their bowel motions? And a bowel motion was certainly on the cards for me, because what happened next was that Mr Adams had to stand and bow deeply from the waist.

It was simple and it was straightforward, provided you had a wig that stayed on your head. My mind scrambled for solutions. All I could think was that I might hold on to the wig with one hand whilst I bowed. But that in itself seemed only slightly less humiliating that having it fall off.

I had to come up with something soon because I was in the front row of the gallery, so if the wig did come off it wouldn't just fall at my feet, but would plummet, to my horror and no doubt to the undying horror and shame of Kerr, the puisne judges and all present, into the well of the Court. Unfortunately by the time my name was called I still hadn't worked out a solution.

My sponsor was present and moved my admission. That was good, but it also meant there was now no escape from the wig problem. I heard:

'Mr Kline, do you move?' It was Kerr's sonorous voice ringing out to me across the centuries.

I still didn't know what to do, but found myself standing and bowing, but a ridiculous shallow bow where I kept my head up, my eyes on Kerr and my upper torso stretched out like a goose across the banister. Even so the wig slid a little and came down over my left eye. But at least it stayed on. And in the end Kerr seemed 'unmoved' by my awkwardness. He just announced in the same bored flat tone he had used for all the previous candidates:

'Let Victor Alan Kline be admitted as a barrister of this Honourable Court.'

That afternoon, Sydney's youngest barrister was in bed in the War Memorial Hospital in Waverly, doped up on pethidine, waiting to have his testicle removed. I lay on my back looking at the rose patterned ceiling, thinking how simple and relaxed life could be. Despite the odds against my surviving, right then, under the golden influence of that drug, I had no doubt I would, thanks to two amazing miracles which had brought me to this point.

First there had been the miracle of the Coogee Hill. Whilst I had spent some time round Coogee as a child I never went there anymore. So it was a miracle I was there at all. And had I not had to break for a car stopping unexpectedly and hold my bike on one of the steepest hills in the State, I would never have felt that searing pain and would never have gone to seek help in time.

This was followed by the miracle of the Royal Sydney Golf Course. I consulted a doctor who completely misdiagnosed me, but just happened to be golfing the very next day with a surgeon who just happened to have operated the week before on a boy with the same extremely rare disease. Remember that Doctor Swain was not an oncologist. He was just a general surgeon. The other boy and I were probably the only two such cases he would see in his entire career. And even then Swain would never have mentioned the other boy had not Doctor Thomas, for whatever reason, decided to talk testicles somewhere round the 14th green.

So there I lay, enjoying the pethidine and contemplating my miracles. I didn't know then there would be far greater miracles to come. For now however the orderly had come for me and was wheeling my bed down the corridor to the operating theatre. Doctor Swain was waiting there for me, as was Agatha's father who had asked to assist. I remember looking up at them and thinking how serious and concerned they both were. I guess they felt it was no small matter for a 22 year old to be losing half his manhood and in all probability his young life. But, whilst I did feel touched by their concern, at the same time under the wondrous influence of the pethidine I also found it amusing.

'Cheer up guys,' I remember saying and laughing. 'It will all be ok.' And for that moment, thanks to pethidine, I really believed it would.

I awoke from the anaesthetic in the middle of the night when everyone else was asleep and the ward was silent. It took me a moment to remember why I was there. But when I did recall where I was and why, I didn't feel sadness or regret or fear. Nor did I even feel any pain. I guessed I must be on some strong drug. But I knew it wasn't pethidine. It felt different.

Dr Swain had told me the first thing they would do in the operating theatre was take a biopsy of my testicle and analyse it while I was still unconscious. In the unlikely event it was not a malignant growth, when I awoke my testicle would still be there. Otherwise of course it would be gone.

I lay there for a moment trying to decide if I should check. Eventually I did, and it was gone. Under the influence of the drug that seemed all right, even natural. I looked about me but the ward didn't feel natural. It was so silent it was as though I were looking at a film with the sound turned off.

Just then the nurse entered the ward. Two things immediately struck me, first that she seemed to be walking in slow motion and secondly that she was the most beautiful woman I had ever seen in my life. I got an erection and laughed out loud.

The nurse heard me laugh and came over to me.

'You're in good spirits,' she said.

'You're beautiful,' I said, but she didn't seem flattered. I thought perhaps she heard that all the time.

I think we talked for a bit, but then I must have fallen asleep. I awoke to a ward full of sunshine and movement, and pain like I had never known before. I screamed and a nurse came running. She injected me with something, maybe pethidine again, and soon the pain started to subside. I looked up at the nurse. She seemed very caring, but unlike the nurse from the night before, was a rather plain looking woman.

'Night nurse gone home?' I asked.

'No,' she said, smiling. 'I'm the night nurse. Last night you were on morphine. Interesting isn't it?'

I felt ashamed, and wanted desperately to say something nice to her.

But it was difficult to get my feet out of my mouth before she left the ward.

The next couple of days I was in and out of consciousness. On about the third day a Franciscan father came into the ward, dressed in the traditional robe and sandals. I watched him talking to some of the other patients. Eventually he came over to me and introduced himself as Father Pacificus.

'Would you like to talk?' he asked.

'I'm not Catholic,' I told him.

'Shouldn't stop you talking', he chuckled. He had a gentle smile and a gentle presence that matched his name.

'I'm frightened,' I heard myself tell him. And I was surprised, because until then I hadn't realised I was.

'Of what?'

'Of dying.'

He sat quietly, waiting for me to continue. So I did and told him all about why I was there. He listened to me. Really listened. Then he spoke but I can't remember what he said. And I don't think it mattered. What was important was that I knew he genuinely cared for what I was going through and what would become of me. And that is powerful.

Here was a man who had spent probably no more than 20 minutes with me, yet he left a very lasting impression. Many years later the memory of Father Pacificus would help incline me positively towards the Catholic Church, despite the many negative things I knew about it in theory.

I had a strange encounter not long after that. A middle aged man was wheeled into the bed opposite me. He was unconscious, but when he woke he sat up in bed, looked at me and said:

'Leon?'

It turned out he was someone who had known my father in Shanghai when he was my age, and his mind had skipped a generation. That brought up all sorts of difficult feelings that never quite made it to my conscious mind, like how much I did resemble my father and what that meant to my mother.

I think it also exacerbated a fear which had been growing in me for some time and which would continue to haunt me for a long time to come. The man in the bed opposite talked a lot about my father, and from what he said it seemed that at 22 my Dad was a slim, a not unattractive and a personable young man. His friend may have been looking at the past through rose coloured glasses, but nonetheless there must have been some truth to it.

So the fear was that even if I did survive, and even if I were slim, not unattractive and personable myself, that was no security. I was at risk of degenerating into the overweight, lazy, cowardly and careless man my father had become.

I think I was focusing on concerns like this to avoid having to address far more pressing psychological needs. The most pressing - how was I going to deal with my childhood and adolescent abuse so it didn't infect and take over my adult life?

I was running away from my difficult memories. Sadly this was not a solution for me, and I'm sure never is for anyone. The memories continue to call to us in muffled voices day and night, getting louder and more frequent as time goes by. Finally we have no choice but to dig them out and listen to what they have to teach us.

Be that as it may, the process of repression, which I had started in my teens, was now all but complete. If you had asked me while I lay in that hospital bed, I would have told you I had a loving mother. I had totally repressed any memory of anything she had done to me, so much so that instead of moving in with Agatha as we had planned, I was now going back home to be cared for by my loving mother. The fact that she hadn't even visited me in hospital apparently presented no problem for the repressive mechanisms of my brain.

After four or five days I was ready for release. Dr Swain visited me and had a suggestion:

'I want you to go and see Leicester Atkinson. He's Professor of Oncology at Prince of Wales. They're trying something new.'

A day or so later I walked through the big double glass doors that took me into the cancer ward at Sydney's Prince of Wales Hospital. The first thing I noticed was the smell of the floor polish. In time I would develop a conditioned response to that smell. Even years later, if I revisited the ward or even smelled that polish somewhere else, I would vomit or at least want to vomit. But for now it was just an appropriate smell.

Professor Atkinson was a dignified, well spoken man in his fifties, relaxed in demeanour, and if not exactly friendly, then certainly polite. He had a dictaphone, which he spoke into as he questioned me:

'I have with me Victor Alan Kline,' he told the dictaphone as I sat opposite. 'Mr Kline is 22 years old and a...' he clicked the dictaphone off. 'What is it you do Mr Kline?'

'I'm a barrister,' I said. I saw a faint smile cross his lips. I'm sure he believed me, but no doubt I did look very young for the job. 'A prosecutor,' I added.

'Ah,' he replied. 'State or Federal?'

'Federal.'

He clicked the dictaphone back on: 'Mr Kline is a prosecuting barrister,' he said, smiling faintly again. 'He represents the Crown in right of the Commonwealth.'

I remember being impressed by that. Phrases like 'Crown in right of the Commonwealth' were well known to lawyers, but few others.

'He has been referred by Dr Swain,' he continued into the machine, 'who has performed a simple orchidectomy of Mr Kline's left testis.'

I remember thinking it was anything but simple from my point of view, but did understand he was probably using the word in the more technical sense of 'standard'. I figured if he could correctly use 'Crown in right of the Commonwealth', I could endure the technical use of the word 'simple' as applied to my extraordinarily painful loss.

He put the dictaphone down: 'You understand the nature of your cancer?' he asked. I told him I did. 'Then you understand that often surgery may not provide a completely satisfactory solution.'

I thought that was the understatement of the century.

'My future father-in-law is a doctor,' I told him. 'He has made it clear what my chances are.'

'Ah, so you're getting married?' This worried him, though at the same time his eyes seemed to tell me he was genuinely pleased I might have someone to love me. 'When were you planning to marry?'

'In April'.

'Ah. You may want to defer that a little.' He said it as gently as he could.

'Because I'm going to die?'

'We are all going to die, Mr Kline'.

'But I may leave a very young bride, is what you think?'

He hesitated for a moment then said, with real compassion: 'You may.' We were silent for a moment, and then he added: 'But there is something we would like to try.' I nodded and he continued. 'We want to try a new form of cobalt irradiation therapy. We believe it may be very effective.'

'You believe?'

'Yes, we believe it will. But we haven't actually tried it yet.'

'And you want to try it on me?'

'Yes we do...with your permission.'

'What are the risks?' I asked.

'Well, it may kill you.'

I couldn't help but smile at the matter of fact way he said that.

'So I have a choice between the frying pan and the fire?'

'Something like that,' he said. 'You see we need to trial it with massive doses. Otherwise we will never know. Most cancer patients are older and would definitely not survive that. But we think because you are young and strong, you may.'

'So would you choose the fire over the frying pan?' I asked him.

'I would choose the irradiation,' he told me in all seriousness. 'To be frank you don't really have much to lose.'

I took his point.

'The fire it is then,' I said.

He cleared his throat: 'Actually that's not all,'

'Yes?'

'After the irradiation therapy, we would need you to undergo some chemotherapy as well. Have you heard of chemotherapy?'

'No I haven't.'

'It's a chemical therapy delivered by a course of injections. We have had forms of chemotherapy for some time, but we are looking at a new combination of drugs, that we think will be far more effective.'

'And you haven't trialled these either?'

'We think the combination of the cobalt therapy and the new chemotherapy is what is needed to treat a virulent form of cancer like yours.'

'If I survive the cobalt therapy, could the chemotherapy kill me?' I asked jokingly. But he didn't laugh.

'Probably not,' was all he said.

I heard myself exhale loudly.

Then he explained to me they first needed to do was a series of x-rays to see if the tumour had spread. If it already had, there was no point going on.

The next day I found myself in a room that didn't seem like an X-ray facility. It was just a big room with glass walls which looked out onto other parts of the hospital. In the middle of the room was a big table where I was asked to lay. A man was there in a white coat. I didn't know whether he was a radiologist or even a doctor at all. But I asked:

'Aren't I supposed to be having X-rays?'

'Umm...yeah,' he said distractedly, 'but first we have to get some dye into your bloodstream.'

I lay there for a few minutes more after which time a very tall well built male nurse entered the room and stood over to one side. Moments later another male nurse came in. He was bigger and stronger looking than the first. Next thing I knew there were four of them and before I could finish wondering why the bruisers were there, they were pinning me to the table, one on each shoulder and one on each thigh.

Then the white coated man came at me with a needle so big he looked like a joke doctor from a Benny Hill skit. He lifted my hospital gown and attacked my right groin with it. The pain of the needle going in was substantial, but nothing compared to what happened next. The dye from the needle ran round my body and hit the inside of my scalp. It was quite literally like I had been hit on the head with a large wooden mallet but from the inside. Simultaneously I felt my whole body involuntarily lift from the table. So powerful was my convulsion that the four strong male nurses could not hold me, and I lifted several inches in the air to come crashing down on my back. Now I understood why they were there.

Things got a little blurry after that. I'm not sure how they determined it, but a few moments later my white coated attacker announced the first shot had not been a success, and they would have to try again. I began to ask whether perhaps there might be another option. But before I could get the words out the nurses had me pinned and the horse needle was again entering my flesh in much the same place as before. This time the nurses leaned on me with all their strength and kept me on the table. But if anything the pain of the dye hitting the top of my head was worse than the first time.

We did this three more times. I don't think I fainted but I wish I had. In the end it just wasn't working and I was told they would have to get the dye in another way. The white coated man apologised for the fact that the alternative method would probably be a tad more painful than the first. Was that possible I wondered?

It was. They told me the only way it was going to get in was if they inserted the needle into the webbing between my big toe and the next. But they assured me they would minimise the discomfort by giving me an anaesthetic. The problem was the anaesthetic took the form of another needle injected into the top of my big toe.

The league table of pain went something like this: the injection in the groin with the resultant clubbing of the inside of my head was worse even than when I had woken from the morphine after my testicle had been removed. However the needle into the top of my big toe was worse than both. And worst of all, because the anaesthetic from the needle in the big toe didn't work, was the insertion of the needle into the webbing of my foot. They say you can't remember pain. But 35 years on I think I can.

Anyway this time it worked, the dye got where it was supposed to go, I had the X-rays and there was no apparent spread. This meant I was free to undergo the delights of the massive doses of radiation and the experimental cocktail of drugs.

I went home to my parents. Nan had died not long before and they had immediately moved into the 'big' room. My young sister was in her first year at University. She had already left home to live with the man she would later marry. I think she did this even before she finished school. I'm sure she felt there was nothing to keep her. There was nothing to keep me either, to say the least. But there I was, installed by my parents in their old room.

Why didn't I just go to my old bedroom? After Pamp fixed it up it was still small, but at least it was light, whereas my parents' room was the darkest place on the planet. It made no sense. When I look back I can't help thinking it was some sort of punishment. How dare he try to come home when he is dying? All right then, put him in the tomb before the tomb.

It was in that room I no doubt developed my craving for sunlight. I quite literally associated brightness and light with survival, and darkness with death. Even today I am much happier when the sun is out. But then it was an obsession. I decided to go back to work sooner than I should have. I guess I just had to get out of that room. So my radiotherapy started the day I started back at work.

The way it worked was I would go out to Prince of Wales on my motorbike every day after work. I would go through the big glass doors and smell the polish before making my way to the waiting room which I shared with representatives of every part of humanity. If ever I had thought to cry out: 'Why me?', that room would have quickly called back: 'Why not you? We've got everyone else here.'

It was not a cheery place. But the nursing staff was always professional and always compassionate. Sister Carter, who ran the ward, always took the time to talk to me, and treat me as an individual. Even after my treatment was over she would say: 'Please come back and see us. Don't forget.' And I knew that was not just politeness.

So I would quietly wait my turn. It was usually a long wait. But eventually I would be taken in to the radiotherapy room and would be put on my back on a large metallic table. The radiographer would focus the machine between two dots which had been tattooed, one in the centre of my chest and one on my stomach. (I still have them as a perpetual reminder of the good fortune of still being alive). Then she would run away behind a wall of lead and the radiotherapy would begin.

It always made me feel a little sick and that got worse as time went by. But the main concern was with the extreme tiredness it created. Because of the massive doses I was having, by the time I got home, I literally had to fall down and couldn't get up till the morning. And even then I went to work exhausted.

I shouldn't have been working, but I needed to, for reasons beyond just the necessity of getting out of the cave. First of all I still suffered from the feeling that if I weren't working I wouldn't be loved, something that no mere deadly cancer would interfere with. But most of all I needed continuity. Despite all the films where the dying character wants to 'live life to the full' before he dies, that's not how it is. The reality is you want things to be as normal as possible because 'normal' implies continuity, whereas 'living life to the full' just reminds you that you are going to die.

So normal for me was going back to what I had left before I got sick. Normal was returning to the prosecutions department. For better or worse, as I had chosen to return, Lou Jarman was going to respect my choice, and start me on the sort of work he had planned for me before I fell ill.

That meant a steep learning curve which would have tired a perfectly healthy new prosecutor, but was of course particularly difficult for me. I started to get more and more depressed. When I returned Lou Jarman had put me in an internal office without a window. It was the only one available. But as the days went by and the depression deepened, the office began to feel like 'my cave away from cave' and I quite literally started to wind down to a point where I couldn't work.

In the end I went in to see Brian Muir in his office which was on the outside of the building with a window over the laneway. It wasn't a harbour view. But there was light through that window. I could have gone to any one of several lawyers in the Department but Brian was only 27 and the next youngest to me, and somehow I thought he might understand.

'Can you give me your office?" I just blurted out as I stood on the other side of his desk. He looked at me curiously but without judgment. 'I think if I stay in the dark, I might really lose it,'

'All right,' he said, after a moment, and there and then began packing up his files and papers to move them into my office. We became very good friends.

So the radiotherapy continued day after day and I got more tired and more depressed. Once a week, every week I would see Professor Atkinson. I started to mention the depression to him, but he brushed it aside.

'It's quite natural,' was all he would say.

Then he would go back to the 'more important' questions surrounding my physicality. I had lost a lot of weight, but I was holding up well, as far as he could tell. The fact that I could work at all was proof of that. And most importantly there was no sign of spread.

Unlike with the nursing staff, I always felt less of an individual and more of a 'test case' with Professor Atkinson. Initially it didn't trouble me. Initially I well understood how incredibly busy he was and the weight of responsibility he was carrying. I felt also he was not uncompassionate. Rather he was just not a very demonstrative man. But as I got more and more depressed I began to lose sight of that, and the feeling I was just an 'experiment' only seemed to add to the depression.

Towards the latter part of the six week course of radiotherapy, emotionally and physically I was in a bad way. I had no energy at all and I was fighting back tears the entire time. Indeed the depression had gone to another level altogether. At night I would stand in the bathroom looking at myself in the mirror, a razor blade in my hand, debating with myself whether it might not be better to just be done with it all. How close I actually came to using the razor, I can't say. But clearly things weren't going well.

I got Dr Thomas to refer me to a psychiatrist. What can I say about that man? Here I was being bombarded with ridiculous and unprecedented amounts of cobalt ray. Naturally that was going to do all sorts of things to my body and mind. I personally was too debilitated, too caught up in it all to be objective, to understand what was happening to me. But he should have been able to. He should have been able to point out the obvious and prescribe me some serapax.

Instead he contrived to build an amazingly convoluted theory for my depression based around my loss of manhood and my grandmother's death. Of course I didn't like losing a testicle, but I had been told I could do anything anyone else could do with my remaining one. And sure I missed Nan terribly. But really! The elephant in the room?

However on the basis of his theory he arranged for me to be admitted as a day patient to the Caritas Psychiatric Centre at Darlinghurst. I don't know what I told Lou Jarman, but two days later I was off work again and parking my motor bike outside the high stone walls of Caritas.

When I entered a rather lean ghoulish looking man 'greeted' me. His name was Horace. When I offered him my hand he looked taken aback, as though crazy people didn't shake hands. Nonetheless he reluctantly took mine and more or less jiggled rather than shook it. Then he sat me down in the foyer and proceeded to explain the house rules. First rule was that I was in for the whole day. I couldn't leave till 6 pm. That's what I had agreed. That's what I had signed up for. There were a whole lot of other rules, but the one that seemed to matter most, even more than the no exit rule, concerned my locker key.

'See this key,' he said, holding it up to the light, no doubt to make sure I did see it. 'This is your locker key. Don't take it home with you. You must not, under any circumstances, take your locker key home. Is that clear?'

'Yes,' I said, 'very clear'.

'So can you repeat it back to me?'

'Repeat what?' I was confused.

'Repeat what you have to do with your locker key.' He sighed.

'I have to not take it home,' I said. 'I have to give it back to you before I go home.'

I think Horace may have almost smiled at that point. Or perhaps he was just quietly passing wind. Either way he seemed satisfied, and so after I had put my bike helmet and leather jacket in my locker, and put the locker key in a safe place, he took me into a room where he introduced me to a nurse, who explained to me the schedule for the day's activities.

First up I was to be part of a group therapy session for new people. About seven or eight of us gathered with a psychologist in a small room where we sat in a circle on hard backed chairs. The psychologist began by suggesting that as he didn't know us and we didn't know each other, we should take a little time to explain why we thought we were there and what was troubling us. That seemed like a perfectly logical suggestion, so when he asked me to begin I was happy to oblige.

I tried to meld in with my psychiatrist's diagnosis and talked a little about the cancer resulting in the partial loss of my manhood. I also explained how much my Nan meant to me and how much I felt her loss. Then I told everyone that I had been feeling very depressed. The psychologist thanked me and then asked:

'Marion, would you like to share a little now?'

'Why?' she blurted. 'Why *should* I? Why?!' Now getting louder and louder. 'Why should I tell *you*? Why do you *want* to know anyway?!!!'

Marion's response filled me with mixed emotion. On the one hand I was shocked at her response. But on the other hand I felt mine had been altogether too tame. And I was definitely in a minority because most of the rest of the group picked up on Marion's approach, launching one wave of verbal aggression after another at the long suffering psychologist. The only relief he got was when one or two refused to speak at all.

Up to the time I went to Caritas one of the thoughts tormenting me, as I sank further and further into depression, was that perhaps I really was losing my mind. After the group therapy session, which lasted for an hour and during which literally nobody said anything that wasn't at best unhelpful and at worst just palpably crazy, I felt a whole lot more sane.

But that was only the curtain raiser. After the group therapy, all the inmates, day and resident, gathered in the big meeting hall. There were perhaps 100 people present. We all sat about in different sorts of chairs arranged at strange angles to the presiding psychiatrist. Many years later as a theatre director, I often thought about what an interesting tableau those angled chairs made. And seated in them was such a variety of humanity. There was every age from late teens to very old, about an equal number of men and women, and an array of demeanours from those who seemed about to fall asleep to those who looked ready to spring. Around the walls stood a number of white coated men.

'Ladies and gentlemen,' the psychiatrist began, 'today we have some important group decisions to make.' I wasn't sure, but despite the apparent innocuousness of his remark, I thought I heard fear in his voice. 'First of all,' he continued, 'as you all know we are going to have this meeting room painted, and I think, as this is such an important room to all of you, everyone should have a say in the colour scheme. So the first thing I want to...'

'Black!' A tall thin middle aged man was on his feet and yelling. 'All black! Everything! Everything has to be black! The walls, the floor, the ceiling, black, black black!!...

He was continuing in the same vein and at the same volume when a woman on the far side of the room suddenly screamed out:

'You bastard! You know it's red. It's always been red, you fucking bastard...'

And then it was someone who wanted polka dots, and someone else who wanted the walls to be invisible. Before I knew it the entire room was involved, some screaming their colour preferences at the psychiatrist, some at their neighbour and some just into the void. Half the patients seemed to really care, I mean really really care, and the other half seemed to care not a jot but were enjoying stirring the pot.

I thought years later how those proportions pretty much mirror question time at the Federal Parliament. I thought too that the level of energy expended relative to the importance of the topic was also reminiscent of some political debates.

Be that as it may, here at Caritas things were threatening to get out of control and the white coated men each made a dash for a different patient whom they physically restrained. I think they must have had a good idea who the real dangers were, because they quickly brought the crowd under control. Once the ringleaders were pinned, the others quickly lost interest and went quiet. Nonetheless the presiding psychiatrist deemed it best to adjourn the meeting for the moment.

Now we were to have half an hour of private time and I went out into the central open air courtyard. It was a beautiful sunny day and I was feeling more and more sane all the time. I was sitting on a wooden bench watching goldfish swim about in a pond when the nurse came over and asked:

'How's it all going then?'

'Bit different from what I expected,' I replied.

'You'll get used to it,' she smiled. 'And now, guess what?'

'What?' I enquired with trepidation.

'Now we're going to do some basket weaving.'

I laughed, assuming she was joking. They couldn't actually have basket weaving. It was too much of a movie cliché of what crazy people did in crazy places like this. But she wasn't joking, and looked puzzled at my response.

'It's great fun,' she said. 'You'll love it. And so relaxing. I'll be back in a minute to assign you to your basket group.'

I was now starting to get nervous. The first two sessions had been disturbing enough. But to be a basket case in my own basket group was a real worry.

As I sat there contemplating how I had managed to get myself into this situation, an older lady came over and sat next to me on the bench. When she introduced herself I thought she seemed very sweet.

'Basket weaving next,' she said enthusiastically.

'Yes, I know,' I replied, trying to find some enthusiasm of my own.

'Do you know how long you're here for?' she asked.

'Just for the day,' I said.

She looked up at me, her head tilting slightly to one side. She smiled wistfully.

'I've been here for 40 years,' she said. 'When I came I was probably just about your age'

Well that was it! I excused myself from the woman, and before the nurse could return to assign me to my basket group, I rushed to the lockers, grabbed my bike gear, and before I even fully knew what I was doing, found myself scaling the 8 foot stone walls of Caritas. The old sandstone was rough and uneven but that gave me my footing, and before the first thread of rattan was handed out, I was over the wall, down the other side, and on to my motorbike.

I spent the rest of the afternoon sitting in the sun in Hyde Park, just enjoying the autumn warmth on my back and the fact that I wasn't feeling depressed for the first time in a long time

When I got home my father said: 'A man named Horace rang. He sounded angry. He says he wants his locker key back.'

The exhilaration of my escape from Caritas kept my depression at bay for a short time. But the worst excesses of that depression, unbeknown to me, were physiologically based. The levels of radiotherapy I was absorbing were extreme and were bound to have extreme consequences, both for my body and my mind. What's more the effects were going to be cumulative.

So as the radiotherapy continued, I sank into a state worse than ever before. I felt as if I were spinning on a fixed axis, searching about for somewhere to run for help. But I was stuck to my pivot point and there was no help to be had.

In the end I decided I had to see Professor Atkinson and I had to see him quickly. I'm not sure if I guessed that the cause of my depression was the radiotherapy. I seem to remember that I didn't. I still hadn't worked out the obvious. I think I just needed to fix the blame for my despair on someone, and in my irrational state, Leicester Atkinson seemed to be the logical choice.

Anyway I turned up at the Prince of Wales early next afternoon and demanded to see him. Sister Carter was understanding but quite reasonably suggested I wait till my normal appointment with him in two days time. But I didn't see that as reasonable. Nothing short of immediate attention was going to do. I insisted on seeing him straight away.

She said it just wasn't possible. At that moment he was in an important Board meeting upstairs. It was then I determined on a course of action which would have made any Caritas resident proud. I stormed up the stairs, found the Boardroom and kicked open the door.

There was Leicester Atkinson, sitting with three or four other men, all of whom, to my addled mind, seemed to look a lot like him.

'I am a human being!' I screamed.

They all stared at me. I knew Atkinson would throw me out, tell me he was in an important meeting, this was totally inappropriate etc. But I didn't care. It was all his fault for treating me like an experiment, like a statistic. Now at least I had told him so.

But to my surprise he excused himself, got up from the table, and came over to where I was still standing in the doorway.

'Of course you are a human being, Mr Kline' he said very solemnly. Then he led me downstairs to his office, where he sat me down, got someone to bring me coffee and waited for me to speak.

'I'm going insane', I told him. 'I'm suicidal and I don't know what to do.' Then I burbled a lot about the psychiatrist and my doubts about his diagnosis and my escape from Caritas, and my sense of hopelessness.

He listened attentively, and when I was finished said:

'The radiotherapy is undoubtedly suppressing your metabolism. That is the cause of your depression. You are not going mad.'

'Couldn't you have warned me at the beginning?' I asked.

'I should have,' he said. 'I am very sorry.' Then he stood up, shook my hand and said: 'If you need me at any time, I will make myself available.' He smiled. 'Even if I'm in a meeting. Just knock.'

After that, whilst the depression continued, at least I knew why. And knowledge is power. I put the razor blades away. When the radiotherapy was finished I had a short break before they started me on the chemo. In some ways this was the most brutal of all. At Prince of Wales they knew I wanted to keep working, so the scheme was that every Friday afternoon after work for eight weeks I would go to the hospital for my weekly injection.

It had to be Friday afternoon because soon after I got home the vomiting would begin, and it would continue all weekend. Every few minutes it would come again. Of course I soon vomited what I had in my stomach and from then on it was all dry wretching, at most a dribble of yellow bile. I literally spent the whole weekend lying on my bed with my head over the side, gagging at a bucket.

It was almost impossible to eat or even drink much, and of course whatever I did consume came straight back up. I only slept in very brief snatches, usually falling asleep with my head still hanging over the side of the bed. By the early hours of Monday morning the nausea would begin to subside and I could go back to work.

By the time mid winter came around I had finished with my chamber of horrors. I looked a little like a Belsen inmate, but I was alive. The treatment hadn't killed me, and so far nor had the cancer.

I asked Atkinson for a prognosis. Of course he couldn't give one, because I was the first. But he thought, given the normal virility of the cancer, if I could survive two years, I would have a very good chance. After that I went back to Prince of Wales initially every week, then later every month for a check up, and every time there was the fear the tumour may have come back. But it never did.

And even though the floor polish made me sick to my stomach, and I would have to stop outside the big glass doors and get myself ready before I went in, when I got there I was treated by Sister Carter and the others, including Atkinson, like a rock star. I was their great success story and they loved to see me and see me alive, still.

For years I went back to visit whenever I could, even though medically it was no longer necessary. There is an amazing bond that builds between you and people who have saved your life. I used to visit Swain too. Whenever I saw him there was always one question in my mind, but it was a question I did not have the courage to ask for a long time. One day, maybe ten years on, I heard myself say to him:

'What about the other boy? Did he make it?'

Swain hesitated and looked away.

'Yes he did,' he said finally.

I'm pretty sure it was a lie. I'm pretty sure the boy didn't make it. Did he go down the radiotherapy and chemotherapy path, but it didn't work for him? Was he too far gone at diagnosis? I would never know. What I did know was that without the boy without a name I would be without a life. That unknown young man was as much an angel to me as Doctors Thomas, Atkinson and Swain.

And I too had become an angel to thousands of others. I had got the wrong terrible illness at just the right time, and so became the vehicle for the healing of so many others. After the success with me, the team at Prince of Wales went on to refine the dosages and expand the treatment to sufferers of all kinds of cancers. My own form of teratoma, which before me had been almost 100% fatal, is these days almost 100% curable.

Because I knew I would be writing this book, I recently did some research on my teratoma and its history. The US articles I came across all seemed to talk about the first experimentations taking place in that country in 1975. That would mean that Leicester Atkinson, experimenting on me, was a full year ahead of the Americans.

Of all my miracles that seems the greatest, because I couldn't have waited till 1975. Atkinson and the hospital he worked from were in my country, in my town. And as a result I may have been the first, or one of the first in the world. That sort of luck is beyond odds, beyond percentages.

It is also wonderful to know that sometimes, through no effort on our own part, but just by being and enduring, by surviving, or perhaps like the young man by not surviving, we can be of benefit to so many others.

I don't know how much I understood at the time. Back then I still had a whole life to get on with and wasn't ready for the necessary reflection. I had a job to do, and in a few months I was going to get married.

8. WILL THE BEST MAN PLEASE STAND UP

When I came out of the fog I had been a prosecutor for six months. Somehow I had managed to keep going and keep learning. And amazingly I had committed no prosecutorial disasters. Perhaps that was because at the Crown I got to learn from some of the best.

There was one QC I worked with who, when I brought a brief to his chambers, would read each page of close legal detail as quickly as he could turn it. At the end of a few minutes, when he may have devoured dozens if not hundreds of pages of law and witness statements, he would begin to question me on all the details needing further argument or information. In court he was known as The Terminator.

He was not the only Sydney barrister who carried an epithet like that. Indeed what distinguished Sydney barristers, especially criminal barristers, from their more gentlemanly counterparts in the other States was that they were tough. They were the street fighters of the legal profession. I remember another QC I worked with who used to subject his own witnesses, in chambers, to the worst possible cross examination they might expect from his opponent in court.

It was a logical approach, but he was so brutal he would traumatise them in advance. I was even present when he reduced a battle hardened sergeant of police to tears. And whilst he waited impatiently for the witness in question to pull himself together he would bark at me or his secretary or the instructing solicitor to go out and get him some more cigars.

This same man had a regular breakfast of two double scotches before court, and another double at morning tea, lunch and immediately after court adjourned. Being tough and working 24/7 needed its fuel.

There was one youngish barrister I often faced off against who was a master of the art of opponent intimidation. Apart from taking every possible objection, and taking it in the rudest, most aggressive way, he would talk to his instructing solicitor in a stage whisper whilst you were trying to cross-examine. Often it wouldn't be about the case but about how stupid or ugly you were. Or he would ceaselessly tap his pen on the desk till it drove you insane. These were only some of the tricks he and his colleauges at the criminal bar got up to.

It forced me to acquire a keen understanding of the laws of evidence, and taught me not just to think on my feet, but in the midst of the whirlwind. It was this which later helped me get the job with the Northern Territory Attorney General. Though originally a Queenslander himself, he had seen the Sydney bar in operation, and was only ever going to have one of those piranhas as his house counsel.

It was a baptism by fire, or perhaps by fire and brimstone. Either way I was learning, and I was coming up against an array of cases. I prosecuted drug importation cases. I prosecuted jewellery smugglers. I prosecuted people under the Excise Act for keeping stills and making hooch. I prosecuted a devout Jewish woman under the Quarantine Act for chipping a piece off the Wailing Wall and bringing it back into Australia.

I was even getting the chance to prosecute some high profile defendants, including Cat Stevens who was picked up at Sydney Airport with a small quantity of cannabis in his bag. Legally it was a very simple case. He admitted possessing the cannabis but denied any knowledge of how it got into his bag. He could only suggest to the magistrate that just before leaving London a young female had made sexual advances to him, which he, being an honourable man, had declined. Perhaps being scorned, she had decided to seek revenge by planting some dope in his bag.

The magistrate believed his story and acquitted him. Perhaps he had been a fan. I certainly didn't mind. I was a fan too. Besides, I think I would have felt like a hypocrite if he had been convicted. It was only the year before when a dozen or so law students, myself included, sat around getting stoned to Cat Stevens music on the same 'illicit' substance I was now prosecuting the Cat for possessing.

But my greatest fame as a federal prosecutor came from a series of cases that provided endless fascination for the media. I was, for a time, a minor darling of the tabloid press for my prosecutions of animal smugglers. Certain protected species of birds and other wildlife could not be taken out of the country. But they fetched a big price in America and Europe if anyone could get them out.

We had people up for trying to smuggle an amazing assortment of parrots and reptiles out of the country. And they used an equally amazing variety of methods to conceal the animals. My favourite was the couple who tried to get a rare python out concealed in a baby's nappy. It was a soiled nappy to boot. I still admire the customs officer who thought to look in the nappy, and who was willing to do the necessaries.

Equally there was a range of animals that couldn't be brought in for quarantine reasons, but which also fetched a good price here. Our most notorious case, which required some amazing detective work, involved an illegally imported snake that escaped, got into the drains of the city, and was discovered by an innocent and horrified resident curled up on the seat of his suburban toilet. Proving the links in the chain that led back to the original malefactor was no mean feat.

I was still going back to Prince of Wales for regular checkups, and would always be met by Sister Carter and the team with warmth and enthusiasm, whilst I tried to hold back the need to vomit because of the floor polish. Every time I sat in the waiting room, I was conscious this could be the time when Atkinson said: 'I'm sorry but we have detected some secondaries.'

But that diagnosis still hadn't come and so I was free to get on with my life and work. Under normal circumstances no doubt I would have settled down to a long career with the Crown. But the problems of my early life, exacerbated as they had been by the cancer, left me restless and confused. I couldn't face the true cause of my pain, so I had a tendency to transfer onto other things.

My beautiful home town of Sydney, for some reason, seemed to bear the brunt of most of my discontent. It is probably one of the most attractive, sophisticated and welcoming cities in the world. But back then I blamed it for most of what ailed me. It was parochial, it was boring, it was responsible for putting me in a terrible school full of anti-Semites, and an equally repressive conservative Law School.

It was nonsense. But an abused person, who can't yet acknowledge his abuse, has to find a scapegoat. I guess Sydney was big and tough enough to take it. The tragedy was mine, not the city's. It meant I was destined, for a time, to seek my solutions outside myself, and to make the classic mistake of thinking I could run away from my pain.

But first, while I was still here I was going to try and escape into a marriage I should not have even contemplated, so young and so damaged as I was. Nonetheless contemplate it I did. The marriage was scheduled to go ahead in September. Agatha's father Mike was amazed I was still alive, but he and wife Margaret threw themselves into the preparations for a wedding in their beautiful garden.

But first I had to deal with the question of the best man. I had two main candidates, Max, my best friend from primary school, and my best friend from High School, Frank. It was a difficult decision because I think both expected the job and both had a good claim.

Frank and I had been great mates in High School and had planned to go to Law School together. But he skipped too many classes to play too much snooker and gamble on too many dog races. In the end he didn't get the marks he needed. After that, although we saw each other regularly, we didn't spend nearly the same amount of time together. Max on the other hand, of whom I had seen little during High School, for some reason became my closest friend through my University years.

In the end the decision came down to the fact that after my cancer diagnosis, when I had hesitated about the marriage to Agatha, it was Frank who had advised me to push on. So given he was in some ways responsible for the wedding going ahead, it seemed logical to give him the gig. It was a disastrous decision.

Frank and I had met during the first few weeks of high school. I think what drew me to him was not only his amazing intelligence and eloquence, but more importantly his gentleness. Frank seemed like an oasis of calm and sensibleness amidst my turmoil and pain.

He was an amateur petrologist, which means he collected rocks. I remember in our first year his giving the class a long and impassioned demonstration of his rock collection, during some sort of show and tell in science class.

Nearly everyone was asleep by the end, but Frank didn't notice. When he was passionate about something, his passion was all consuming, in its own quiet way. I liked that about him too. His advice to marry Agatha came from that same place. He believed in true love and he was going to make sure his friend didn't miss his chance.

What happened after that, and in such a short time, I am at a loss to even begin to understand. Over the previous couple of years his drinking and gambling had increased, and everyone was encouraging him to cut back on both, but neither was at a point where anyone felt there was a real problem.

It all seemed to begin when Frank went to see the Clint Eastwood film *Play Misty for Me* where Eastwood is a DJ who gets involved with an obsessed female fan and a lot of knives get flashed around. Afterwards Frank was very disturbed and was having trouble sleeping. He told me he was haunted by the images in the film. But as if in some perverse attempt to ward off the evil of the movie, he started carrying a knife himself.

Not long afterwards I got a call from his father. He told me Frank had come over to their house drunk, and had threatened all the family, including his younger siblings, with the knife. They didn't know what to do. They didn't understand. Nor did I. It happened again a week or so later and this time one of the younger children had to sneak off and call the police. I don't think Frank was actually arrested, but the police did make a very firm point of advising him against wielding a knife at his unsuspecting family.

I tried to talk to him about this, but he just kept blaming the film, like it had somehow possessed him. So I spent hours with him analysing the minutiae of *Play Misty for Me*. Clearly the film was touching off something else, but to this day I have no idea what it could have been. At the time I was just totally confused, so much so I didn't even think to advise him to get help.

This was partly because he still came across as so plausible, as an intelligent young man who, despite everything, still had control of his life. We would finish our long sessions and he would thank me and make sure I knew everything was going to be all right.

'Thanks mate,' he would say, 'I'm on top of it. ' As he spoke he was still the organised little rock collector I had always known and believed in. So I believed in him still.

But then next thing he was calling me over to his flat in Newtown where he was in bed with his girlfriend of the time, and telling me that as he loved us both so much he really thought I ought to have sex with her. She was a sensible girl, but such was his ability to entwine people with his false logic, he had managed to convince her, at least partially, of the wisdom of his idea.

I didn't take them up on the offer, and it made him angry. No doubt his girlfriend was very relieved. In any event their relationship didn't last much longer. When they broke off he took up immediately with a flamboyant redhead whom he also wanted me to sleep with. But here I was even less keen, because between the two women a lot had intervened.

It started when he rang me one night round midnight. His voice was pretty much as calm as always, but what he had to say didn't fit the tone.

'See, mate, I've turned the knife on myself.'

'What?!'

'I've stuck it in my belly.' I felt sick. 'But it's ok for now. You remember what we learned in cadets.'

'I wasn't in the cadets,' I reminded him, trying as hard as I could to keep calm.

'Oh yeah,' he said, almost wistfully. 'You should have been, it was fun, and we learned a lot about...'

'Frank!'

'Oh sorry, yeah, well you know, it's not the 'going in' that's the problem, it's the 'pulling out'. You know like when you shoot a parrot.'

'Parrot? What?'

'Like when you shoot a parrot, there's just a tiny hole in its chest where the bullet goes in, but a big bloody hole in its back where the bullet comes out.' I couldn't speak. 'So it's not really a problem when you put the knife in, it's when you pull it out that everything gets ripped up.'

I waited a moment to catch my breath then said, as gently and lovingly as I could:

'Frank, please don't pull the knife out.'

'I don't know, mate,' he said. His voice was childlike. It was as though

I were talking to the little petrologist again. Then suddenly it got hard and angry and very grown up: 'I think it'll be real good if I pull it out.'

I talked very fast after that. I don't remember what I said, but in the end I managed to convince him to wait where he was without extracting the knife. I would be right over and in the meantime I would call an ambulance.

I needed to ride across country from Maroubra, so the ambulance got there much quicker than I. Frank let the ambulance men in, but then held them at bay by threatening to pull the knife out if they got any closer. When I arrived the two ambos were sitting together on the couch with Frank in a chair opposite, the knife sticking out of his stomach. It was the most macabre Mexican standoff.

'Goodaye, mate!' he smiled at me. 'Just waiting for you to get here. OK boys I'm ready.'

And he surrendered himself to the ambulance men. What happened after that is a blur to me. I know he was taken to emergency at RPA and the attending doctor there must have, not surprisingly, decided he needed psychiatric help, because once the knife was removed and he was stabilised, Frank found himself committed to Callan Park.

A few days later I went over there to see him, but he had been discharged. He had managed to convince the head psychiatrist he was no danger to himself or anyone else. We all thought it was amazing. No-one talked their way out of that place. Except Frank. Frank talked his way out.

It was then I began to realise how dangerous his phoney plausibility really was. I started to worry about a best man who might decide to take charge:

'And now, ladies and gentlemen, the bride and groom will *not* cut the cake. I have a much better use for the knife!'

At the same time I still clung to the belief maybe something could be done to bring him back from the spiral he was descending into. After his release from Callan Park there was a period when everything seemed to return to normal. And of course he told me how he had learned his lesson, how Callan Park had snapped him back to reality.

Then one night he called again: 'See mate, I don't want to be any trouble. I *am* going to cut my wrists, but I've laid out paper everywhere so there won't be any bleeding on the rugs or furniture.'

This time when I arrived the ambulance men were waiting outside. Frank's reputation had preceded him, and they weren't going in till I got there. So the three of us went in together, and sure enough, there was Frank, in a beanbag, holding his bleeding wrists out sideways to bleed on the paper he had laid down.

I can't remember if he was sent to Callan Park this time or not, but if he were, he talked his way out again. Now the wedding was only a couple of months away, and Frank's behaviour was getting harder to ignore, to say the least. Why I hesitated to sack him as my best man, I can't really say. I just couldn't let go of someone whom I had loved and who had always been the very antithesis of what I was now witnessing.

Whatever the cause of my hesitation, I justified it by telling myself Frank was no danger to anyone else. He was only a danger to himself. However unfortunately, or perhaps fortunately, that was all about to change.

Again I was called over in the middle of the night but this time Frank's weapon of choice was different. He was sitting up in bed with a shotgun across his lap and he started talking to me about how I needed to sleep with his redhead. I guess he could see I was more focused on the gun, so he decided to leave the sex and concentrate on the violence. He lifted the gun so the barrel was pointed at his mouth and said:

'I'm just going to blow my head off.' Then slowly he turned the gun around till it pointed at me. 'But first I'm going to blow you away,' he added.

I still cannot explain why, but I felt no fear. The amazing thing is that whenever in my life I have been confronted with 'clear and present danger' I have always been quite clam. Ironically on the other hand, because of my background, I have wasted a lot of my life in terrible fear over phantoms that not only did not exist, but could never hurt me even if they did.

But here, confronted with a very sad sick boy, who was quite capable of very real violence, and who was chillingly about to turn that violence on me, I was not afraid.

'No,' I said, 'you won't'.

And I walked from the room with, I assumed, the gun still pointed at my back, opened the door, and without looking back, closed it behind me.

Now there was the real possibility that Agatha or members of her family would be in danger. The wedding was only three weeks away and I needed to act. I rang Frank and told him, given all that had happened, I couldn't risk him as my best man. In fact, I told him, he wasn't to come to the wedding.

'I'm very disappointed, mate,' he said. 'I don't think you've given me a chance.'

So now I was without a best man. Full of embarrassment I asked Max if he would step in. To my amazement and to his credit, he showed no resentment at being asked second, and took on the task with gusto.

The wedding went off beautifully, thanks to Mike and Margaret, the only real hitch being when the priest caught my sister's fiancé running a poker school for some of the old aunts. We had a short driving holiday for a honeymoon and then moved into a tiny rented apartment above the fish and chips shop on Bronte Beach, where we stayed for six months before moving to a house in Hunter's Hill.

Agatha was now enrolled in an MA, but she never went to lectures. In fact she never went anywhere, just stayed in the house, doing not much at all. She did cook some nice meals whilst we were there, but most days she would ring me up at work and ask me to bring home take away. When I look back I have no doubt she was suffering from depression. After all she had married someone with a lot of problems, which would have been impacting on her in ways I couldn't begin to consciously know. What's more she had problems of her own. I was to discover these much later on. They were perhaps not so different from my own. Damaged people will find each other, much to their mutual disadvantage.

I started to become very restless in my job. Lou Jarman retired at the end of my first year, and whereas his replacement was a good boss and a good lawyer, I didn't have anything like the same rapport with him. My past was tapping at my unconscious but I didn't want to let it in, not yet, not for a long time. So I decided the solution to my unease was to make a change.

I started searching the employment ads and one Saturday morning I found a job for a barrister in the Northern Territory, resident in Alice Springs.

'Want to go to Alice Springs to live?' I asked Agatha.

She seemed enthusiastic. Maybe she was hoping to run away from her pain too.

The ad didn't give many details, so I rang up the employment agency in North Sydney to find out more. They asked me to come in for an interview. They told me the job was as 'house counsel' with Everingham & Co. Paul Everingham was the Northern Territory Attorney-General and his law firm had branches in Darwin, Tennant Creek, Katherine and Alice Springs. His idea was to employ someone who would take briefs exclusively from the various solicitors in all the branches of his firm, someone who would travel about doing the court work for the firm in all the towns of the Territory.

He had advertised in Sydney because he wanted a pen tapping, insult mumbling, 'object to everything that moves' type of barrister, and he knew Sydney was where he would find that. His theory was that because most lawyers in the Territory were schooled in the gentlemanly practices of the Adelaide bar, if he could get hold of a nice aggressive bastard from Sydney, he could cut a swath through his opponents.

He was particularly looking for a criminal barrister, as I was to discover later, because he knew they were the meanest of the mean. So my experience, limited though it was, gave me an advantage there. In fact only a few days after the interview, the agency called me in to offer me the job. I was very excited, not only because of the adventure of going to the outback and the challenge of the job, but because it was offering a salary of $15,000. That may not sound like a lot now, but if you know in those days I was on a salary of $4,990 per annum at the Crown, then you can see it was around three times what I was currently earning. However the agent was about to resile from that.

'You would be taking briefs in every area of legal practice,' he said, leaning back in his chair and rolling the words around his cheeks. He was very pompous. 'Now clearly your experience is limited to criminal law. And of course you are *very* young. Your value is therefore...how shall I say...limited.' He paused to make sure his pearls had been effectively cast before the swine. 'So of course you can't expect to receive the salary as advertised. Nonetheless Mr Everingham is prepared to make you an offer of $10,000 per annum.'

I politely declined. It seemed to me either I wasn't right for the job, in which case I shouldn't be offered it at all, or if I were right, I should get the salary they advertised. If I took less I would be telling myself I wasn't quite up to it, wasn't quite worth it, and that would be a bad way to start a new career. The interviewer dismissed me with a wave of the hand.

I went home and forgot about it. In some ways I was relieved. Alice Springs would have been an adventure, but in those days when communications were not as they are today, a very big adventure in a very remote place. And I was worried I wouldn't have the knowledge and experience to tackle the responsibilities of the job, especially the broad range of law I would have to cover.

But the following Saturday morning I got a call. It was Paul Everingham. He had flown to Sydney to see me. He had the employment agent with him. Could they come over and meet with me now? Half an hour later the flamboyant figure of Paul Everingham was sweeping into our little house with a somewhat chastened looking agent following in his wake.

Everingham was short of stature but large of presence. He was a rough diamond orator, one of the few politicians Australia has produced who could walk the world stage with confidence, had he been given the chance. He later became Chief Minister of the Northern Territory and later still entered Federal Parliament on the conservative side. This worried the Labor Government very much. They saw Everingham as the inevitable leader of the Liberal Party and someone they would not be able to match. They were so worried that when he first got up to speak in Parliament they abandoned, for the first time in nearly 200 years, the Westminster convention of not interrupting a member in his maiden speech. They heckled and attacked him as though he were already leader of the Opposition.

And here he was sitting in my lounge room with a big smile on his face.

'What do you mean knocking back my job?' he laughed.

'I just thought...' I began, but he interrupted.

'Well I want you to take the job.'

I was very flattered he had come all this way to try and talk me into taking the job. Still I said:

'I've been thinking about it, and your agent does have a point. All my experience is in criminal law. I'm not sure...' But he interrupted me again:

'A case is a case,' he insisted. 'Same deal. You just got to get on top of your opponent. A gun Sydney barrister like you won't have any trouble beating the shit out of the 'gentlemen' up in the Territory.'

'I think you've got me confused with some of our defence counsel,' I said. 'We at the Commonwealth Crown are more at the gentlemanly end.'

'Look here,' he said, abandoning his larrikin tone and getting serious, 'when I went to Alice Springs, Brian Martin made mince meat of me in every case we fought. I just kept losing. But I was young and I had to learn. Maybe you don't know much about workers' comp or family law just yet, but you'll learn, and if Brian carves you up a few times while you're learning, that's ok with me.'

He had spoken with such open sincerity, he really was difficult to resist. But there were some things I still needed to know. To begin with we were worlds apart politically. How would that work?

'I need to tell you I'm a socialist,' I said, very self importantly.

'Are you now,' he laughed. 'I have two partners. One is President of the Labor Party, and the other is even worse: he's a swinging voter. I think we can tolerate a socialist as well.'

Then there's the question of the salary,' I said. 'Maybe you don't think I'm worth the 15 grand you advertised, but the way I see it...'

'I'll give you 17,' he said.

I was shocked into a long moment of silence, finally saying:

'But your agent said you...'

'He's an idiot,' he said, with the man sitting right there. 'I didn't give him permission to offer less. Just thought he was doing me a favour, didn't you Bruce?' And he turned a big smile on the agent, whose mixture of anger and humiliation melted away.

'That is a good offer,' I confessed.

'Glad you approve,' he said. 'By the way, we can pay you the last two grand as perks so you don't pay tax on it. Motor vehicle expenses. Rent.' Then he smiled again. 'Unless of course that offends your socialist sensibilities.'

I told him the socialist within would survive, and the deal was done. I was heading for the wild west.

9. AN UNEXPECTED ANGEL

It was September 1975 when we arrived in Alice Springs on the Old Ghan, a magnificent 1920s German built train with sleeper carriages all polished brass and porcelain, waiters liveried in white for breakfast and black for dinner, a dining car like something out of Agatha Christie, and a lounge car just for sitting and watching the desert go by.

It was probably the slowest train in the world at the time. The tracks could not be fixed to the shifting sands of the desert floor, so they just lay there subject to the caprice of the weather. It meant at times the train needed to go so slowly you could get out and walk alongside. And when it rained the tracks just got washed away and the passengers found themselves stranded. The trip was supposed to take two days from Adelaide to Alice Springs, but there was no real timetable and the journey could take three or four. The record for the slowest trip (which admittedly did include a track washout) was over one month.

I would lie on my bed in the sleeping car or sit in the lounge and just watch the changing landscape. Going south to north across the Australian continent means a change in the desert and its vegetation every few minutes. For 1500 kilometres I had enforced leisure, which was something I knew I needed because I had some hard work and a steep learning curve ahead of me.

We were met at the station by Everingham's partners (he himself was then running the Darwin Office). John Reeves, President of the Labor Party, was not much older than me, maybe 25. He would go on to become the Federal member for The Northern Territory and later a Federal Court judge. The other partner in the firm Peter Howard (the swinging voter) was much older, probably pushing 30.

It was a young person's town. Everingham himself was only 32. Most of his solicitors were under 30. The oldest lawyer in town was Brian Martin who had achieved the Methuselian age of 40. He was a top practitioner, as I would soon discover. He would go on to become Chief Justice of the Northern Territory.

As we drove in John Reeve's car to the flat Everingham had arranged, John was already briefing me on my first case. It was the beginning of the deluge. I would come to understand that being house counsel for Everingham meant you were going to earn your money. However I wouldn't be the only busy lawyer. They were all incredibly busy, and this is why:

Almost everyone of European descent in Alice Springs was from somewhere else. And most were running away from something. It was Australia's equivalent of the French Foreign Legion. And like the Legion, whose traditional home is the North African desert, Alice Springs was a desert community as far away as you could get from wherever you lived. It was right in the centre of Australia, over 2000 kilometres from Sydney. Even the nearest town, the dusty little mining town of Tennant Creek was 500 kilometres away.

Like the Legion too, the community was tiny. The town was no more than 14,000 people. If you included outlying cattle properties and Aboriginal settlements, the whole area for several hundred thousand square kilometres would still have had no more than 20,000 souls. And yet, because they were mostly escapees from something or someone or just from themselves, they were not the typical law abiding cross section of your typical law abiding community. Even the Northern Territory Police had members with criminal records.

In my first year the 20,000 people of greater Alice Springs managed to commit more murders than the whole of the city of Sydney with its population of over 3 million. And that's only the statistics for the most serious crime. Being the sort of people they were, the residents of Alice Springs were always doing something dodgy to one another, be it criminal act, tortuous malefaction or contractual breach.

Alcohol played a big part. At the time the Northern Territory consumed about 2000% more beer per capita than any other State. People would drive from Alice Springs to Darwin with several dozen cans of beer which they would consume on the way. They would just throw the empties out the window. It meant that throughout the whole 1500 kilometres, it was not possible to find a piece of roadside that wasn't covered with cans. Sometimes whole trees were surrounded with a mountain of empties rising 2 metres up the trunk, where successive people had stopped to take a break.

Even the simplest social event was alcohol sodden. The etiquette was you couldn't just drop in on a friend for afternoon coffee, without bringing two dozen cans of beer with you. And most times the coffee was forgotten and all two dozen were consumed. So the town was awash with drink driving cases, drunken assaults and drunken domestic violence, not to mention contracts people had unwisely entered into under the influence of alcohol.

Part of the process of running away often involved starting a business that the person was ill equipped to run, or which was economically unsound or just plain illegal. This too gave rise to lots of litigation. And because people drove so wildly, even when they were not drunk, motor vehicle injury cases abounded.

So litigation was everywhere, and at least as far as Paul's firm was concerned, it was all about to funnel down to me. At the age of 24 I was going to have to run an array of cases which, in the cities, would only be handled by very experienced counsel; murder trials, million dollar damages suits, complicated divorce proceedings, mining claims, workers' compensation cases. The volume of work, the amount of new learning required, and the responsibility for all those peoples' lives and liberties and fortunes, was going to put a burden of work and emotional strain on me I could not have imagined.

And that didn't even include the cases I would have to run in Tennant Creek, Katherine and Darwin. But I guess when I look back, it was all perfectly designed to achieve what unconsciously I wanted to achieve. My 'foreign legion' posting was going to be a very efficient way of avoiding what I needed to face and what I needed to do. It would also be the nascent beginnings of a workaholia I would exploit as the very best way not to look at myself and my past.

And so long as I was super busy, I not only wouldn't have to listen to the cause of my emotional pain, I would be able to blame the pain on the busyness. The law firm of Everingham & Co would easily succeed my school and university and home town, as the new cause of my fears and discontent. It could easily become the new culprit.

But whoever you erroneously try to blame, life always finds a way of knocking at the door of the unconscious. The Universe moves you on and says: 'Take a look at this! Take a lesson from that!' It had tried to move me on a few times already and was about to try again.

I was sitting in my 'chambers' one day not long after arriving in The Alice. 'Chambers' is perhaps too grand a term for the room underneath Everingham's Office, which used to be a garage and which I now shared with the local Building Society. I was staring at the pile of briefs I had already inherited, all neatly wrapped in their pink ribbon, each calling out to me for immediate attention, wondering which one to attack first.

Then Ross Clifford came in. He was my age, had worked in a criminal law firm in Sydney's notorious Kings Cross, had been a leading light in the

Young Liberals there, and, of all things, wanted to be a Baptist Minister. He
had a passion for life.

'Attempted murder case, mate!' he beamed at me, throwing a brief on
my desk. I looked at him and then at the brief. 'Well open it! We're on in
two days.'

'How can that be? What about the committal and...'

'That's all happened. Someone else was looking after him. But he
sacked them. Said he needed a Jew. Said only a Jew would understand him.'
He hesitated for a moment. 'You are Jewish aren't you? I told him you
were.'

'Sort of,' I mumbled, completely confused. 'My Dad was Jewish.'

'That's got to be close enough,' Ross smiled.

'Why does he want a Jew,' I asked, finally starting to focus. 'Is he
Jewish?'

'I don't know. Maybe.' He thought for a minute. 'Actually I don't think
he is. I'll get you in to see him and you can find out.'

'Shouldn't I read this first,' I said, indicating the brief.

'Look, if you really have to,' he laughed. 'I'll get you in round two then.
Enough time?'

'A whole hour to read a big fat brief,' I said. 'Sure. That's starting to
feel like luxury in this job.'

The case was The Crown v Joseph Ember. The accused was a man in
his fifties who, whilst living in a mining camp near Tennant Creek was
alleged to have stabbed one of his fellow workers. He had been charged
with attempted murder, and there was a back up charge of unlawful
wounding.

It seemed that Ember was a Czechoslovakian Catholic who had risked
his life hundreds of times during the War smuggling Jews out of Nazi
Germany and Czechoslovakia. In the mining camp there was a group of ex
German Nazis, including a man by the name of Baeker who was the one he
had stabbed. They would taunt him constantly for being a 'Jew lover', and
sing *Deutschland Uber Alles* under his bunkhouse window when he was trying
to sleep. Ember didn't deny the stabbing, but said it was in self defence.

When I met with him in the cells, the first thing that struck me was
Ember's gentleness. He was a small quiet man, almost serene. It seemed
impossible to believe he could be capable of an unprovoked attack.

'As a Jew you'll understand,' he said to me, his gentle eyes full of trust.

But did I understand? Did having an anti-Semitic mother and a Jewish
father help me understand, especially when I was doing my best to repress
all memory of that? All I knew was that I felt very uncomfortable and didn't
want this brief.

'I'm not really Jewish,' I said in the end. 'My Dad was Jewish, but my
Mum wasn't and that means I can't be.'

'Technicalities,' he said. 'You understand what happened in the war?'

'Perhaps I understand something about it.'

'I can see in your eyes, you understand all I need you to understand.'

'Mr Ember,' I said, 'you are facing a very serious charge. You could go to gaol for a long time. I'm only 24. We could brief someone more senior, get someone experienced up from Sydney.'

'I don't want experience, I want someone who cares.'

'It's not about caring. It's about good advocacy?' I heard an edge in my voice I didn't like.

Ember was a man of vast life experience. He couldn't possibly have known what was happening in my mind, especially when I myself didn't know. But he knew something was happening. He walked over and put his hand on my shoulder

'Yes it is,' he said very softly. 'It is always about caring.'

I heard myself sigh deeply

'Why *did* you do it?' I asked.

'I had to. He had a knife. He would have killed me.'

'I'm sorry,' I said. 'I didn't mean that. I meant why did you do what you did in the war, with the Jews. You weren't a Jew. Why did you take such terrible risks for them?'

'I couldn't not,' he said quite simply.

And now, for all the unwanted thoughts this man was already bringing to the surface of my unwilling conscious, I too 'couldn't not' defend Joseph Ember.

The case, though serious, was quite simple from a legal point of view. Baeker said Ember had attacked him, unprovoked. If the jury believed that they would convict of attempted murder. Ember said Baeker came at him with a knife, they had struggled and in the struggle Baeker had been stabbed. If the jury believed that they would acquit Ember on the basis of self defence. If they believed Ember's story, but felt he could still have avoided stabbing Baeker, they could convict of the less serious charge of unlawful wounding. It really just came down to whom they believed, and that in turn would depend heavily on what I could do in the cross examination of Baeker.

I was not at my emotional best leading up to the trial. I was 'too close to the case' as lawyers say. I admired Ember for what he had done in the War and for the sort of man he was, and I had no doubt he was innocent. I was to find over the years I could never distance myself enough when I believed a client to be innocent and when his liberty was in my hands. Then of course because of my own background and abuse, with its sick anti-Semitic overtones, I was way too close in another way.

On the day, as I sat at the bar table, with Ember behind me, waiting for the judge to enter, it was all I could do to stop from shaking. Then we were all standing as Mr Justice Muirhead took the bench. Jim Muirhead was a judge I would appear before many times over the next three years. I would come to admire his erudition and his understanding of human nature. But for the moment this was my first time before him and that made me nervous too.

The first thing we had to do was empanel the jury. I had no real reason to challenge anyone until I heard a juror called by the name of Mueller. I turned to see a young man, maybe 25 years old, big and solid with red hair. Obviously with a name like Mueller there was a chance he was German or German origin and might be biased against my client. As soon as he was called I rose on my still shaky nervous legs to make the challenge. But Ember was on his feet too, tugging at my barrister's gown. I turned to him.

'He's young,' Ember insisted. 'He won't be like the last generation.'

I tried anxiously to argue with him in the short time we had as the young Mueller crossed the floor of the courtroom.

'Maybe,' I said, 'but why risk it.'

'Because unless we risk it, who will? We have to stop it in this generation. We have to trust!'

And that was it. Mueller had the bible in his hand. Too late to challenge. This amazing man, who had seen the very worst of the German race, was going to risk his own liberty to prove the goodness and resilience of humankind. So Mueller was empanelled as a juror, and was, to my great discomfort, made foreman of the jury.

Nonetheless, even if I doubted the wisdom of Ember's decision, his courage had the effect of taking my nerves from me. As the prosecutor made his opening address, I started to feel I might be able to do what I needed to do for my client.

In cross-examination of Baeker I managed to punch all sorts of holes in his testimony. It really wasn't very difficult because he hadn't thought through any of his lies. I didn't doubt most of the jurors could tell his evidence was a fabrication.

When Ember went into the witness box he was as believable as Baeker was not, and the prosecutor could do nothing to shake him. And then the first day of the trial was over. The next day we gave our final addresses and the jurors retired to consider their verdict. The Clerk of Courts in those days was a young man named Peter Campbell. As the jury was filing out he said to me:

'Well done, mate. I reckon you're home.'

I went to say something back but he held up his hand to stop me:

'Can't talk now', he smiled. 'Got to go and listen to the deliberations.' And he followed the jury out.

I had no idea what he meant. Was there some sort of obscure Northern Territory rule where the Clerk of Courts got to sit in with the jury? The prosecutor explained the jury room was a tin shed out the back of the Supreme Court. It was not at all sound proofed. It was the Clerk of Court's job to guard the jury by sitting outside the shed. He could not help but hear everything they said. That was, as far as I know, a phenomenon unique to Alice Springs and one that I suspect has not been repeated elsewhere in the common law world. At least I hope not.

The jury was out for nearly six hours. Had they gone over the six hours, under Northern Territory law they would have had to be discharged and a new trial ordered. As they took their seats I felt my nerves return in full force. I tried to tell myself we were in a good position. Baeker had come off badly, Ember very well. And the Clerk of Courts was looking across and smiling at me.

Now the judge was back and the Clerk was on his feet facing Mueller who was also on his feet. Campbell was saying:

'On the charge of attempted murder, do you find the accused Joseph Ember guilty or not guilty?'

There seemed now to be such silence and not just because no-one was speaking. It was a profound silence a lot like the silence when I'd woken from my operation. In the end I don't think I heard Mueller's voice. I just saw a brief twisted 'smile of despair' cross his lips and then I read those same lips as they pronounced the one word:

'Guilty.'

I felt sick, and in slow motion turned to my client, whose voice came out of the fog to me, deep and distorted, as if also in slow motion:

'It is all right. You did your best,' he was saying.

And now the judge was dismissing the jury and adjourning the sentencing till the following day. Ember was being led away. I watched him leave the courtroom and then I caught sight of the Clerk, looking surprised and confused. He was talking to one of the juror's at the door of the court. He kept looking across at me. Soon he was heading my way.

'I've got something to tell you,' he was saying. 'I shouldn't. But I will.'

He then recounted a story I found it hard to take in at the time. I'm sure I would have found it hard to take in at any time, but especially the way I was now. The shock and disappointment of the verdict, because of my own personal unconscious concerns, had left me feeling deeply responsible, almost culpable.

Campbell, as usual, had heard all the deliberations. Apparently right from the beginning the jury had split 9-3. Nine were absolutely convinced of Ember's innocence and wanted to acquit outright. The three others, led by the foreman Mueller, wanted to convict of the principal charge of attempted murder. Their arguments for conviction, it seems, had little to do with the evidence. They ranged from things as logical as the suggestion that Ember had shifty eyes, right down to the fact that if he were such a Jew lover he must be a communist and therefore had to have initiated the violence with Baeker.

Fortunately the quality of their argument only served to make the majority more determined to acquit. The debate raged for near on six hours with neither side making a dint in the other's resolve. However once they were at risk of being discharged, Mueller came up with a compromise suggestion. He pointed out that if they were discharged a new jury might see the sort of 'sense' he and the other two had been arguing, and the majority wouldn't want that, now would they?

So his deal was they should convict Ember of the far less serious backup charge of unlawful wounding. That way the majority would probably keep him out of gaol and the minority would have the satisfaction of not seeing him get off scot free. The majority were not happy with this as they felt Ember was not guilty of anything. But equally they didn't want to risk him being convicted of attempted murder at a re-trial. So just before the six hours ran out they agreed to Mueller's compromise.

Campbell knew all this and that's why he had smiled at me. If my shock had been substantial, imagine how he felt when Mueller got on his feet and double crossed the majority by announcing a conviction for attempted murder. Campbell knew one of the jurors personally, as is often the case in a small town. So once they were discharged he got hold of the man and tactfully questioned him. Of course he couldn't admit to listening outside the shed, but said:

'That's interesting, mate. We all thought he might go down on the backup, but we were sure you wouldn't convict of attempted murder.'

'We didn't,' the man said in surprise.

'Yes you did!' Campbell told him.

It seems that in the mix of high drama and legal formality, not one juror had the wherewithal to notice they had been double crossed. Not one realised they had just been party to convicting a man on a charge they were determined to acquit him of.

So now I was faced with a legal conundrum I couldn't begin to unravel. One thing I did know was that it was unique in Australian jurisprudential history, and probably the jurisprudential history of the Western world.

In those days an appeal from the Northern Territory Supreme Court went straight to the High Court which is the ultimate court of appeal in Australia. I needed to appeal to the High Court, but how, and on what basis exactly. The problem is that with criminal trials usually the only basis for an appeal is on a point of law or a point of misdirection of the jury by the trial judge.

It is almost impossible to launch an appeal that impugns a jury's verdict, because by definition the jury's deliberations are in secret and therefore there is nothing known which can be impugned. However here we did know the jury didn't want to convict because we heard what they had said. I could see myself getting up before a bench of three or five largely conservative High Court judges who had never been outside a city, trying to tender an affidavit from the Clerk of the Supreme Court in Alice Springs saying he had been listening at the tin shed out the back.

And would Campbell be willing to give such an affidavit when it would certainly mean his job? Could I even ask him? Could I instead approach the jurors and ask them for affidavits? Would that be ethical? And even if it were, wouldn't the first question from the High Court judges be why I had even thought to talk to the jurors?

It all seemed so impossible. But I had to make it possible. I could not let Joseph Ember go to gaol just because he had put his faith in a young German man who had failed to honour that faith in the extreme. But before I could address any of this, I had to prepare my plea in mitigation of penalty.

I stayed up late that night struggling to perfect my arguments. In the morning I addressed Muirhead for around an hour, mostly detailing the amazing courage Ember had shown in the war. Muirhead gave me a very hard time, especially when I spoke about the taunting by Baeker and the others and their singing of *Deutschland Uber Alles*.

'I heard them sing that in restaurants when I was there last year,' he snapped at me. 'It means nothing. You don't try to kill someone because you don't like their singing.'

At the end of my address Muirhead retired for a short while and when he came back he asked Joseph Ember to stand. I stood next to my client as Muirhead talked directly to him, taking some pains to stress how serious was the charge with which he had been convicted. It wasn't looking good. But after about fifteen minutes, he started to move onto some of the details of Ember's past life, and then it seemed we might be lucky enough to get a sentence at the shorter end of the range. In the end he concluded with:

'Men like you are rare, Joseph Ember. They deserve a chance.'

But I had no idea even then how big a chance he was about to give my client. He took the extraordinarily unusual step of releasing someone who had just been convicted of a very serious crime of violence, on a two year good behaviour bond. I felt a huge smile cover my face. Then I heard Muirhead say:

'Mr Kline, what we need from young barristers in our court system is men and women who care. You are one of those. I congratulate you for it.'

As the court adjourned, I turned to Ember and now it was he who was wearing the huge smile.

'Is it appropriate to say "I told you so"?' he laughed.

'It is appropriate,' I said.

It was a miraculous result. But I still had the jury question on my mind. Over coffee with my client, now a free man, I told him about what had happened in the tin shed and about Mueller's double cross at verdict time. He looked disappointed.

'We can go to the High Court if you want,' I said, 'to try and remove the conviction against your name.'

'I don't care about that. It's Mueller I care about. He has done himself a great disservice.'

I didn't know what to say to that. I was too young to understand the wisdom of the remark. I understand it now however. At the time I just said:

'But you're on probation for two years. Are you all right with that?'

'Of course,' he smiled. 'I've been on probation all my life.'

And as he said that I realised I had been on probation all my life too. We all have. He was a wise man, Joseph Ember. In the short time I knew him he taught me many things. He showed me how dazzling real courage was, in the face of real adversity. Not just his courage in the war, but the courage of trusting his liberty to a raw young barrister with nowhere near the skill nor the experience needed, just because his instincts told him that young man cared.

He also led me to an understanding of the power of forgiveness. As far as I know Ember was not a practising Christian, but his attitude to Mueller was pure 'love thine enemy'. As I said, at that time I didn't understand, at least not intellectually, though perhaps my own instincts felt the power of it. But over my lifetime I would often recall Mueller's sick twisted smile as he pronounced the verdict and Ember's serenity as he received it, and that told me a lot about the person who does, and the person who doesn't forgive. Over time I came to understand you forgive your enemy not for their sake, but for your own.

But most of all, though it would take me years to understand it, by allowing me to represent him, this man helped to loosen the grip of my abusers, and further the process of bringing the truth back to my conscious mind. My mother had been an anti-Semite. Joseph Ember had fought against such people. I had fought for Ember. Therefore I had struck a blow against my mother and a blow for my own freedom. For all this I have to say Joseph Ember qualifies as one of my major angels.

10. THE WILD WILD WEST

Though I have compared Alice Springs to the French Foreign Legion, the jury's tin shed was probably more like the Wild West. Many things in Alice Springs were. Take for example the case of Peter Dean, a solicitor who worked for Everingham. One day just after my experience with Joseph Ember, Dean set off to argue a case in the Supreme Court. He was up against a lawyer named Ted Skuse. Only a few minutes after he left, the office had a visit from one of his former clients, a man by the name of Prus Gryzbrowski. I can't remember what Prus' legal problem had been, but he didn't like the way Peter Dean had handled it, to say the least.

He arrived in the upstairs reception wielding a pistol and demanding to know the whereabouts of Dean. The receptionist showed remarkable courage and cool, and just told him she had no idea where Dean was. But Prus was not to be deterred. He barged into the office, running about, waving the pistol, getting more and more agitated and screaming at everyone to tell him where Dean was. Finally he got hold of one of the secretaries and pinned her to the wall with the gun to her head. Under that sort of pressure she understandably told him where Dean had gone.

And so Prus was off, thundering down the stairs, and heading for the Court. Though I had heard some commotion upstairs, I had no idea what was happening till I saw Prus flash by my downstairs office flailing his gun in the air. Peter Howard and others followed him at a discrete distance. At the bottom of the stairs they headed in the opposite direction to get the police.

Unfortunately they were never going to have time to get the police and still beat Prus to the Courthouse. And in those days security was an unknown concept. So Prus just walked into the back of the court. Sitting at the bar table with their backs to him were Dean, Skuse and two other lawyers waiting for their cases to be called. The problem for Prus was that as they were all seated and as they were all wearing wigs and gowns, he couldn't tell one from another.

Now he might have walked up to the front of the court so he could see which one was his intended victim. Even better perhaps he could have re-thought the whole scheme. Unfortunately he did neither of these. He decided instead to take a one in four chance and just fire in the general direction of the bar table. He hit Ted Skuse in the back.

As Skuse slumped to the floor, I'm not sure if Prus realised his mistake, or if, having fired one shot he was satisfied, whoever he hit. Anyway after the shot he dropped the gun and strolled out of the court into the waiting arms of the cavalry who were arriving just that little bit too late.

Fortunately for Prus and even more fortunately for Skuse, the shot was not fatal. Prus was sent to Yatala Prison in Adelaide for a long time. For Dean and for the rest of us, it was a pretty graphic reminder that in Alice Springs, if you are going to lose a case for a client, do your best to stay on good terms with them nonetheless.

Alice Springs was the sort of place however, that when Agatha and I were looking for an ironing lady some twelve months later and Mrs Prus applied (Prus' wife was not known as Mrs Gryzbrowski but as Mrs Prus), we didn't hesitate to give her the job. But we were always careful to compliment her on her work and pay her on time.

Social life was like the Wild West too, licentious and alcohol sodden. In fact it was hard to find a part of life in which alcohol didn't play a part. When Ross Clifford moved to Tennant Creek, and I was up there, I would sometimes go to watch him play cricket. In temperatures well in excess of 40 degrees centigrade, the locals felt they could best keep themselves hydrated by drinking a continual stream of beer. So all the fielders stood in position can in hand. And of course they needed to go to the toilet quite a lot. So a rule was developed that a fielder could leave the field at any time, but had to put his beer can at the spot where he was fielding. The game continued and if the ball hit the can on the full the batter was out.

My best remembered 'but for the alcohol' event involved a hard drinking lawyer by the name of Graeme Houston. He was in the Alice when we arrived but about a year later he took a job in Darwin. The next time we were up there he asked Agatha and I and a few other Darwin lawyers to go for a sunset sail on his boat out of Darwin Harbour. Even though it was the wet season, it was an unusually clear night. None of us knew anything about sailing, but Graeme assured us he did and could handle the boat himself.

So we set out with the sun going down on a beautiful calm Darwin evening. When we had first boarded we saw Graeme had had quite a bit to drink already. But that was neither unusual nor surprising. Once on the boat however he started to put away the bundies at a rate that surprised even us. Nonetheless the sailing was smooth and we weren't worried. We sailed due north for about an hour, out into the Timor Sea, and now a broad starry night had fallen. In the warmth of that tropical night, it was a magical feeling.

Graeme was at the tiller. At one point he stood up and started to walk towards the front of the boat. No-one really paid any attention. We were leaving the sailing to him, whatever that may mean. Then suddenly I heard Graeme emit a tiny noise and as I turned to see, he fell forward on his face on the deck. We rushed over and turned him on his back. There didn't seem to be any major injury

'Are you OK?' one of the others asked. No reply.

She shook him. But still there was no response. It didn't take us long to realise he was dead drunk.

Even now we didn't worry. The boat was still heading north, but at a slow pace driven by a gentle southerly wind. We figured Graeme would wake up soon and turn the boat around. So we sat there drinking and enjoying the night as the unmanned boat continued to head north.

An hour later Graeme was still unconscious and we were starting to get a little concerned, especially as the gentle southerly breeze started to turn into a howling gale, much more typical of the season.

'Things can sure change fast at sea,' someone unhelpfully yelled above the gale.

Most of us had never even been on a sailing boat. As the gale caught the sails and drove us at remarkable speed, and the boat tilted from side to side, we reasoned it might help to bring the sail down. But for the life of us we couldn't work out how to do that. People tugged and pulled at ropes but to no avail. As the wind pushed us further and further out into the Timor Sea, the waves got bigger and started crashing over the side of the boat.

By now we had serious thoughts of dying and redoubled our efforts to furl the sails and to wake Graeme. But we failed at both, and were close to a point of panic. Finally someone managed to loosen the sail which then proceeded to tangle itself about the mast and throw the boat in all directions. Once it was finally down we calculated we had been driving before the wind for well over an hour and could easily be half way to Dili. Certainly we had left Australian waters far behind.

And still Graeme would not be woken. As we couldn't sail, we decided to try and get ourselves back to Darwin by mechanical means. The boat had no motor but the lifeboat did have an outboard. So a couple of us lowered the dinghy into the dark waters, climbed in, tied a rope from the back of it to the front of the sail boat and started the outboard. The idea was to tow the sail boat by the dinghy back into Darwin Harbour.

We got about ten metres before the strain of trying to pull something many times its size caused the dinghy, outboard motor and all, to sink to the bottom. We swam back to the main vessel. Now we had no way of getting back, and sat helpless and at the mercy of the fates.

Around one in the morning Graeme woke up, looked about him,

realised what had happened and started abusing us for letting things get to this state. Of course several people vied to point out his part in the disaster. Nonetheless under Graeme's direction we steadied the ship, and by two in the morning, when the main force of the gale had died down, we started on the long trip back. We finally made Darwin Harbour around seven. Now here was the problem: most of the people on the boat were lawyers who were due in court in a couple of hours. There were no docks in Darwin Harbour. You simply dropped anchor out in the harbour and went ashore in your dinghy. Of course we no longer had a dinghy.

Nor could we swim ashore. The distance was not far, but we were in the wet season and the harbour was infested with deadly stingers and anyone who tried to swim that distance would probably be stung and would probably die. We thought our salvation was at hand when we started to see, on the other side of the harbour, the fishing boats coming back from their night fishing. We screamed and waved to them, but they just thought we were being friendly and waved back.

It was almost ten o'clock when one fisherman finally realised we might be in trouble. He rescued us, took us ashore and we jumped a cab straight to court. We did not have time to go home and change. So the various court rooms in the Darwin court complex, though they were used to more informality than in most courts, were treated to various lawyers dressed in thongs and shorts, begging His Worship's pardon and trying to explain why they were appearing without benefit of tie or trousers.

Despite the town's obsession with the booze, there was some non alcohol dependent experiences to be had in Alice Springs, including a visit from the heir to the British throne, HRH the Prince of Wales. Charles was a bachelor then, and all the 'joys' of his marriage to Diana were ahead of him. So he was still young and relatively carefree and made a very funny speech to the whole town in the main street, standing with the mayor on a hastily erected and very wobbly platform.

When he had finished, the mayor announced it was the Prince's birthday, and he thought it would be a fine idea if we all sang him 'Happy Birthday'. It was a bit of a cringe moment, especially as the tone deaf mayor led off, solo and unaccompanied. However we all joined in and things were fine right through:

'Happy birthday to you, happy birthday to you, happy birthday dear...'

And then everyone stopped. There was total silence, because nobody knew what we should call him. I don't think even the Palace etiquette book could have helped. Which honorific *do* you to use in the middle of 'Happy Birthday' sung by the populace of an outback town?

The options that flashed through our collective minds included, 'Charles', 'Charlie', 'Prince', but none seemed quite right and so we all just stood there in agonising silence. Finally in his high pitched tone deaf quavering voice, the Mayor blurted out all by himself:

'Your Royal Hiiiighness'.

Later that month the Mayor lost the mayoral election to Brian Martin, but I refuse to believe his singing had anything to do with it.

In the afternoon of the same day, I had a call from the Mayor, inviting Agatha and I to a reception he had planned that night for the Prince. He tactfully explained how he was rounding up all the lawyers and other professionals because he couldn't trust anyone else in the town not to make fools of themselves. Flattered though I was, being a 'socialist' and therefore by definition an anti-monarchist, I politely declined.

I immediately rang Agatha to say how funny it was that we, of all people, should be invited to a reception for the heir to the British throne. Agatha was, by her own assertion, at least as dedicated a left winger as I.

'Did you accept?' she asked.

'Of course not,' I said, laughing.

'What?!' she yelled. 'What?!' There was silence. I was confused. 'Ring them back!' she demanded. 'How dare you deprive me of a chance to meet the Prince'.

So I rang the mayor back and explained my wife was very angry with me, and could we come anyway. He was delighted as he was still having problems finding enough responsible people to fill the room.

That night we arrived a little late at the 'reception venue', which, until two days before, had been an animal breeding laboratory. The Prince was already there and mingling.

I have to say for all my anti-monarchist ideals, I found myself, against my will, being quite impressed by the man. He did seem to have the common touch, and was quite comfortable with everyone he talked to.

He even kept his composure when Miss Alice Springs Runner Up literally pinned him to the wall with her outstretched arm on his shoulder and said:

'G'day Prince! How's it goin'?'

'I'm really well!' he replied in that crisp well known accent. 'And yourself?'

'Bit of a shit day,' she said. 'But can't complain.'

She then proceeded to tell him most of her life story culminating in the tragic injustice of only getting second place in the Miss Alice Springs contest.

Later that evening, no doubt due to the fact the animal breeding laboratory had not been properly scoured before turning it into a catering venue, the entire party, the Prince included, was struck down with *Shigella flexneri* dysentery. This particular strain was severe and several townspeople were hospitalised. One or two were even on the critical list.

Agatha and I were leaking badly and got to a point of nausea and weakness so debilitating we literally couldn't get out of bed. We really just had to lie amidst our leakings for almost 24 hours.

I remember that night turning on the television and seeing Prince Charles addressing a reception in Perth. We could barely move, but there he was, not just standing upright, but talking and smiling to boot. Either he had enormous *sang froid* or a medical team far superior to anything we could find at the Alice Springs Hospital.

I played some sport in Alice Springs. There was cricket for one of the local teams. I once almost got a century, but threw my wicket away in the nineties, because the custom was century makers were awarded a keg of beer, and more or less expected to drink it. I decided I hadn't survived deadly cancer, a runaway sail boat in the Timor Sea and Dysentery with the Prince, just to die from alcohol poisoning.

The most interesting sport, which many of us played for the 'cultural contact', was baseball. The US Space Base at Pine Gap was just outside Alice Springs, and several of the men who worked there had been minor league baseballers in their day. Whereas they were forbidden even to talk to us for fear of letting slip classified information, they were allowed to play in the baseball league.

So although I never got to have a conversation with anyone from Pine Gap, I had the pleasure of being abused by them on the baseball field. We cricketers, who were used to the gentlemanly conduct of that game, were surprised, to say the least, when we stepped up to bat and had to hear not only that we were 'no batter' but also that our penises were of inadequate length or that our girlfriends gave blowjobs to sailors.

Later when I worked for Legal Aid I defended protestors who had invaded the Pine Gap facility. They were, of course, against the idea the Americans could have a base on Australian soil, the activities of which were a secret even to the Australian Government.

One day I decided to go out to Pine Gap to see if I could get in to talk to someone or interview someone. I didn't really expect to be allowed. I just wanted to see how I would be received. I parked the car several hundred metres back from the main gate and approached on foot.

I didn't even get to ask. When I was still a hundred metres away the guard turned his sub machine gun at me. As always, though I lived a life where fear of the unseen was always with me, when confronted by real danger I felt no fear. I just kept walking. He raised the gun more threateningly. But still I came towards him. When I was about twenty metres away he said:

'If you take another step I will shoot you!'

I stopped. Still I felt no fear, but the logical part of me said he just might do what he was threatening. I wonder if he would have? I turned and went home, still never having had a conversation with an American.

But an aspect of our alliance with the US impressed itself on me that day. It was that whereas my clients the protestors were subject to prosecution, I myself, as an Australian citizen, could very well be gunned down on my own soil, by a non citizen who might not even be called to account for it.

Pine Gap was a big issue for left wing voters in those days. In fact many believed Gough Whitlam's threat to close down the base may have had something to do with his Dismissal. Whether or not that is true, overall these were politically volatile times. And as I found myself working in a firm with, and living two doors down from the President of the Labor Party, John Reeves, this seemed like the time to put my socialist money where my mouth was. So I joined the Party. And it was soon after that I turned up for my first Party meeting at John's flat.

In the mid seventies the Labor Party in the Northern Territory did not hold one seat in the Parliament. So the Party was in a state of demoralisation and the meeting was small, with only a few faithful present. I was looking forward to my first branch meeting and expected some lively debate on a range of social and philosophical issues. But all anyone wanted to talk about was how to get some seats in the Parliament. That was understandable, I told myself, given the party's parliamentary absence. But I was just a little surprised by the way the conversation went.

John Reeves began by making an impassioned speech about how the Party had compromised itself my moving too much towards the centre, making it difficult to distinguish, in the voters' minds, from the governing conservative Country Liberal Party. He suggested a bold across the board shift to the far left.

When he had finished another member of the Executive raised a series of counter arguments as to why that would not get them any more seats. At the end of his speech it was clear he had convinced John his 'far left' plan was not the answer.

'OK,' said John, after a few moments' thought. 'How about we move to the far right instead and beat them at their own game?'

I laughed out loud. Sadly I was the only one. They all stared at me for a moment, but I was of no account, and was quickly forgotten as they all rushed to congratulate John on this stroke of genius. Fortunately or unfortunately I realised very early in my political career that I may have been a tad too idealistic. So that career came to a shuddering end on the very night of its birth.

But politics, Prince poisoning and open court lawyer slaying notwithstanding, the thing that really marked out Alice Springs at that time was, unfortunately, its racism. Very few people in modern Australia have any idea what it was like in those days for the aborigines of the Centre.

The depth of the racism was easily on par with the worst excesses of the deep south of America. Lynchings were not uncommon and a non-official but just as horrifying de facto slavery, though gone by the 1970s, was not long gone. One pastoralist I met proudly showed me a photo of the 'good old days'. To my horror it was of a group of six Aboriginal men, shackled at the neck, pulling a heavily laden cart, exactly as if they were oxen.

Perhaps the most horrible example of which I was a part, took place after I had left Everingham's and gone to work for the Australian Legal Aid Office. A white man came to see me. He had been charged by the police. The conversation between lawyer and client went something like this:

'So we had the spotlight on this big bugger...'

'Sorry, what do you mean spotlight?'

'You know the big spotlight, on the front of the truck.'

'Ah, you were kangaroo shooting.'

'Boong shooting.'

'Sorry?'

'Boong shooting. We were boong shooting.' He looked amazed that he had to explain this.

I stared at him. Was he trying to make some sort of very bad joke? Apparently not.

'You were out on your truck trying to shoot Aborigines?'

'Sure, Friday nights. Get us some boongs.'

He said it with such calm. I looked for any sign of guilt or regret. There was none. He might as well have been telling me about his fly fishing trip.

'Anyway we're in the Todd and we're just getting the light going and this silly bugger runs straight into it. Startled he is. Stands right there in front of me, startled!' He laughed. 'Talk about a sitting duck. So I figure at that range I can plant one right between his eyes, but just as I pull the trigger me mate bumps me, and I end up shooting the bugger's ear off.'

So I have a man who has tried to murder someone, just sitting in my office. I have to ask myself how he even managed bail? I get him to give me his charge sheet. I look at it dumbfounded. The police haven't charged him with attempted murder, they haven't even charged him with some form of grievous wounding. The crime for which I have to defend him, is nothing more or less than common assault.

'You're charged with assault?' I hear myself say.

Of course what I mean is 'you're *only* charged with assault'. But he doesn't take it that way. He thinks I want to know why he has been charged with anything at all.

'Yeah, it's me own bloody fault,' he says. 'And the cop's right. That close to town. What if I'd missed and the bullet'd gone into someone's house.'

From this and from a little further questioning I come to understand the police have only charged him to teach him a lesson. They know all about the Friday night 'sport'. They just want to make sure he keeps it further out bush where no-one (no-one 'human' that is) could accidentally get hurt.

It was one of my darkest moments in Alice Springs, and at the same time, perhaps another world first. I'm sure other police forces have chosen not to prosecute murderers they should have prosecuted. But I would be surprised if any Southern Sheriff or SS Officer had prosecuted an attempted murderer for common assault, just to alert him to the need to be more disciplined in his murdering.

As a lawyer I had an ethical duty to defend anyone who came to me for help. It was perhaps the one time I just wanted to throw that duty out the window. Nonetheless I went to court for him where he pleaded guilty and was fined $10 (the equivalent of $100 in today's money).

I remember another case where I represented a young Aboriginal man charged with malicious damage. The police alleged that on the night in question, around midnight, he had thrown a brick through a shop window at the end of an arcade. The arresting officers said they had been driving by the arcade and saw him do it. Under cross examination I forced them to admit that at the speed their car was travelling they had less than one third of one second to see 100 metres up the narrow unlit arcade and make a positive identification of an aboriginal man on a moonless night.

After the case I said to the prosecuting police sergeant Jerry Benedict:

'You knew they couldn't have seen him. Why did you let them lie?'

'Because we know he did it,' was Jerry's answer.

That was more than enough for him, but not for me. He saw my disquiet, and was worried. Like so many of the white racists in town, he was quite capable of feeling the whole range of human emotions, provided blacks were not involved. He saw me as a colleague who was disturbed and that disturbed him.

'Look, Vic,' he said with great compassion in his voice. 'You don't understand how it works here. You haven't been in town long enough.'

'What's that got to do with it?' I snapped. 'Would you do that with a white man? Would you give false evidence just because you thought he did it?'

'Of course not.' He looked at me in amazement. 'But this is very different.'

'Why is it different?' I demanded.

'Because we have a duty to keep them under control.'

'Is that why your guys just drive around on a Friday night picking up Aborigines at random, even if they haven't done anything, and keep them in the cells till Monday morning?'

It was a notorious fact of Alice Springs policing, and being angry, I was going to take the chance to throw it up at Jerry. But he didn't even try to deny it.

'That's it,' he said, as though finally I was getting the message.

It was hopeless.

'You talk like they're not part of the human race, like they're wild animals,' I said.

'Not all of them,' he said.

'You must really hate them,' I said, starting to walk away.

But he followed after me and stopped me by grabbing hold of my arm.

'I don't hate them at all,' he said. He stood there for a moment thinking, as though determined to find some way to help me see the light. 'It's like this,' he finally said. 'You know how kittens are really cute. But when they grow up into cats, you've got to find a way to keep them under control. If you can do that, fine. If you can't you're better off tying them in a sac and throwing them in the river.'

'And you want to avoid the latter if possible?' I asked, hearing the sarcasm rise in my voice.

But Jerry didn't seem to notice. He just smiled a big smile and said:

'That's it. You've got it.'

It has been said most people who do evil things, aren't setting out to do evil. They genuinely believe, for whatever twisted reasons, they are doing what's right. I guess Jerry may have fallen into that category. I don't know. But it didn't help me.

'My problem is I don't see them as animals,' was what I told him.

'That's because you haven't been exposed enough,' he said.

'I don't think so,' I said, walking off again.

But this meant a lot to Jerry and he wasn't about to let it go.

'Here's an idea,' he said, calling me back. 'I have to go out to Yuendumu settlement tomorrow. Fly out with me. I'll arrange everything. Meet some of them. Then you'll see what I mean.'

And now I was in the crazy position of feeling the need to accommodate someone whose views I abhorred, just because the man cared enough for me and my 'education' to go to the trouble of flying me out to an Aboriginal settlement. I reluctantly agreed. But later I was very glad I did.

So the next day I was in a light aircraft with Jerry Benedict flying low over the amazing multi coloured Tanami desert North West of Alice Springs. As soon as we got to the settlement Jerry told me he was going to take me to meet one of the elders, a man named Jabaldjari.

The man was tall, lean and dressed in European clothes. He could have been anywhere from 40 to 60. I couldn't tell because his face was so weathered by the desert life.

G'day Jab,' Harry bellowed at the man though he was only inches away from him. 'Brought you someone. This is Vic. He wants to ask you some questions.' He had slowly enunciated every syllable as if Jabaldjari were a child.

Jabaldjari looked at Jerry with something half way between fear and disdain. He said nothing. Just stared at Jerry, who now smiled at me as if to say: 'See. What did I tell you? This is one of their elders, one of their top men, and he can't even speak when spoken to.'

'I'll leave you two to get acquainted,' Jerry said, and walked away shaking his head and smiling to himself.

'I *would* like to ask you some questions,' I said to Jabaldjari, 'if that's not too much trouble.'

But now Jabaldjari just stood there staring at me, looking into my eyes. There was silence for a very long time. My logical side told me he didn't want to talk or couldn't talk to me. My logical side told me to just go off and find Jerry. But as the seconds turned into silent minutes, though I was very uncomfortable, my instincts would not let me leave the man. Finally he did speak, in a deep clear and gentle voice.

'I think you are a lawyer,' he said.

'Yes I am.'

'I'll tell you 'bout our law.' And a faint gentle smile crossed his lips.

'I would like that,' I said.

'But we'll go sit. We'll go under a tree. It's hot out here.' And now his smile was bigger.

So we sat under a tree and crossed our legs and talked. We talked for near on five hours, much to the annoyance of Jerry Benedict who finished his own work in under two and was keen to get back. He kept coming over and signalling me. But I sat there and listened to what Jabaldjari had to say.

I did learn many things about their tribal law, its strictness and its complexities, and how much of it conflicted, for them, with what white law required them to do. Some of this I knew already, but Jabaldjari spoke with such clarity that I came to understand subtleties I would never have acquired talking to the white lawyers in town.

But more importantly I came to understand something of Jabaldjari himself, how he thought, and how his people thought. Early on in our conversation he had said to me:

'You people got to answer right away. Doesn't matter what you say, the answer's got to be now. We like to think first. We like to give the right answer, not the quick one.'

And I understood that was why he had taken so long to speak to me. He wanted to look at me first, to work out what kind of person I was. Then he would talk, and he would know what kind of talk to make.

By his acceptance of me and his willingness to share with me, I came to understand that in sharp contrast to their antagonists in the Alice Springs police and others, for Jabaldjari's people each white person was innocent till proven guilty. No matter what had been done to him and his tribe by the whites, when Victor Kline came to visit, it was not assumed I was there to injure him, even though I had come under the auspices of a man who would not even grant him human status. He looked into my eyes long enough to decide I was ok. After that I had his trust, which was then for me to lose.

And this ethic ran deep, even with the urban Aborigines, some of whom had been so much more degraded by their contact with the whites. A few weeks after my meeting with Jabaldjari I was in a petrol station when a very drunk Aboriginal man came my way armed with the jagged remains of a broken glass flagon in his hand. He got so close to me I could smell the stink of his breath.

He raised the jagged glass as though he were about to bring it down into my face. But I remembered what Jabaldjari had told me and I refused, even under these circumstances, to assume his guilt. I looked in his eyes and I smiled. And because of that he lowered the glass. So we stood looking at each other for a while, much as Jabaldjari and I had done in the desert. Eventually he smiled too. Then he moved on, touching me in a brotherly way on the shoulder as he passed.

During my time in Alice Springs I had a lot more to do with the Aboriginal people, both through my work and because of later living in The Gap, the black area of town. I developed a deep respect for their history, their lifestyles and their wisdom. Where I could, I sought out their company. I hope I never became unduly romantic about the Aborigines and their way of life. I hope I never lost touch with the reality that their law, in our eyes, could sometimes seem harsh, just as our law could often look obstructive and irrelevant to them.

Nonetheless I had no doubt we had a lot to learn from them, as they did from us, and I regretted that often we didn't listen to their wisdom. Even more I regretted that, with some notable exceptions, black and white travelled on parallel paths in Alice Springs, and when those paths did cross, more often than not they crossed in misunderstanding or even in violence. I had a yearning to bring the peoples together. I still do.

But right then I had some more medical problems to deal with. Not long after my time at Yuendemu, I developed an infection in my groin where the surgeon had entered to remove my testicle. I went to the only private doctor in town, Paterson MacPhee, a man of great good humour.

He diagnosed that some of my internal stitches had failed to dissolve and had risen up towards the surface, causing the infection. He said it was pretty straight forward. All he needed to do was give me a local anaesthetic in the groin and dig out the offending stitches. So he did give me an anaesthetic and then started to dig. Problem was the anaesthetic did not do what anaesthetics are supposed to do. I felt everything. I screamed. He stopped.

'Can you feel that?' he asked, surprised.

'Yes!' I managed to blurt out as he dabbed away to stop the bleeding.

'Ah,' he said, 'better get the nurse in here. Eunice!' he called.

The middle aged woman who doubled as his receptionist came in. I had met her several times, and even talked to her about her career as a theatre nurse in World War II.

'Bit of a problem with the anaesthetic,' he told her. And he got her to take over the swabbing whilst he fetched another anaesthetic injection and whacked it into my still throbbing groin.

'Should be fine now,' he told me in his usual cheery tone.

But when he started to cut, again the anaesthetic gave me no help. Again I screamed. He instructed the nurse to hold me down.

'Just hang on mate,' he said to me, 'I'm sure I've almost got it.'

And despite my protestations he continued to cut and probe. After a moment the nurse had to run to the wash basin to throw up. I don't know exactly what he was doing down there, but if it could make a war nurse vomit, it couldn't have been good.

'Hm,' he said. 'Maybe you need to have this done under a general.'

So the next day I flew to Sydney where a surgeon removed what needed to be removed and cleaned my infection under a general anaesthetic.

Two days later, when I was released from hospital I went down to the Prince of Wales to pay a visit to Leister Atkinson and Sister Carter. They were obviously happy to see me, especially as more than two years had now passed since the original diagnosis.

I told Sister Carter what had happened with the groin infection.

'You haven't had much luck,' she laughed.

I almost laughed too, but not quite. What I did say was:

'Two years have passed. I'm still here. I think I've had my share of luck.'

'That's true,' she said, gave me a hug and took me in to see Atkinson.

They had learnt a lot since my treatment, and although there was still much guesswork involved, he was even more confident survival for two years meant a fine chance of a long life.

Back in Alice, Agatha and I started to talk about the possibility of having a family. We hadn't wanted to try before, but now the two year milestone had passed and Atkinson was so confident, we felt the time had safely come, or safely enough. Agatha suggested I go and get a sperm count done, just in case the radiotherapy had knocked me about.

I wasn't keen to go back to Paterson. But about that time a new 'itinerant' doctor had come to town. He was a man in his fifties with a bushy grey beard and a twenty year old anorexic girlfriend. He had set up his 'surgery' in a shop front with a desk, a stethoscope and not much else. The waiting room had three plastic chairs and in the middle of the room was a big cardboard box filled with Playboy magazines. That was all.

It didn't inspire confidence, but then again nor did Paterson. So I went to see Doctor Sleezebone. He spoke with an educated smarmy accent, talking slowly in measured patronising tones. He sent me off to the public toilet to give my sample.

'Now you have to ejaculate into this little plastic jar here. Don't miss and put in on the floor now will you?' And he allowed himself a tiny chuckle. 'Aha. Aha.'

I managed to get my sperm in the jar, and a week later came back for the results.

'You don't actually have any sperm at all,' Sleezebone smiled.

It took me a moment to take that in.

'What none at all?' I finally said.

'No none. Radiotherapy knocked it for a loop.'

'But they didn't tell me that could happen," I said.

'Well there you are.' He was starting to wind up. He had given me the news. Now I really should be a good fellow and let him get on to his next patient. But I wasn't ready to leave just yet.

'Is there any chance the sperm could regenerate?' I asked.

'Not really.' He smiled again.

I found it hard to believe the radiotherapy could have so comprehensively destroyed my sperm.

'Is it possible,' I asked, 'that it has nothing to do with the radiotherapy? Could I have been born with a nil count?'

'If it makes you feel better to believe that,' he oozed, 'you just go right ahead and believe it.'

That statement from Dr Sleezebone still ranks as the most careless, most useless and most condescending remark I have ever had the misfortune to be the recipient of.

I remember afterwards walking down the main street of Alice Springs and being surprised just how much not being able to have a child mattered to me. Of course it would matter to anyone. But I think on a deep unconscious level I always felt my healing lay in being able to raise a child in love and security, to redress the balance of what had been done to me.

I went home to tell Agatha. I expected her to be upset. But what I got was something different. She didn't cry. She didn't really say anything. But as I explained what Sleezebone had told me, I watched as a kind of metaphorical film covered her eyes. And then she went cold on me. Physical affection and physical contact of any kind virtually disappeared. Our sex life diminished overnight to almost nothing, and even that became formulaic and unenthusiastic.

At first I didn't worry too much. I understood how profound Agatha's disappointment must have been. After all I felt the same way myself. And of course the link between my infertility and our sex life was obvious. News like that couldn't help but inhibit normal affection and normal sexuality for a time, even for a long time. The problem was, that as time went by, I began to realise the change in Agatha wasn't just temporary.

Very shortly after that I received some news that most people would have considered very exciting and somewhat of a counterbalance to the bad news of the sperm count. Peter Howard called me into his office to tell me he had met with Everingham and Reeves and they would like to offer me a partnership. After only a year or so in the firm it was surprising and flattering. Unfortunately in my personal life I was very unhappy and very confused, and so I couldn't see it for what it was.

Ideally this would have been the time to listen to my unconscious which knocked ceaselessly with its irrational fears and its gruesome nightmares. Ideally I should have been able to trace life backwards and realise not only that Agatha's coldness had been caused by the infertility but that the infertility had been caused by the cancer which in turn had been caused (literally or metaphorically) by a childhood of sexual and psychological abuse.

But I was still too young and obviously still too frightened to face my reality. Indeed I was so far from understanding the truth that I was sending my parents a generous stipend every month as some small token of thanks for all they had done for me.

So instead of acknowledging what I needed to acknowledge, I blamed all the wrong things. Everingham & Co was my major scapegoat. They worked me too hard and they were just some sort of capitalist conspiracy that stifled my compassion and my socialist ideals. They were the ones responsible for the fear that gripped my chest during the day, the nightmares, and the sick feeling in the pit of my gut when I woke in the mornings. If I were to accept a partnership with them I would be selling out and shackling myself for ever more to my own misery.

Clearly all would be better if I just 'moved on' again. Going overseas would obviously be the best idea, but I didn't yet have the money. So I would take a job with the Australian Legal Aid Office whilst I saved up. At least there I would be able to escape my capitalist torturers and help the downtrodden.

Objectively it was a good idea to go and offer my services to the less fortunate, and I think I did help some people who otherwise wouldn't have been helped. But it was my unacknowledged and subjective motivation that was suspect. It was my 'running away' again that was not very helpful to either Agatha or myself. So somewhat ungraciously I refused Peter

Howard's offer and applied for the position of senior legal officer that was going at the Australian Legal Aid Office. I got the job, resigned from Everingham and Co and went to work under the Principal Legal Officer Jack Cranshaw.

11. THE BLACK SIDE OF TOWN

In those days in Alice Springs there were two legal aid services, The Aboriginal Legal Service, and the Australian Legal Aid Office. To qualify for the former you needed to be black and to qualify for the latter you needed to be poor. If you were black and poor you could choose. Tribal people tended to go to the Aboriginal Legal Service which was much better set up for their needs, and those Aboriginal people who lived closer to the European end of the spectrum, especially those who lived in The Gap, tended to come to us.

So we acted for poor whites and poor mostly urban blacks. As I said before, Alice Springs society was riven with problems and, as there was only the two of us in the office, it was a busy practice. Probably half of what we did was criminal law, often involving very serious crime. A lot of the rest was family law, and then there was a scattering of things like workers' compensation, and a range of personal injuries claims.

My boss Jack Cranshaw had a good legal mind and I learned much from him. He was also easily the most eccentric person I have ever met. He was about 5'4" and quite fat. He wore shorts, long socks and a sleeveless shirt to work. Nothing he wore ever looked like it had ever formed an acquaintance with an iron. I think he wore clothes for a while and when they were so wrinkled he couldn't tell the shorts from the shirts, he just threw them out, unless of course he could engage in some creative salvaging. I remember one day he came in with the hem of his shorts hanging down. Not that he would ever have noticed, but one of the secretaries pointed it out to him.

'I can fix that,' he said, taking hold of her stapler and stapling the hem back into place with about 30 staples all the way round his leg.

His filing system involved the avoidance of the filing cabinet. Every piece of paper relating to every case he was handling was on his desk. As he was, at any given time, handling a large number of cases, his desk was covered in a mountain of papers about a metre high.

So the way Jack would work was that he would come into his office in the morning and stare at the mountain of paper, and say:

'Ok nothing today.'

But then as he went to sit down behind the mountain, his eye might catch the corner of a red summons sheet sticking out near the bottom of the pile, and he would say:

'Oh no shit! I'm supposed to be in Court.'

And he would rip the piece of paper out of the mountain, sometimes causing other pieces of paper to dislodge and float to the floor. Then he would rush out the door bearing the red summons. I remember thinking at the time that clients whose cases, for whatever reason, involved colourful paperwork, were much more likely to be attended to quicker.

The mountain did get sorted one day, but not in a way you might imagine. We had a very serious and complex murder case, and Jim had rightly decided we should brief a QC from Sydney. So one morning Jack came in with eminent senior counsel who was looking a little culture shocked, which is not surprising as he had just been picked up from a tiny dusty outback airport by a little man in a dirty old ute who was wearing crinkled shorts with the hem stapled (yes Jack was so taken with his own tailoring he kept the shorts).

'Let's go into my office and run through this,' Jack was saying as they came through the door.

Of course the secretaries and I, aware of the state of Jack's desk, followed closely behind to see the QC's reaction. It was priceless. He looked at the stack of papers, then at Jack, then at us. Clearly he was wondering where they might find a space to work, and how he was going to carry on a conversation with his instructing lawyer if, as is normal and traditional, they sat on opposite sides of the desk, because then they would not be able to see one another over the mountain of papers.

It took Jack a moment to realise what the problem was. The he said:

'Oh shit, sorry!'

And he walked over to the desk, leant down to the right hand edge of the mountain, and with super human effort, using both arms, he swept the pile off the desk. It was really quite beautiful watching the hundreds of pieces of paper, being of different weights and wind resistance, fluttering to the four corners of the room. When all the papers had finally settled, Jack, with a huge smile of satisfaction, pulled out a chair for the QC to sit on, only to find it too was covered with paper.

'So that's where those little buggers got to,' he said matter of factly, as he brushed the last offending documents to the floor.

Miraculously though, in the year or so I worked with Jack, I never knew him to miss a court date, or a meeting or to fail to file a document on time. He had his system, and however chaotic it looked to the rest of us, it worked for him.

I did some pretty gruesome cases in that first year with Jack. One murder client had disposed of his victim by pushing his head through a brick wall. Whether because of the hardness of the victim's head or the determination of the offender, the *actus reus* actually made a head size hole in the wall.

Another client, who earned his living decapitating chickens, decided to use his skills to settle an argument over football with a friend. He grabbed hold of his friend by the hair and sawed his head off with a breadknife, only to dispose of it by throwing it over the fence where it landed in his neighbour's barbecue - while he was barbequing. He did confess to me later he had employed a reverse decapitation.

'See with ya chooks ya cut from the back to the front, that way ya sever the spinal cord quick and the little bastards don't feel much after that. But with Billie I cut from the front to the back so the prick would feel the lot. That was mean of me, wasn't it?'

But the implication was there was nothing wrong with killing Billie for his football supporting malefactions. It was only the method he used that made him feel guilty. As he talked to me in the cells he kept saying things like:

'Soon as this silly stuff is over, I think I'll take meself up North Queensland for the cane cuttin'.

The Alice Springs Office was also responsible for Tennant Creek which was 500 kilometres 'up the road'. So as the junior member of the team it was my job to go there once a month for the local court list. I liked going because I could stay with Ross and Bev Clifford who had by then moved there to open a new branch of Everingham and Co.

Ross already had a strong faith. In those days however, I saw myself as an atheist. Like many militant non believers I had a deep yearning which embarrassed me because it didn't fit with the logic of the world as I saw it. So my militancy was a reaction to that, perhaps an overreaction.

As a very small child at school, maybe only five or six, I had been told by a scripture teacher that if I felt frightened in my room at night I need only ask for God's protection and it would be given. It was a simple message that would not withstand the logic of a 'rational' adult mind. But my childhood room was a frightening place and I wanted to believe there was some protection somewhere. Despite what was happening to me, I did believe and it did help me through.

All that had been forgotten but the fear was still with me, and it would come out via irrational anxieties in my waking moments and in nightmares whilst I slept. And here was Ross whose faith seemed so effortless and who seemed so comfortable in his own skin. So I always wanted to talk to him about how it was for him.

If possible I would give him a hard time about his faith. It was all part of my defensive militancy. I remember one night when I went for the jugular. Ross was a Baptist and came from an evangelical background. Therefore his fellow believers would have seen it as part of his 'brief' to convert whoever he could. But Ross never did that. And it was that very quality I admired, which I used against him.

'Am I your friend?' I asked.

'Of course.'

'And as your friend, do you care for my well being?'

'Sure.'

'And isn't part of my well being, perhaps the biggest part, my spiritual salvation?'

He was starting to see where this cross-examination was going, but had to say:

'It is.'

'Then if you love me,' I taunted him, 'why don't you make an effort to save me? Why are you willing to let me just go on in my darkened state?'

I was having fun, but I saw a look of guilt and tragedy cross his face. From his perspective that was just what he knew he should be doing, and wasn't. And now he had been caught out by the very person he should have been trying to help. He had no answer for me and hung his head.

When I saw that I felt terrible. It was so tactless of me. And when I look back I can't help wondering how much truth was in my jest? How much did I really want him to do what I was teasing him about?

Ross and I almost went into partnership together in Tennant Creek. We would have done very well financially because it had always been a town starved of legal representation. Before Ross got there they had no-one, and short of travelling to Alice Springs, they had to sort things out for themselves.

There was one famous 'case' where, for want of a lawyer, a would-be divorcee drew up a list of all her husband's malefactions and her demands and nailed the 'petition' to the door of the courthouse, asking the town to be her judge. The husband then prepared his own document in reply and nailed it to the same door next to hers. The townsfolk then duly read both documents, weighed the arguments, took sides and the whole thing ended in a brawl.

In the end the partnership idea didn't eventuate. Even the five years or so needed to make our fortunes seemed like way too long in that dusty barbaric place with its fierce heat and a level of violence that made Alice Springs look like a nunnery. Besides, what Ross really wanted was to return to Sydney to study for the Ministry. I of course didn't know what I wanted, but consciously or unconsciously, I did know I would need to move on again soon.

For the time being however, Agatha and I had bought a house amongst many of my clients in The Gap. Alice Springs houses were cheap but if you were willing to live in the black area, they were very cheap. We had a bedroom the size of the house I now live in and three other bedrooms to boot. There was an enormous yard with fruit trees and a grape vine and an above ground plastic swimming pool that all the local kids would play in all the time. We were very popular amongst the local kids.

They were delightful, noisy but gentle and polite, and above all fun loving. One very affectionate little eight year old made me an Easter card once which I still cherish. It had a drawing of a big white cross bearing a rather jolly looking red faced Jesus, and she had written in wobbly letters:

'Have a Happy Easter and a very good Friday'.

Our street was like a bustling bazaar. The house on the corner had an Italian family with about 15 kids. They made a lot of noise, and there was always music of some sort coming from their house, albeit not always totally tuneful. Across the road were the only other whites, an elderly German couple called Harry and Hilde Klein. It was a sad day for the Kleins when we moved in because my clients were often in urgent need of help and often not at the most accommodating hours. So they would ask where the Klines lived and someone would tell them Kraegen Street. The subtlety of the different spelling would be lost on them and they would be banging on Harry and Hilda's door at two am.

The aboriginal families really adopted us as one of their own. So much so that on two or three occasions when one of their number died and they had to choose a mourning ground they chose our front yard. It was a great honour, but the first time it happened we got quite a shock when at six in the morning a dozen people started wailing at the top of their voice on our lawn.

Of all the people with whom we became friends, my favourite couple was Charlie and Audrey. Charlie was much older than his wife. He was probably well in his sixties when we knew them and she only in her forties. They had a very loving relationship, but when they had been drinking things could get rocky. We were told that in the past Charlie had occasionally been known to be violent to Audrey, but now that he was getting older and weaker, she was getting her own back.

She would come over to our house regularly to report how she had 'taught the old bastard a lesson'. Her eyes would twinkle with delight as she described how she had given Charlie a thrashing he would never forget. My suspicion was that Charlie, older and wiser, and regretting his past behaviour, let Audrey get in a few good ones, to boost her self esteem and to keep their marriage strong. However I may be doing Audrey a disservice.

She may really have had his measure. Wherever the truth lay, it did keep their marriage vital, and Charlie was Audrey's greatest defender.

One night however he didn't get a chance to defend her. Agatha and I came home from a night out to see a pool of blood outside our front gate which turned into a trail of bloody streaks and footprints leading up to our front door. There we found Audrey lying on the doorstep, barely conscious. It turned out Charlie had been out somewhere and she was home alone when burglars broke in and bashed her. She had crawled all the way from her house to ours only to find we were not home.

I called the ambulance and rushed her to Alice Springs Hospital where they took her into emergency. But there we struck a problem that I saw in so many guises on so many occasions in Alice Springs. The attending doctor came out into the waiting room and said:

'You might as well take her home. There's nothing I can do.'

'What do you mean,' I said. 'She'll bleed to death.'

The doctor let out a deep sigh of disapproval.

'These people,' he said, 'they just don't know what's good for them.'

Of course when I got 'these people' from someone I knew what I was dealing with.

'Please just tell me what the problem is,' I said.

'She won't let me touch her. How can I fix her up if I can't even touch her?'

'Did you ask if you could touch her before you tried to?' The doctor just stared blankly at me. 'Look,' I said, 'will you let me talk to her?'

'What's the point?' he barked at me. 'I've tried! The nurse has tried! What the hell do you hope to achieve?'

'Please.' I tried hard to remain calm and respectful.

Reluctantly the doctor let me follow him into the emergency room. I went up to Audrey who had her eyes closed.

'Audrey?' I said softly, bending right over her.

She slowly opened her eyes.

'Yes, darling,' she said in a soft voice.

'I've got the doctor here,' I explained. 'He's very worried about you, and wants to fix you up. Do you think you could let him touch you so that he can fix you up?'

She looked up at me from the bed and struggled to give me a smile.

'Is that what you want?' she asked

'Yes,' I said. 'Very much.'

'All right then, darling.' And she reached up and put her arms around my head. 'No worries.'

An hour or so later the doctor came out and announced that Audrey was out of danger. But there was little doubt he was very angry with me.

At the end of my first year at Legal Aid, Jack Cranshaw resigned to

VICTOR KLINE

take a job as a magistrate in Fiji. I never got the chance, but would have given anything to see how he conducted his court. The bureaucracy took its time to find a replacement for Jack, and in the meantime I was made acting Principal Legal Officer. It was an honour but at the same time I was aware I was almost certainly the only Principal Legal Officer in the country to have a staff of zero lawyers under him.

After I had been running the office for nearly nine months, the Attorney-General's Department finally appointed a new Principal Legal Officer. His name was Howard Havas and he was a Melbourne barrister. Howard was the exact opposite of Jack. He was organised and efficient with a quiet sense of humour best exemplified by a framed sign which he immediately hung on his office wall, and which read: 'Eschew Obfuscation'.

He was Jewish but was married to a German Nazi. At least he said she was a Nazi. At any rate she was German and the love of her life was not Howard. It was a big black Rottweiler called Hans. When we visited their apartment she would sit on the floor and Hans would lie on his back partly on top of her and she would stroke his genitals.

Howard's rather unusual home life in no way affected his abilities as a lawyer and I enjoyed working with him. He didn't have Jack's 'flair', but in all honesty that was sometimes a relief. We became close friends over the six months we worked together. That friendship perhaps reached its highest point one morning when Howard came into the office his face bruised and his eye blackened. He had been attacked the night before by his drunken neighbour.

Howard naturally enough wanted to launch a suit for assault against the man and asked me to represent him. It was a great compliment because he could easily have got someone with much more experience like Brian Martin, or even someone from Melbourne.

So I issued a summons and a day or so later was in court cross examining our defendant. I gave that cross examination all I had. In fact I would have made some of the Sydney razor gang proud. The man ended up confessing to everything and indeed making matters worse for himself by showing his unrepentant anger and aggression in the witness box. Though in the end he only got a fine, that didn't matter to Howard who felt that he had been avenged. He was very grateful to me.

After the court adjourned I left the bar table and, turning around, saw our secretaries in the back of the court. They didn't normally come to watch, but naturally this was a case in which they had a direct interest. To my surprise I saw my secretary was looking quite pale and sick.

'Are you ok?' I asked.

She just stared at me for a moment and then said:

'I had no idea you could be such a bastard.' She paused and shook her head. 'In the office, you're such a nice man.'

At first I didn't understand what she meant but soon realised she had been shaken by the roughness of my cross examination. She was glad I had fought hard for Howard but at the same time was shocked at seeing a side to me she could never have imagined existed.

Her reaction was to be the final piece in the jigsaw of discontent I was completing against Alice Springs and against the practice of the law in general. My unaddressed problems remained unaddressed and so I needed to find new scapegoats for my anxieties. Alice Springs was isolated, parochial, and racist. The law was a pointless waste of my time, where everyone was always a loser and there was nothing I could do to help anyone. Now, worst of all, I was allowing it to turn me into some sort of monster.

Apart from these imagined ills, my marriage to Agatha really had got much worse. Not that we ever fought. Perhaps it would have been better if we had. Instead we just lived together and did things together whilst the coldness got colder and the distance between us got greater. An objective observer would have suggested I leave Agatha not Alice Springs, for both our sakes. An objective observer would have said I didn't need to leave the law. I *was* helping people and it was ok to be a tough cross examiner provided I didn't let that toughness spill over into my ordinary life. Clearly I hadn't done that yet or my secretary wouldn't have been so surprised. And there was no reason to think I would in the future.

Nonetheless there was no objective observer to tell me all that, and if there had been, I wouldn't have listened. The solution, as I saw it, was to leave the law forever and do what I would have done two years before if I had had the money. Agatha and I would go to London and Paris and parts beyond and that would fix everything.

12. THE INTERNATIONAL LANGUAGE CLUB

Alice Springs had been expensive and I hadn't saved as much as I would have liked. So we decided to stay at The International Language Club in Croydon on the southern edge of suburban London. I had booked it in advance, relying on the popular budget travel guide of the time: *Frommer's Europe on $10 A Day*. The guesthouse was described as a series of houses set on a square where the multi-lingual proprietor Mr Driscoll hosted people from all over the world who came to speak many tongues and exchange cultural wisdoms. It sounded perfect.

Regretfully almost nothing of Frommer's description was anywhere near the truth. There were no languages spoken other than English, no cultures avowed other than those arising naturally out of South London and the houses were not even on a square. They were in a row. We had expected to be met by Mr Driscoll but instead got the housemaid Florey who was straight out of Coronation Street, spotted scarf, missing front tooth, cockney accent and all. Due to flight problems we were two days late.

'We thought as ya weren't comin',' she said, accusingly. 'So we gives ya room away.'

We had been awake for over 60 hours, had endured a trip that was a shade less than luxurious, it was now ten o'clock at night and we were freezing.

'Isn't there anywhere you can put us?' I asked.

'Mrs Driscoll!?' Florey yelled over her shoulder.

A little old lady came out of the kitchen and shuffled down the hall to meet us. She was wearing slippers and an old apron and carrying a large metal spoon.

'You'd be the young couple from Australia,' she said in a thick Irish accent.

We noticed that her head was bent to one side, dragged down by the weight of a huge swelling we later learned was a tumour she refused to get treated.

I enquired after Mr Driscoll.

'Ah,' she said wistfully, 'he'd be in another place.'

I wasn't sure if she meant on this earth or indeed somewhere better. We later learned he was just at their other guesthouse at The Elephant and Castle.

'I tells 'em as 'ow we gives their room away.' Florey explained.

I then launched into a tale of woe designed to melt Mrs Driscoll's heart. I was careful to include the fact that my Catholic wife (of Irish extraction) hadn't slept for some time, and worse still, because of the flight delays, had been forced to miss Sunday mass.

My craven plea worked a treat. Not only did we get a room, but Mrs Driscoll gave us the best room she had. It was the one over the kitchen in the main house which was reserved for her special guests.

We soon realised why the room was so sought after. None of the rooms had heating but ours got the natural heat rising from the kitchen below. It also got the kitchen smells, some of which were appetising but some of which were not. We had a bathroom across the hall with a real bath that even produced a limited amount of hot water each day, something not available to most other guests.

I remember early in our stay, a man from one of the houses a few doors down, sneaking into our house one night with a couple of buckets, quietly stealing into our bathroom and filling his buckets with our hot water. He must have crept quietly up and down the stairs because we didn't hear him even though he had to go right past our door. We were only alerted when, struggling under the weight of the water, he inadvertently banged the downstairs front door. I looked out of our window to see him running down the street spilling water from the two steaming buckets.

I stuck my head out the window and yelled at him, words I am confident I have never had occasion to utter before or since:

'Come back with our hot water, you thieving bastard!'

We were the instant envy of all the residents, many of whom were in awe of our meteoric rise to the best room and the favour of Mrs Driscoll. We met most of them over breakfast the first day. There wasn't one foreign language speaker amongst them. Apart from the occasional itinerants like us, most of the residents were long term and were infirm, insane or otherwise unemployable. They handed their pension or dole cheques to Mrs Driscoll each week in exchange for unheated rooms with limited or no hot water and two wholesome but limited meals a day.

We met and came to know Phil who spoke with a lisp, had a trick hip and was fanatical about not wasting food. Each morning and evening Mrs

Driscoll gave him an extra piece of bread so he could scour his plate for any remaining gravy or other residual food flakes. Phil was also interested in weapons and was a self appointed expert on The War.

This annoyed The Commodore who actually was in The War, or at least claimed to have been. Phil was too young to have served. The Commodore had a very cultivated accent and was spoken of by the others in whispers. It was generally assumed he must have undergone some tragedy to come so far down in the world. My secret guess was he was an out of work actor reprising the David Niven role from *Separate Tables*.

Despite the fact they rarely spoke to one another, except for the occasional mumbled critique, Phil and The Commodore always sat at the same table. It was the most prestigious table because The Commodore was the most prestigious resident. It gave us an early insight into the almost psychopathic need of the English to create hierarchies, even in a place like The International Language Club. Even in a world of misfits, one had to have superior class misfits and inferior class misfits.

Though we were colonials, and that worked against us, the imprimatur of Mrs Driscoll and the Upper Room was enough to get us an invitation to join The Commodore's table. It was an honour we shared also with Old George who was so old it took him fifteen minutes to walk from his house to the main house for dinner even though it was no more than 50 metres away. I would often look out our window just before dinner to see Old George shuffling along the street from his house. 'Shuffling' is the only word I can think to use, but it implies a rapidity Old George couldn't muster.

The final member of our table was a tall well educated man of about forty named Brian. At first we couldn't understand what Brian was doing there. He was intelligent and funny and seemed to be of sound mind and body. Later we discovered he suffered from agoraphobia, and had lived the last twelve years in the limited world of the distance between his house and the main dining house.

Brian was my favourite resident and became a friend. The friendship was of course limited by the fact I couldn't go anywhere with him, but I spent many evenings in his room, which was stacked to the ceiling with books, talking about literature and life. The saddest moment in my relationship with Brian came one evening a short time after Genevieve arrived. She was a very beautiful and elegant young French woman who had had a big fight with her millionaire boyfriend Jeremy. He was one of London's leading makers of television commercials. Whatever the fight had been about, Genevieve had just walked out and went to the last place she thought Jeremy would look for her, Croydon and the International Language Club.

Naturally The Commodore invited her to join our table. She stayed at

The International Language Club for several weeks and we all got to know her well. She took a special liking to Brian. Eventually she found herself an apartment near Victoria and on the night before she was to move she invited Brian to come up and see her new flat the following night. I will always remember the tragic look on Brian's face. Of course he wanted to go. He clearly liked Genevieve a lot. She was a beautiful intelligent woman and he wasn't going to get offers like that every day at the International Language Club. But he also knew he wasn't going to be able to find the courage to do it. It was painful watching him trying to make excuses that of course made no sense to Genevieve.

The following night at dinner, when he could and should have been with Genevieve, Brian was unusually quiet. Before the end of the meal he told us he had had enough to eat and excused himself. Everyone went on talking but I sensed something was wrong, so after a few minutes I excused myself too, and went down the street to Brian's room. I knocked on the door but he didn't answer. So I knocked harder and harder and then, sensing something was very wrong, started yelling for him to open. Eventually he came to the door looking very groggy and I could smell the gas from the little stove Mrs Driscoll let him keep to make tea.

'You must have dozed and forgotten the gas.'

'Yes, yes,' he said. 'How silly.'

After we had left the International Language Club I always meant to go back and see how Brian was. But I never did. Perhaps I was too frightened I wouldn't find him there.

The only other guests we had in our couple of months at The International Language Club, had a lot in common with one another: they were all young men, all Irish, all unshaven and all stayed for just one night. This was a time of high IRA bombing activity in London, and although we had nothing but circumstantial evidence to go on, it was an amazing co-incidence that every bombing in the Croydon area coincided exactly with the arrival of one of these Irish guests at our guesthouse. Mrs Driscoll appeared to be a mild mannered old boarding house owner, but perhaps she was a covert operative in disguise. Anyway that's certainly what most of us liked to think.

The International Language Club gave me time to think. And whereas I was not yet ready to face my past, I did have one really useful thought. It occurred to me Doctor Sleezebone could have been wrong. In fact given the sort of man he was, perhaps there was every chance he was wrong. Where had my sample been sent for analysis and how? Down south to Adelaide bouncing around with the dogs on the back of a ute till the desert sun evaporated any sperm that was there? And even if there really were no sperm, how could he be sure it wouldn't regenerate? What did he know of the effects of a hitherto untried radiotherapy treatment?

For over two years I had accepted Sleezebone's diagnosis as gospel. Well not any more. Here I was in one of the world's great cities with its peerless medical reputation. I was going to get a second opinion. Belated though it was, it was going to come from a real doctor in a real surgery with actual furniture and medical equipment who probably didn't have an anorexic 20 year old girlfriend. When the idea came to me I rushed to tell Agatha. But she was not enthusiastic.

'I don't think you should.'

'Why not?'

'I don't want to have to think about it again.' She spoke with finality.

I was surprised by her attitude but clearly I was not going to convince her. Still I couldn't let the idea go. So I decided to get the medical advice without telling her. I went to a real doctor who told me I did have sperm and quite a bit of it. My count was at the lower end, which could make falling pregnant a little difficult, but provided we maximised our chances by timing sex to ovulation, there was every possibility we could have a child.

It is hard to describe how the new diagnosis made me feel. I think it must be a little like a blind person getting their sight back or a deaf person being able to hear again. A whole crucial functioning part of myself, which I thought I had lost forever, was suddenly gifted back to me. Obviously I was going to tell Agatha.

When I got back she was reading a book. I remember rushing into the room and feeling the words bubble out of me like a silly child. I don't think it was till that moment, as I heard myself babble, that I realised just how much this mattered to me. Of course it would matter to anyone. But beyond the normal healthy desire for a child, I think I desperately needed to have someone I could love and care for and not abuse, just so I could break the chain that bound me to the people who abused me and didn't love and didn't care for me.

It wasn't till much later in life I understood the chain can only be broken by facing the truth and finding the courage to do what is necessary to deal with it. Having a child is wonderful but it has to be with the right person and for the right reasons. But for now I saw it as the solution to my ailing relationship with Agatha and to all the other aspects of my pain.

'That is good news,' she said with a half smile. Then she went back to her book.

But I couldn't just leave it there.

'So we just have to really go for it around the middle of your cycle,' I explained, dragging the book away from her.

'Yes of course,' she said. 'I understand. But let's not get too excited. There are no guarantees.'

'I know. I know. But we should give it a real try, shouldn't we?'

'I said of course.' She took her book back and began to read again.

But then it didn't happen that way. Every month in her fertile period Agatha was unwell or had women's issues or was just not in the mood. Our sex life had dwindled to even less than in Alice Springs and when we did have sex it was always as far from the middle of the cycle as possible.

Nothing quite added up, and all these years later still doesn't add up. If Agatha's disappointment over not being able to have children knocked the guts out of our marriage and our sex life, surely learning that we could have children would revive both. And if the trauma had been so great she could never recover, never find me attractive again, then she should have left me. What was the point of hanging around in a relationship with someone you didn't desire and had no affection for, only having sex when it was certain not to produce children?

As I say, I still don't know the answer, but my best guess comes from looking at myself at that point in time, and asking, why didn't I leave Agatha? Once it was clear I could not make her happy, and once it was clear our empty marriage was going to stay that way, what kept me around?

I think the answer is that I had been taught by my parents that I was unlovable, and having a failed marriage would just be more evidence of that unlovability. So I couldn't let that happen. The irony of course is that by staying in a marriage without love and affection I was sending myself a daily message that I was unlovable. Yet I clung to the lovelessness. After all it was what I had always known. It was what I had come to expect of life. It was what I was 'comfortable' with.

And maybe Agatha was just a mirror image of me. Maybe she stayed around for a similar sad set of reasons. Many years later when I had faced my demons and was on the road to healing myself, I mentioned to Agatha I thought perhaps she had been sexually abused as well. Several things she had said and done over the years were recognisable and led me to think it was a real possibility. She astounded me by saying yes she thought she had, but that she wasn't going to look at that. It was much easier, she said, just to ignore it.

Of course there was no way I was going to penetrate or unravel any of this at the time. I just stayed in the marriage, observed that my wife was unhappy, heard her say, despite her actions not matching her words, that she still wanted children, and blamed myself, not only for our general unhappiness but also for our childlessness.

By now we had been about six weeks at the International Language Club, and our financial situation was getting dire. I needed to find a job. So I went down to the local Croydon Labour Exchange to see what might be available. The woman there was quite confused as to why a qualified lawyer was not going off to be a lawyer. But in the end she asked me if I would consider working in a new cane furniture emporium which was just about to open in Croydon.

'It's a cash and carry,' she said.

'I'm not sure I know what that is,' I told her, and hard as it is to believe, perhaps because they didn't exist in Sydney yet, or I had been locked away in Alice for three years, I genuinely didn't know what she meant.

She looked at me with pity in her eyes that seemed to question how I could have got a law degree at all.

'Well,' she said, slowly and indulgently, 'you pay *cash* and then you *carry* away what you've bought.'

Despite my 'slowness' she arranged for me to meet the owners of 'Fulham Trading', a father and son team named Arthur and Eddie. We were to get together at their Fulham shop, the success of which was the reason for the expansion of the Arthur and Eddie Empire into Croydon.

The owners were both what would then have been called 'cockney wide boys'. The two generations had grown up in poverty in the East End of London. When Eddie left school at the age of fourteen, father and son formed a team, and through years of hard work and other wide boy activities centred on their market stall, they scratched together the capital to start Fulham Trading.

Arthur was about 50 and his son in his late twenties. They had a pragmatic and ironic view of life which was perfectly explicable given where they had come from and the struggles they had had to undergo. They both had a cheekiness that reminded me a little of Pamp.

At the meeting father and son were happy to employ me. Unlike many Australian employers who would have said I was overqualified, they loved the idea of having a barrister work in their new shop. They explained to me that Arthur's younger son Evelyn would be managing the store.

To begin with I would be the only employee, till the business started to take off. The next day I turned up to the premises of Fulham Trading Croydon, only to find Evelyn had not yet arrived. So I was forced to stand out in the snow. Half an hour later I was still there, so decided to find a public phone and ring Arthur.

He didn't say much, only that Eddie would be over as soon as possible to let me in. That day I was alone in the store. Evelyn never did show up. It was all right because we had very little stock at that point and hardly anyone came in. At around five Eddie came back and gave me the keys to lock up.

The next day I arrived at opening time, let myself in and waited. Evelyn arrived around midday. He was nothing like his father or older brother. He was small and hunched and refused to make eye contact. But what was most surprising was he spoke with a private school accent. Obviously once he'd made his money, Arthur had decided to give his younger son the benefits he'd not had himself and hadn't been able to afford for Eddie.

So Evelyn didn't say much and we both stood about in the store wondering what to do. After an hour or so he went out to get himself some lunch.

'Anything special you want me to do?' I asked when he came back around four.

'No, not really,' he said.

So the second day of my career in cane and rattan furniture came to an end. We went on much like that for two more days. We were expecting the first big deliveries of cane furniture to arrive from the Philippines and Thailand, but as yet almost nothing had come. We had a large floor space with a few cane flower pots and a couple of chairs scattered around it.

There was a little room in the back where we hung our coats and bags. At the end of the fourth day I collected my coat and bag and set off through the little snow covered park I had to cross to get back to the International Language Club. At the other side of the park I decided to stop and buy some chocolates to take home.

When I reached into my bag to get my wallet it was gone. I rushed home and emptied the bag on the bed, but still no wallet. I tried to think things through. I knew I had the wallet when I hung the bag on the hook in the back room that morning. I had been nowhere with the bag since. We had almost no customers in the shop and it was inconceivable any could have gone into the back room without one of us noticing.

I had to come to the inescapable conclusion Evelyn had stolen my wallet. Apart from the annoyance of having lost my last forty quid, I could see I was also in a very difficult position. I couldn't go on working for someone who robbed me. But at the same time it was going to be tricky suggesting to Arthur his son was a thief. In the end I decided I had no choice but to give Arthur the facts, and resign.

'Look, Arthur, this is very difficult,' I said into the phone in the hall at the International Language Club, with several of the inmates finding an excuse to be nearby. 'I'm not going to be able to work for you anymore.'

'Why is that, mate?' he asked quite calmly.

'You're not going to like this,' I told him, 'and I don't expect you to believe it, but Evelyn has stolen my wallet.'

I was ready to launch into an explanation of how I had irresistibly arrived at that conclusion, but Arthur didn't give me the chance.

'Yeah,' he sighed, 'the li'l bugga does stuff like dat.' There was silence on the line for a moment before Arthur said: 'Look 'ere, Vic. I'm making you the manager. I'll sack the li'l prick. Eddie'll bring ya wallet back tomorrow.'

And so it came to pass, that after only four days of extremely limited experience in the retailing of cane and rattan furniture, I had shot to the top. I was a manager but without staff to manage, and a virtually empty store. Still I had the glory of my new executive status, I was getting ten quid a week extra, and I had my wallet and its contents back.

Then the deluge hit. Vast quantities of furniture started arriving in huge trucks and I had to try and work out where to put it all. And I didn't know how to account for any of it as it all came without paperwork. Whatever the reasons for this I didn't enquire. But I did know, if I had wanted, I could have robbed Arthur blind, because no-one could be sure what stock had and hadn't arrived. I tried my best to keep it all neat and properly displayed but when Eddie came over to help he just laughed and explained that wasn't how you did it with this sort of retailing.

'Pile it all up, mate. Stick the shit all over the place. If the punters have to search through to find something, they'll think they've got a prize.'

The furniture was very cheap and so it drew the crowds. It was also rubbish. Over the time I worked there I had a lot of trouble with customers who had paid their *cash* only to find the merchandise hadn't been worth the *carry*. One particular big circular recliner had a tendency to collapse under the first sitting.

However for the moment my most urgent need was for another staff member. Agatha worked for me for a day, but decided that was humiliating and took a job at Berlitz language school instead. So I employed a pleasant woman in her early forties named Maggie.

Maggie lived with her boyfriend Jasper, who was a few years older than she, in a big four bedroom house in Sanderstead, which was a village in Surrey just a few minutes' drive south of Croydon. How they came to own such a large house was something I never worked out. Maggie was a shop assistant and Jasper was a 'novelist' whose one novel had met with limited success back in the 1960s. And he appeared to have no other means of support.

Maggie gave me a copy of Jasper's novel to read. I didn't get round to it for a while, which was a shame, because had I read it, I would not have accepted her offer to rent us a room in their house. I had met Jasper briefly and had been a little spooked by his sharp blue eyes that seemed suspicious of everything. He didn't seem to fit with the gentle good humoured character who was Maggie. But I had no reason to think much about him.

However the author of the novel, who jumped from the page with lurid and twisted psycho-sexual descriptions, would not be someone you would rush to share a house with. But as I say I hadn't yet read the novel at that point, and Agatha and I felt it was time to move on from the luxuries of the International Language Club. Now we were both working we could afford a real room and so we took Maggie up on her offer. The room itself was a beautiful attic that looked over the village, and during the first evening we congratulated ourselves on having made such a smart move.

We were forced to reconsider when at dawn the next morning we were woken by a fast thumping sound we couldn't possibly understand or locate. When I was awake enough I realised the noise was coming from just outside our room. I opened the door to see that Jasper had a punching ball on a hook on our door frame. I tried to reason with him above the noise, but without stopping he just let us know it was his house and he could hang his punching ball wherever he chose. It was not a good start, and an appeal to Maggie didn't seem to have much effect. I came to understand over time she was actually quite frightened of him, and not surprisingly.

That same morning when we came down to breakfast, I noticed there was a small circular hole cut in the glass of the kitchen windows. I was soon to discover why. When Jasper came down he was armed with a shotgun. He went straight to the window, shoved the barrel through the hole and started blasting away at the birds in a nearby tree. He brought one down and later that morning, as Agatha and I were walking down the lane behind the house, the same dead bird fell at our feet. Jasper, who had been hiding behind the hedge waiting for us to go by, had lobbed it at us. He thought it was very funny.

Now we were in a difficult position. We were sharing a house with a man we shouldn't have been sharing a house with, and what's more it was his house. It would take time to find somewhere else to live and in the meantime who could guess what Jasper might get up to.

I decided the only possible solution was to work on the assumption that Jasper, like all bullies, was a coward. So I sought a private audience with him, pointed out I was very unhappy, was 20 years his junior and, despite his punch ball training routine, clearly fitter and stronger than he.

Given my smoking and lack of exercise, it was a bluff. But luckily it worked because after that, though he would shoot the odd bird when we weren't there, he never did it in our presence, and the punching ball disappeared altogether. He retreated into a kind of sullenness and we rarely saw him. It is interesting why he didn't just kick us out. Perhaps it was because even though they owned the house they needed the income from our rent. Perhaps he felt, for obvious reasons, he wasn't good at keeping tenants, so he better hang on to us.

What surprises me, when I look back, is how I could be so sublimely confident I had completely neutralised him. How could I have been so sure he wasn't quietly plotting some horrible revenge? But, young and confident, we just stayed on. And when Maggie told us they wanted to rent one of the other rooms as well, we didn't have any hesitation in recommending it to one of Agatha's colleagues from Berlitz, a teacher by the name of Peter Branxton.

Peter was a delicate young gay man with pale skin and curly hair that made him look quite cherubic. He came from aristocratic stock but his own branch of the family had come down in the world because his father had inexplicably chosen to marry a Welsh commoner.

His parents didn't have much money and lived a quiet life in a small historic town in Norfolk. Nonetheless they had managed to send Peter to a fine school and after that he had won a choral scholarship to Oxford. He did have a most amazing tenor voice. The sound of it coming from the room next to ours as he accompanied himself on his clavichord was a whole lot better than the punching bag.

Peter too was a novelist, though unlike Jasper his books were gentle miniatures that reflected his own gentle character. He had written three when we first met him, none of which had been published. He eventually went on to write seven unpublished novels before he finally gave up on his literary dreams, and on England in general, and went to live permanently in Nice.

However for the moment he still lived in hope. It was a 'literary' household because, freed from the time devouring practice of the law, I had started to write the novel I had always wanted to write.

I became very close friends with Peter, and we would sit up late into the night smoking cigars and discussing all manner of topics. I think he was pleased to have me in his life because he was a lonely character. He found it hard to make friends for the very simple reason he couldn't free himself from the indoctrination of his class. He so wanted to be a democrat, but when confronted with anyone who wasn't from his own class he just didn't know how to talk to them. Unlike HRH Prince Charles he was not comfortable with anyone other than his own.

Unfortunately he didn't have the money to keep regular company with his own, so basically that meant he was restricted to the events one just couldn't afford to miss. Once a year he would put on his dress clothes and go to Henley on Thames and once a year he would put on his dress clothes and go to Ascot. But the rest of the time, on his modest Berlitz salary, he found himself alone.

I think as a colonial I was outside the system and so he could spend time with me in comfort. In fact I think in the end the reason he went to France was so he could get outside the system altogether and just relax. I have since discovered that many impoverished English upper class people have done the same thing over the centuries.

I remember one night Agatha and I were about to go to a party in South London with a group of teachers, all of whom were university educated people but from the lower-middle and lower classes. It was before I came to understand the full extent of Peter's class bound problems. He came into our room as I was ironing a shirt.

'Out to a party?' he said.

'Yes, up in Streatham.'

'Aha. Aha.' He hung about. 'Well have a fine time.' And he went to leave the room.

'Why don't you come?' I said as he was leaving. He turned back to me, surprised and with a look of confusion in his eyes.

'Yes...no...well, look I don't think I should.'

'It's not a problem,' I said. 'It's pretty much an open party.'

'Even so...I...I'

'Oh don't be a drongo,' I said.

I figured using 'drongo' might win him over. He loved Australian slang and was always asking me to teach him new words. In fact 'drongo' was his favourite term, though he had no hope of pronouncing it properly. From time to time I would hear him walking round the house practising, but it never came out better than a sort of high pitched pucker 'dronko'.

The 'drongo' did win him because he stopped and said very solemnly: 'Yes, I should, shouldn't I. It would be good for me.'

I had no idea what he meant by that, but came to understand later. In the struggle to turn himself into a functioning democrat it really would be a good idea to expose himself to the other half.

So we went to the party and it was typical of South London parties of the late 70s and early 80s, a shared household with lots of beer and the four gas jets going on the cook top to keep the place warm. As soon as we got there however, Peter's democratic resolve left him. He remained all night, his back glued to the wall, a trembling hand holding a small gin, gazing out over the hordes in horror.

We were all educated and interested in similar things. Peter was a great talker with a fine vocabulary, a range of things to talk about, and he even worked with some of the guests. Yet despite all this, whenever anyone came over to him, he would choke up and could utter only conversation terminating monosyllables.

The three of us lived together for several months in Jasper's house until one defining night when Genevieve came to dinner with her now reconciled Jeremy. They arrived in Jeremy's Rolls Royce, and Jasper was horrified.

'Why didn't you tell me her boyfriend had a Rolls?' he demanded.

'What does it matter?' I asked, perplexed.

'Because if I'd known,' he responded indignantly, 'I would have had time to prepare, time to dress.'

So from that we discovered Jasper was not just a bully and a coward, but a snob as well. And the fawning he did over Jeremy during dinner was close to unbearable, for all of us. Ironically, though the bullying hadn't made Agatha and I feel the need to move, the grovelling did. Or rather it was the final straw. We just couldn't look at him anymore. Peter felt the same. So the three of us moved out and rented a house together deeper into Surrey at a place called Shirley, which was just a penny's throw from Purley.

The house was owned by a Miss Bottomley, whom the real estate agent told us was a fine upstanding spinster (yes he used the term 'spinster') and a missionary in India. He belonged to Miss Bottomley's church, and being a great admirer of her work, he did the agenting for free. He wanted equally upstanding people to rent her house. I'm not sure Agatha and I would have qualified, but Peter, with his patrician bearing and background, was clearly the right stamp of a man, and so we got the place.

The only relic of Miss Bottomley that remained on the premises was an old bicycle that looked like it came from the 1920s. The agent asked us specifically not to ride Miss Bottomley's bicycle. Of course we rode it everywhere, imagining ourselves as the children of The Vicar enjoying our 'salad days'.

The summer was coming on and Shirley was in bloom. Fulham Trading Croydon had become a modest success for Arthur and Eddie. We now had a small staff, a regular turnover, and the stock had even started arriving accompanied by paperwork. Nonetheless I was beginning to feel my days as a cane furniture store manager were coming to an end.

I applied for and got a summer job teaching English to European teenagers which was due to start in June. I handed in my notice to Arthur who insisted on taking me to lunch as a kind of thank you for getting his shop up and running. We had a very pleasant meal somewhere near Croydon. During the sweets Arthur said to me:

'You done a great job, Vic. But the thing I'm most grateful for is ya didn't rob me blind when ya could 'ave.'

'How do you know I didn't?' I said.

'I'm a good judge a character,' he told me. It was a nice compliment from an 'honourable' man.

And so I became a teacher. I had no training and no qualifications, but the Language School was more interested in people who were free over the summer and especially who didn't expect to be paid much.

The branch of the school I was to teach at operated out of a beautiful eighteen century house overlooking a classic English park in Surrey. Most of the students had wealthy parents who not only wanted their children to learn English, but in some cases (especially the Italians), who wanted to get them out of the way of groups like the Red Brigade. It was very active at the time kidnapping the children of the wealthy.

I still think the job at the Language School was the best job I've ever had. For starters it was a beautiful mild English summer and the setting for the school was idyllic. The arrangement was we would teach in the mornings and in the afternoons would take the students on 'educational' sightseeing tours to places like St Pauls or The Tower of London to see the Crown Jewels. In the mornings I would more often than not choose to wander through the park with my students conducting my lesson like some sort of latter day Socrates.

Most of my class were incredibly sophisticated and well educated with, in some cases, almost impeccable English. The way I won their respect was to treat them as the adults they were, to treat them as equals. A trained teacher might say that is the worst thing to do in most teaching situations. But it was the only thing to do here. And I determined to follow through with it no matter what. I remember one day, while I was trying to teach, a good looking Italian boy named Paulo was telling a risqué joke under his breath to a Dutch girl he was interested in. I picked up bits of what he was saying because of course they had to communicate in English.

'I missed the beginning, Paulo,' I said. 'Let's hear the whole joke.'

'No of course you don't want to hear it,' he said, just slightly embarrassed. Embarrassment was an emotion almost unknown to him. So this was a good start.

'No I do,' I said. 'I'm sure the others would too.' I was careful to keep any trace of sarcasm from my voice, to make it sound like I was genuinely interested.

Of course the rest of the class jumped in to insist he tell us the joke, which in the end he had to do. It really was quite funny.

'That's great, Paulo. Excellent use of English idiom,' I said, making sure I kept a perfectly straight face.

I saw Paulo's chest swell out. He was very pleased with himself. After that he became my biggest supporter. Later than day after class was over I went to the local pub with the other teachers and who should be there but Paulo, holding court with some of the girls from the class. He came over to our table and just sat himself down.

'What would you like to drink?' he asked me.

'Paulo, you're only seventeen. You're not allowed to drink in England, let alone buy drinks for your teacher.'

He just smiled his big charming smile and said: 'We won't worry about that. Now what is it you're having?'

I went to protest, but he just held up his hand: 'I'll take the liberty of bringing you a double scotch.'

And he did, and it was a quality whiskey too. Then he sat down again and started telling us all about his home town of Venice. Meanwhile the girls had drifted over to our table. I think only one of them was of legal drinking age. So there I was in flagrant breach of the licensing laws, listening to Paulo's lyrical descriptions, rendered in flawless English, of the glories of his city.

'You must go there,' he was telling me. "I think it is a city which would suit you. And you would suit the city too.'

As we were leaving the pub, later that afternoon, Paulo called out to me: 'Remember Venezia!'

It was to become almost a ritual form of farewell between us. At least once a week over the summer, as he was leaving, Paulo would fix me with his dark eyes that were never quite serious and say: 'Remember Venezia. Remember to go.'

'I will,' I would smile back at him.

I never have gone, but I think it is somewhere I really must go before I die.

Paulo was not the only one in my advanced class with excellent English. Most of them were close to bilingual speakers. One Belgian girl in fact was so good I would play games with her for the amusement of the class. I would throw incredibly tricky English locutions at her to try and catch her out. But she always came back with an impeccable explanation or paraphrase. The only time I got her (and the rest of the class too) was when I gave them four words of almost identical spelling (tough, though, through, trough), explained they were pronounced four different ways and asked them to give me those pronunciations. They couldn't, and when I told them the answer a whistle of disbelief echoed round the room. And so the teacher kept his nose just above water line, thanks to the sublime idiocy of the English language.

With a class like that I knew standard grammar lessons would be a waste of time. So each morning I would come in with a new and different poem by someone like Christopher Isherwood, John Betjeman, Wilfred Owen or some other archetypal English poet I had got Peter to recommend. I would start by reading the poem. Then I would ask them to comment, in any way they liked, not just on the poem's literary worth but on its philosophy or even just the facts it revealed.

And when the first student did comment I would question that comment or take it in some tangential direction. I used my skills as a cross examiner to tease and taunt all sorts of ideas and opinions out of them. Not that they needed much teasing as most were confident and loved the chance to express their views on anything that came up. Soon a debate would be raging across the classroom which would take all sorts of directions that had nothing to do with the poem. And that was the idea. Within a few minutes the poem would be forgotten, but the conversation would ebb and flow till morning tea time, full of excitement.

If needs be I would correct their English, but not often. The aim of my game was to get them using the wonderful English they already had in ways they hadn't thought of. It was exhausting for them but they loved it, and often would be reluctant to get on the bus for the afternoon excursion till every burning coal of their disputation had been extinguished.

The trips to London every afternoon were delightful. Not only did I get to see all sorts of attractions I hadn't yet seen, but got to observe the often hilarious cultural exchanges between my students and the unsuspecting London public. Most people found the openness of my students, especially the Italians like Paulo, a refreshing change. The only real problem we ever had was one hot day when the students decided they wanted to buy ice cream. There was an ice cream van, I think it was in Trafalgar Square, and it was busy. In fact there was a long queue stretching back maybe ten metres. The English of course value their ability to form an orderly and civilised queue. And that's what they had done here. Although the counter was quite wide and three quarters of it was vacant, the English had formed their queue stretching back from just one end.

However the only thing my students could see was a big vacant area of counter that no-one had thought to approach. The long snaking queue, especially for the Italians, made no sense and was thus worthy of being dismissed from their minds. For them it would have been as inexplicable as if drivers in Rome had suddenly all decided to drive down the street on the same side one behind the other.

The French students probably understood what was going on, but felt if the English were stupid enough to get in a long skinny queue and leave the rest of the counter vacant, then that was typically English and worthy only of scorn. Either way they all just rushed up to the vacant part of the counter and started putting in their orders.

Well, there was rioting in the ranks. The English in the queue were horrified, and began articulating that horror to the van operators and to me in particular. I understood how disturbing this was to them, but I didn't know what to do about it. I tried dragging my students away from the counter, but once the queuers started baying at them they just thought it one big delightful joke, and redoubled their efforts to get their ice creams ahead of the English.

I turned to the queue and tried to explain the cultural differences and why that might lead to such a flagrant breach of etiquette. But one big North Country man was not about to be mollified. He actually took the unprecedented step of leaving his place in the queue to come and tower over me.

'I don't need no bloody foreigner to teach me 'ow to queue,' he bellowed.

I wasn't sure whether the 'bloody foreigner' was me or the student body. Either way it was looking ugly. Fortunately Paulo came to my rescue. He realised what was happening and yelled at his fellow students to quit the counter. They obeyed immediately and the day was saved.

Paulo knew I was Australian. As we walked away from the ice cream van he linked his arm in mine and said with a twinkle in his eye:

'Victor, the English are a strange breed, don't you find?'

It was not the only time Paulo was to come to my rescue. Normally each afternoon three buses would turn up, one for each class, to take the students up to their London excursion. But one day a few weeks after the ice cream incident, only one bus arrived.

We didn't know what to do so I decided to ring Yvonne de la Mer, the head of the school, to see if she could sort it out. But she just told me to put them all on the one bus. I explained that was impossible. It would be illegal and very dangerous, even if we could squash them all on. She insisted. Again I explained the difficulty. She told me she was coming down.

Half an hour later Yvonne arrived looking very put out:

'Get the children on the bus,' she barked at me.

'I'm not prepared to do that,' I said.

Yvonne raised herself up to the fullest possible height of haughtiness, and looking down her sleek elongated nose, serenely informed me I would do as I was told.

I informed her that I quit.

She said that was a fine decision.

I collected my stuff and went home. An hour and a half later I got a phone call from Yvonne. She was nauseatingly pleasant. In fact her voice sounded strangely tortured and almost unrecognisable. She was forced to admit the students had gone on strike until things got sorted out with me. I could hear it was killing her to tell me this. But I could also hear she didn't feel she had a choice. So of course I came back to the school, and they all gave three cheers and Yvonne looked like she wanted to kill me whilst saying how glad she was I'd decided to come back.

The next day I got the full story from the other teachers. Apparently Paulo, once he learned what had happened, and having observed the tactics of the workers in his father's factory, immediately raised the metaphorical red banner, and organised the other students into a sit down strike in the park. He told Yvonne de la Mer that unless she apologised and got me to come back, they were certainly not returning to class. Furthermore they would leave for their home countries forthwith to tell their parents what a shabby school they had been sent to. They would make sure, he said, no-one else would ever come to her school again.

So I kept teaching my 'Bolsheviks' for the rest of the term and then we all said goodbye. It was a tearful occasion, that last afternoon in the park. I did see one French boy, Pierre, again not so long after. The others have all gone their own ways. I think of them often.

I remember once using for our discussion starter Macbeth's soliloquy: *Tomorrow and tomorrow and tomorrow, creeps in this petty pace*...and asking them whether life was in fact as hopeless as Shakespeare's character would have us believe. Their answers didn't surprise me. They all said it was not hopeless at all and they were about to prove that by going off and becoming all the things their dreams called them to become.

One was going to design tall elegant city buildings which would be his lasting testament, another was going to heal the entire continent of Africa, and I think Paulo was going to reform the Italian Parliament from within. I like to think they are well on the way to doing all those things.

Paulo and the other students were a great antidote for someone who had grown up not feeling wanted. Their enthusiasm and their joy in class had made me feel very wanted. And the strike made me feel wanted like I had never been wanted before. For those gifts I will always think of them as amongst my more memorable and dynamic angels. They were certainly my friends.

After the Language School I took another month full time in Shirley to finish my novel. Holding the finished manuscript in my hand was an amazing feeling which I'm sure everyone experiences who has actually completed something that big and that daunting for the first time in their lives. I can't remember what it was called, nor even what it was about. No doubt it had a big lashing of 'coming of age' in it, and was ill thought out, lacking in honesty and cliché riddled. At least that was what Agatha believed, and she was probably right. It has long since disappeared, no doubt cast into the fire in a drunken moment of artistic despair - or maybe I just lost it. Anyway agents and publishers were spared the need to read it.

13. MADAME MASSE AND THE KITCHEN TABLE

I'm not sure when I first developed the idea I had been a French lieutenant in the Franco Prussian War of 1870. I suspect it was in Year 10, along with a whole range of other romantic Francophile notions. At 15 I had felt myself misplaced and imagined everything would have been different if only I had been born and raised somewhere else, somewhere more cultural, more intellectual, more romantic, which of course, as I was studying French, had to be France.

I was the best student in the class, or at least I could do the best French accent. Where had this natural ability come from, this affinity with all things *Français*? Clearly I must be drawing on past lives, and what better past life to have than to be on the losing side in that ever so romantic war? I think I even developed scenarios of being trapped behind German lines and being sheltered in a farmhouse by a beautiful young *fräulein,* who despite being my enemy, was overcome by the instant passion between us, and couldn't bring herself to turn me in. That French lieutenant lived on. And now here I was in a queue at the French Embassy in London, waiting to get my visa to 'return' to my spiritual home.

We had applied for student visas to study French in the special course for foreigners at the University of St Etienne. We had to have every possibly relevant document translated into French and then we had to swear the equivalent of a statutory declaration that under no circumstances, on pain of instant expulsion, would we accept paid work whilst there. Now we were armed with these several dozen pieces of paper, standing in a very long queue, and I was reminded that the word 'bureaucracy' is a French word.

I noticed that everyone in the line ahead of us was a black African, obviously from ex French colonies. In fact we were the only white people in the room. Now the clerk at our window seemed to be waving to us to come to the head of the line. We looked about. Were we mistaken? Was he waving to someone else?

'*Allez-y! Vite!*' He was calling to us. 'Let's go. Hurry up.'

It took me a moment to absorb this dilemma. We had maybe 12 people ahead of us in the queue. They were all black. The clerk was signalling us to come up and be dealt with before them. It was hard to avoid the idea that our special treatment had something to do with the colour of our skin.

In that short moment I realised we had two choices. On the one hand we could refuse to be a party to this flagrant act of racial discrimination, stand our ground, have a very long wait whilst everyone ahead of us had their dozens of documents scrutinised, and then in all probability be given a hard time by the clerk for refusing his offer of preferential treatment, and perhaps even have our documents rejected. On the other hand we could just go to the head of the queue. Whilst I would like to say we took the loftier option, in fact we just went to the head of the queue.

We took our old Volkswagen fastback on the cross channel ferry and landed on French soil at Calais. It was a long drive to St Etienne which was near the Massif Central about 50 kilometres from Lyon. Unfortunately this was a dark time in the history of Anglo/French relations known on both sides of The Channel as the *Guerre de Mouton* (the Mutton War). I forget the details but think it had something to do with the English stockpiling mutton and undercutting French sheep farmers.

The practical problem for us was that driving through the countryside could be dangerous. Many French, especially sheep farmers, when they saw an English car, would pelt it with rotten fruit or garbage or hose it as it went by. So often I would not be able to see out of the windscreen and would have to pull over, which only made us an easier target for more rotten fruit. Of course I would try yelling out things like:

'*Nous ne sommes pas Anglais. Nous sommes Australiens. Nous détestons les Anglais. Vive les moutons Français.*' (We are not English. We are Australians. We hate the English. Long live French sheep).

Sometimes this would work, but more often than not they would just think we were cowardly English trying to avoid our fate by claiming to be Australians and they would redouble their pelting.

On top of that the French student body was also protesting something at the time. I can't remember what it was but it had nothing to do with sheep or the English. So they had no problem with us per se. But again their mode of protestation had practical problems for us as we went through the towns. What the students would do would be to run down the road alongside a row of cars waiting at traffic lights. They had their protest posters and a pot of glue. They would slap glue on the poster and then slap the poster on the front windscreen of the car on the passenger side.

The problem for us was that in our right hand drive car the passenger side was the driver side. The protesting students, in their rush, wouldn't notice and so I would have a huge poster stuck on the windscreen in front of me and couldn't see to drive. I would have to pull over in heavy traffic to remove the poster and that rarely made me popular with the other drivers.

Perhaps my most glorious driving moment however was in Paris when I chose to go the wrong way down the four lane *Boulevard Périphérique* and managed to bring what looked like the entire city to a halt. It is a frightening experience to be facing that many cars head on with nowhere to go. It was at that time I learned my first French obscenity:

'Et ta soeur!', many of the drivers yelled at once. It means literally 'And your sister', which at first blush seems harmless enough, until you learn that *et ta soeur* is just shorthand, being the final words of a long and very pornographic insult.

Somehow, despite snapped accelerator cables, several more cases of driving on the wrong side of the road, and several more attempts to stigmatise my sister, we finally made it to St Etienne. On the outskirts I stopped and went into a shop for something. It was to be my baptism by water. The shopkeeper covered me in spittle as he spoke. Naturally I thought he had a speech impediment. But after I had been into several shops, I began to realise the chance of them all having the same speech impediment was highly unlikely, and I learned to converse at a distance. I came to understand that the local accent, known as *l'accent Gaga*, demanded a good healthy spray. It was not a feature I could, or really wanted to master, and it certainly made understanding difficult. Mind you, in the long run it is a great training ground. Months later when we went up to Paris, after spending time with Les Stéphanois, the notorious Parisian accent was as clear as a bell to me.

We found a place to rent quickly, an apartment in a little village called St-Priest-en-Jarez, at the end of the tram line at the southern end of St Etienne. We were on the third floor of a building with paper thin walls and wooden floorboards that, if you walked in shoes on them, created an echo chamber in the flat below.

Our downstairs neighbour, whom we knew from her name on the letterbox to be Mademoiselle Y. Youillon (or 'Eegrek' as we called her - Eegrek being how the French say the letter 'Y'), rushed upstairs the first time we brought shopping home, ranting about the noise we were making. At first we couldn't quite understand what her problem was, as she used an extreme form of *Le Gaga*. So we just smiled and nodded. But from the intensity of her distress we finally got the message that you had to leave your shoes in the hallway at the bottom of the stairs and walk up in your socks. Next time we obliged, only to find our shoes got stolen.

Later on Eegrek also took the trouble to explain to us that the custom, when you moved in to a new apartment, was to have your name engraved on a small gold plaque and have it attached to your letterbox. She took us to the letterboxes and showed us how everyone did that, stressing that the gold plaque was really the way to go. Other options, such as the one we had chosen, of scrawling our names on a torn piece of paper and affixing it with scotch tape, were not acceptable.

We should have listened to her advice. This was a conservative provincial community. They had their ways of doing things. But we felt the torn paper would serve our purpose well enough. We didn't even take the hint when we saw written in French underneath our names on the same piece of paper what might be best translated as:

'May I suggest you acquire a gold plaque. Warmest Regards, Your Postman.'

When we didn't comply with his kind suggestion, he forced down the window of our car and threw the mail on the front driver's seat. This he continued to do till the plaque was affixed.

Meanwhile I had started on the business of our bureaucratic requirements. I was obliged, within the first week, to present myself, with all our translated documents, and our visas, to *Monsieur Le Préfet*. The office of the 'Prefect' is a purely French institution. He is neither a police official nor a member of local government, but runs parallel with both, and in many ways has authority over both. He would best be described as the representative of the President and Central Government in the town in question.

Whatever his exact functions, everyone in every French town outside Paris knows that the Prefect is the big cheese, and nothing is allowed to happen unless he authorises it, including the settlement and university enrolment of a visiting Australian couple. When you think that St Etienne was a town of half a million people, and that the Prefect had to personally scrutinise our documents, you realise just how centralised French administration is, and how busy the poor Prefect must be.

So I duly presented myself to *Monsieur Le Préfet*. He was an overweight red faced man, but someone who seemed surprisingly relaxed for all the responsibility he was carrying. He took some time looking over our documents, and told me they seemed fine as far as they went, but of course I would be required to have them all translated again by a local translator.

At first I thought I hadn't understood his French. In Anglo Saxon terms that just didn't make sense. We had had our documents translated by a translator authorised by the French Embassy in London, which was satisfied enough to give us a visa. What could possibly be gained by having them translated again? The answer was it would satisfy the will of the all powerful *Monsieur Le Préfet.*

So off I went to the local translator, who was very excited to discover I was a lawyer. There were very few people in St Etienne who could speak English at all and certainly no-one who knew anything about English law. And yet he always had legal documentation that required English translation. Would I be interested, he asked me, in working for him, translating these documents?

I was presented with two problems here. First of all, as the statutory declaration he currently held in his hand indicated, I had sworn that I wouldn't work. Secondly my French was woeful. I could barely order lunch, let alone translate legal documents. He, like many others, obviously thought my French was better than it actually was, because I could affect a good accent.

The irony of how the first problem had arisen, did not escape me. If the Prefect hadn't insisted on a totally unnecessary second translation of our documents, I would never have had the opportunity to meet the man who was now making me a job offer. This fact, plus a general lack of any sense of moral obligation to the French immigration laws, enabled me to believe it wasn't really a problem at all.

The second problem was a little more concerning. However here too I managed to convince myself that I would pick up the necessaries as I went along. After all, the translator had a specialist French/English legal and commercial dictionary, and that would have to be a big help. Besides I would be able to work at home, which meant he wouldn't need to see me struggling for hours over every line. And what better way to improve my French?

I had always hoped I would be able to pick up a little work in France. We didn't have nearly enough money to stay long term unless I did. But I hadn't expected a chance to come so quickly and in such an 'interesting' way. In the end I did feel the need to point out the obvious to the translator, which was that he was about to translate a document whereby I swore that under no circumstances would I work. But when he just waved his hand as though that were some technicality we could overlook, I agreed to take the job.

Over the following months I was to translate a number of legal contracts for him, and the process certainly did improve my French. But I have to admit there were large slabs of almost every document where I had severe doubts about whether I had accurately rendered the parties' contractual agreement. I fear I may have caused long term confusion in, if not damage to, certain Anglo/French commercial relations.

Be that as it may, I now had a second local translation of our documents (charged at mates' rates by my new employer), which I duly took back to the Prefect. This time he barely looked at them before assuring me that all was in order and we were free to stay and start our course.

Then as I got up to leave he motioned me to sit down again. He was obviously searching for the right thing to say:

'Monsieur Kline,' he began in a tone which was half way between guilty and cheeky, 'my daughter is at High School. She is studying many interesting subjects, including English.' Her paused to look at me. He was clearly trying to gauge my reaction. But I had no idea what I was supposed to be reacting to.

'Does she enjoy the English?' I asked, hoping I was on the right track.

'Ah well,' he sighed, 'there we have the problem.' Clearly I had been somewhere near the right track. 'Whilst she admires the beauty of the English language, she is having some trouble coming to grips with it.'

'Ah,' I said, 'yes it can be tricky.'

'Indeed. Indeed. And of course I want her to do well in her exams.'

'Of course.'

'And I would be more than happy to arrange a tutor for her, to pay for a tutor.' He paused to look at me again.

'Of course?' I repeated, hesitatingly.

'But alas, here in St Etienne we have very few people who speak English, and none who can teach it.'

'That is a shame,' I said. Could this be going where I thought it was going?

'Monsieur Kline?'

'Yes, *Monsieur le Préfet*.'

'I notice from your documents that you have taught English in London, and that you are an esteemed advocate.'

'I have taught a little English,' I confessed.

'Then do you think it might be appropriate if I were to offer you the position of English tutor to my daughter.' At this he bestowed a huge warm smile on me.

'*Monsieur le Préfet*,' I said, 'I would be honoured to accept.'

And so, as part of the same process of ensuring I didn't work during my time in France, I acquired work teaching English to the daughter of the principal upholder of the law in St Etienne. After that I felt I was in a somewhat protected position and proceeded to advertise as an English teacher in the local paper, as a result of which I picked up a lot more work.

Meanwhile we had begun our French course at the University of St Etienne. It was a motley concoction of classes including one grammar teacher who seemed to go out of his way to make a dry topic dryer, setting us one dreary example after another, whilst employing the slowest most monotonous voice I had yet heard in all of France.

The funny thing was that when the class was over he would chat to the English speakers in perfect American English which he delivered with verve and enthusiasm. I often wondered why he couldn't bring the same approach to his own language and the teaching of it. Did he change cultures when he changed languages?

Our literature teacher was a young Jewish woman who spent a lot of time talking about the horrors of the holocaust and how we should never forget what had happened. We sympathised with her but often wondered how she kept finding segues to that topic from the poetry of Verlaine and Rimbaud. Nonetheless her classes were fun and we did learn quite a lot about French literature.

Meanwhile I had become friends with a local GP by the name of Madame Masse. Her son Pierre had been in my class at the Language School in London, and one day a couple of months after we arrived I had run into him in the street. I was amazed at the co-incidence, but he behaved as if nothing could be more normal, and immediately invited us home to meet his mother. We went over the next afternoon and had a delightful chat with her. Or rather she had a delightful chat with us.

Madame Masse was a single mother, a woman in her early forties, and a dynamo. She would talk to us at a speed we couldn't possibly hope to follow. It was either flattering she thought we could follow French at the speed of light, or else she just didn't care. I suspect the latter. She loved to talk, she loved to talk fast and she loved to talk continuously. We may not have understood everything or even much of what she said, but we understood what was being said was being said with passion.

At the same time she made us feel very welcome. When she invited us to dinner, as she did on several occasions, she went all out. One Saturday night she had decided we were going to have fondue but because she felt the local cheese merchants of St Etienne were inferior, she drove to Geneva to get the cheese.

I think it may have been that night I 'made the mistake' of seeking a medical opinion from her. For a couple of weeks prior I had been feeling pain in my remaining testicle. Now it had been explained to me the chances of getting the cancer in the other testicle were ridiculously slight. Because the two testicles operated on separate circulatory systems, the cancer literally could not spread from one to the other. For me to get the cancer in the other testicle I would need to suffer a separate and independent contraction of the disease. As the chances of getting it once were 100,000 to 1, the chance of getting it twice were 100,000 x 100,000 or about 10 billion to 1.

Nonetheless when you go through something like my cancer treatment, it is very difficult to re-assure yourself with statistics. I had pain, it felt like the pain I had originally had in the other testicle and I was worried. So after dinner, when Pierre had gone to his room, and we were alone with Madame Masse in the lounge room I asked her if I might come to her surgery on Monday for a consultation. She said that would be silly. If I had a problem, consult her now. So I did and explained my concerns.

'Let's have a look', she said in her rapid fire French. 'Come in the kitchen.'

So I followed her into the kitchen. She made me take off my trousers and lie on my back on the kitchen table, where she gently manipulated my testicle. Unfortunately in the middle of her examination Pierre decided he wanted a drink.

'Maman, is there any coke in...' he said as he came through the door, only to be stopped in his tracks by the sight of his mother apparently playing with his ex teacher's genitals on the kitchen table.

But Madame Masse was not fazed. She turned to him, and without even the faintest attempt at an explanation, said simply:

'Get out'.

And after a long moment's hesitation her shame-faced son retreated backwards out of the kitchen. I'm not sure if she ever bothered to explain to him what she was really doing.

Madame Masse's diagnosis was delivered in a French no less rapid than anything else she said. As a result I didn't get hold of everything. However she seemed to be saying there wasn't a problem, but just to be safe she thought I should see her specialist friend at the St Etienne Hospital. Perhaps if my French had been better or if she had spoken just a little slower I would have fully understood what she was suggesting. As it was I went like a lamb to the slaughter.

The specialist met me at reception, assured me he had been fully briefed by Madame Masse and thanked me for agreeing to come. I thought that last was very polite indeed. He took me down the hall and we went into a room which I expected to be his consulting surgery. Instead the door opened into a very big empty space with an examination table in the centre. He asked me to take my trousers off and to lie on my back on the table. He then left the room and I did as I was told.

I lay there for a few minutes wondering why he needed to examine me in such a big space. But then things were always just a little different in a foreign country. After a few minutes more I was surprised when a young woman came into the room. I didn't know who she was, and was of course embarrassed to be lying there without my trousers. She smiled at me, a little embarrassed too, and went and stood near the door with her back to the wall. Soon after that a young man, of about her age, entered and stood near her, his back also to the wall.

Then as dozens more started flooding in, I came to finally understand. This was a teaching hospital, these were medical students, and they were going to be present at my examination. As I lay there, wearing no trousers, with perhaps as many as 30 young people staring at my genitals, I questioned the wisdom of having consulted Madame Masse.

The doctor took his time in coming back, which heightened both my embarrassment, and as far as I could see, the embarrassment of many of the young students. They were trying to look professional, but most couldn't quite pull it off. After all there was a man, naked from the waist down, lying silently in the middle of the room.

Eventually the doctor did come back and began lecturing them on my form of cancer. Then he explained that he was going to show them how to examine the testicle to see if there was a tumour. They all crowded round. He leant over me and in very beautiful French said:

'First of all you must be careful never to do it like this.' And he grabbed my testicle and squeezed mercilessly.

I screamed.

The students all murmured. 'Aha, oh yes, I see.'

'Nor,' he continued, 'should you do this.'

Again I screamed as once more he brutalised my private parts. More murmuring from the students.

Eventually, when I could clearly endure no more, he showed them the right way to do it, and I was released to put my pants back on.

Afterwards I asked him if everything looked all right. He didn't seem to understand what I meant.

'My testicle,' I said, 'is there any chance I have the cancer in my testicle.'

He looked at me surprised:

'Of course not. To get it in both testicles would be a 10 billion to one chance.'

Well, at least I had advanced the cause of medical education in St Etienne. He thanked me again and I hobbled back to the car.

A couple of months after my adventure at St Etienne's teaching hospital we got an invitation from Jane Lydbury, a friend from London. She was asking us to spend a week in Paris with her. Her sister and brother-in-law were journalists, foreign correspondents, who lived on a boat which was permanently moored on the Seine, right near the Pont Alexandre III and the Champs- Élysées. They were both off doing stories in the Middle East and the boat was free.

It was a unique experience to live for a whole week on a boat in such a romantic locale. Six of us had gathered there on the *Bateau Almeria*, which was an ex Admiral's pinnace. Jane's brother-in-law and sister had bought and fitted it out as a home, so they could live out their dream of residing in a part of Paris otherwise reserved for millionaires.

In the day we would sit on the deck drinking pastis and watching the traffic on the Seine, or the people who wandered along the bank, the lovers arm in arm, the brisk business people and the wide eyed tourists. Or we would wander up for coffee on the Champs Élysées. At night the gentle rocking from the current of the river gave me the best sleep I have ever had before or since.

We got to know some of the extensive ex-patriot English speaking community who lived permanently on the Seine. They were an interesting *demi-monde*, people who had lost a lot of their own culture without having integrated into the one in which they lived. I found their language fascinating. It was thoroughly English but included a wide range of French words which reflected their immediate environment. They had no conscious idea they were using French words. It was just part of their Parisian English dialect.

Our neighbour, that is the man who lived on the boat one down the river, was an American ex CIA agent, who had been retired from the service after suffering a massive heart attack. He had come to Paris to live out his days in peace. And I came very close to spoiling his dream.

About the third day we were there he came onto our boat and asked us all to crew for him. He was taking his boat down river to the confluence with the Marne. We protested we knew nothing about boats. I protested the loudest, remembering the experience of the last time I had been part of an untrained crew in the Timor Sea. But he was insistent. This was a motor launch. This was a river. Nothing like that could happen here. Just relax, he told us. He would show us what to do.

So we agreed to crew for him and had a very pleasant day sailing the Seine and the Marne Rivers. Towards evening we motored back towards the mooring spot, and he told Jane and I that we would be responsible for helping him tie up the boat. We would be throwing the lines to him on the dock. Jane would throw the bow line, and I would throw the stern.

As we pulled in to the dock he cut the motors, jumped off and waited for our throws. Jane threw hers and he tied the bow. But when I came to throw mine I realised I had somehow got hold of the wrong rope. When I tried to throw it my arm jerked back because the rope was only a couple of feet long. I scrambled around looking for what might be the right rope, the CIA agent yelling incomprehensible things at me all the time.

But now, driven by the current of the river, the untethered stern of the boat was starting to swing out into the Seine. We all realised it would keeping swinging round with the current until it had done a 180 degree turn and the side that was formerly abutting the river would be abutting the dock. That wouldn't have been such a problem except for the fact that the owner's very expensive fibreglass dinghy was attached to the side that used to be abutting the river. The dinghy would be crushed against the dock as the current swung the boat into its 'new mooring'.

I watched in horror as the poor owner rushed to the stern and desperately tried to hold the boat away from the dock with his bare hands.

His face was red as a beetroot. 'Don't subject yourself to stress,' the cardiac specialist had told him. I thought he was going to die. I thought I had killed him for sure. But eventually he could hold the boat no more, and it crushed the fibreglass dinghy to pieces. He stood there weeping but alive. By the time we left Paris he was still alive. I did not enquire beyond that.

A week or so after we returned to St Etienne I got a letter from the government department responsible for inland waterways. It told me my application for the job of boatman on the Loire had been successful. It remains one of the great mysteries of my life. I had no recollection of putting in for such a job, and can't imagine why I would have. To teach English to the Prefect's daughter on a wink from him was one thing, but to become a full time employee of the regional government was quite another. However there was no doubt about the offer. It had my name and details, the salary I was to be paid and when I could start.

Of course this meant we could stay in France as long as we liked. It is something I very much wanted to do. I had settled well into life in St Etienne and was starting to make real progress with the language. But I was still a long way from fluency. The jobs I had had so far were irregular, not to say illegal. But now, with this full time job, we would have the money and the security. This was my chance to achieve what I had come here to achieve and in comfort.

However it was also a chance to avoid dealing with the fact that nightmares remained my constant companion. I was of course still trying to run away. But no-one can run forever. The breathless attempt to stay ahead of the pursuer, may keep the fears at bay, somewhat, and for some of the time. But in the nights and in the quiet moments, they will catch you. The unconscious comes tapping. And going home was always going to raise the threat of having to acknowledge the unthinkable.

Unfortunately, or perhaps fortunately, Agatha had never really settled into life in St Etienne and wanted to go home. The job offer brought that all to a head. In the end we decided home it would be. We said goodbye to *Monsieur Le Préfet* and his daughter, Pierre and Madame Masse, my ever tolerant translator, our fellow students at the University and all my own English students. I politely refused the job offer of boatman on the Loire. We drove our Volkswagen back to London, gave it to a friend and flew back to Sydney. It was to be many years before I would be back in France again, and that would be under very different circumstances.

14. AUNT EUNICE AND THE PARTY LINE

'Everything old is new again'. Or is it 'everything new is old again'? Either way, after five or six years' absence, in places as different as Alice Springs, London and St Etienne, coming back to my home town was new and old all at once, and quite disorienting. Agatha's great Aunt Eunice had gone into permanent care, so the idea was we would rent out her flat, at mate's rates, whilst getting the money together for our own place. Aunt Eunice's flat was a 'unique residence' within a unique community. Five sisters inhabited three houses in a row. In the first was Agatha's widowed grandmother. Next to her was a profoundly deaf great Aunt with her equally profoundly deaf husband. Then in the third house, three more widowed great Aunts had lived. Two of these three had decided the third, Eunice, was impossible to live with, so they built her a flat of her own on top of the house. There she lived for some years before deciding to take herself off to one of Sydney's premier private hospitals for permanent care. Hence the vacant flat.

The first thing I learned when we moved in was we could not play loud music. It didn't bother the great aunts underneath, but it was very troublesome for the deaf couple next door. The first time we did it, he came over with a note pad.

'The vibrations!' he wrote.

'Sorry,' I wrote underneath, 'we'll keep it down.'

The problem was, after that, whoever played loud music in the neighbourhood, he assumed it was us. Clearly he could feel the vibrations but couldn't tell where they were coming from. So regularly he would turn up on the doorstep with the note pad, and I would usher him in so he could write:

'The vibrations!'

And I would write underneath: 'It isn't us.'

At which point he would look suspiciously around the living room. But when he saw there was no light on the record player and nothing spinning on the turntable, he would leave, casting a sidelong glance at the bedroom, just in case we had another secret vibrating implement stashed in there.

Eunice's flat was tiny. It had one small bedroom, with a single iron frame bed, a combination lounge/dining/kitchen and a bathroom that was so narrow you had to slide in sideways. If you were a man, you could find nowhere to stand properly and so had to pee at a very dangerous angle, or pee sitting down. It was during my first venture into the bathroom I came to suspect, just possibly, the flat had been built without council approval.

The biggest practical problem however came from the downstairs great aunts. They never left the house and lived in the few remaining square feet not taken up by stacks of newspapers and Women's Weeklies dating back to the 1930s which were piled in rows down the hallways and round the walls of all the rooms. They were always friendly when they saw us and quite liked our music. But they were on the other end of a party line.

A party line was a phone line that was shared by two or more parties. That is to say they were not extensions but separate phone numbers that used the same line. It was cheaper for each user that way. So when Eunice had moved upstairs she had got her own number but for the sake of saving money they had all agreed on a party line. Again it made little sense given she had plenty of money. But the great aunts had all been through the Depression, and like many who had, they were curiously frugal.

I was amazed they could even get a party line. I thought they had disappeared in Australia just after the War. But nonetheless there it was, and there was my problem, because when one 'party' was talking on the line, any other 'party' could listen in, or in the case of the aunts, join in. So I would be applying for a job and would be talking to some prospective employer, trying to sound professional, when one of the great aunts would jump on the party line and, in her high pitched broad country accent, would interrupt with something like:

'Hello dear. Would you mind having a look to see if Eunice's frilly bloomers are still in her drawer? They're so comfie, and she always lent them to me when I had a rash.'

In an attempt to dodge the party line, I went down to the Sydney University job centre. The employment officer was enthusiastic:

'What about ASIO?' he said, as his very first suggestion. 'They're always looking for smart young things. Could get you a job there for sure.'

'Don't you need some sort of security check?' I asked, amazed he could so confidently guarantee a job with the Secret Service.

'Not really,' he said with a wave of the hand. 'Uni graduate, Australian citizen. You're a shoe in.'

"I don't actually believe there should be a secret service,' I told him.

'Pity,' he replied philosophically. 'But then most grads feel that way.'

I wondered how many graduates he had to try before he could 'sell' an ASIO job.

'Ok then,' he said, 'what about Reader's Digest?'

I laughed. There had been rumours for years that Reader's Digest, with their headquarters in the macabrely named Pleasantville USA, was just a front for the CIA. We had thought it a joke. But could it be true? Was the next job offer after ASIO always going to be with the Digest? Anyway, again politely I declined.

I went on applying for jobs but was having trouble finding work. I was determined not to go back into the law. I still believed it was the cause or part of the cause of my unhappiness. Plus I wanted to write and I knew the law allowed for no other master. Nonetheless Agatha's father Mike had a friend who was a judge on the Industrial Court in New South Wales. I had met him, and had liked him very much. He was smart and down to earth. Mike had discovered he needed a new Associate and suggested me for the job. It was something people usually did straight out of law school, but it would be a great way for me to ease back in, and maybe learn about a new area of the law, which would help if I did decide to go back into practice.

The judge told Mike he would be happy to see me for an interview. There wasn't much doubt the job would be mine if I wanted it. In the circumstances I really thought I ought to give it a go, so an interview was set up for one o'clock the following Monday. The judge would see me in chambers when the Court was in recess. He was even going to arrange for lunch to be brought in for us.

The night before the interview we went to bed around midnight. Agatha was sleeping on the single bed and I had a temporary mattress on the floor. There was nothing special about the night. We hadn't drunk anything. We hadn't taken any sleeping pills. We had been back for a couple of weeks so jet lag wasn't a problem. Nonetheless we slept for 13 hours and woke just before one o'clock.

I had never slept 13 hours straight in my life. I had never slept anything like 13 hours straight in my life. And now what was I to do about the interview? Even if I left immediately, unshaven and undressed, I would still be an hour late. These were not the days of mobile phones. I couldn't ring and claim to be caught in traffic. Besides traffic jams in the middle of the day in Sydney in the early 1980s were rare. I couldn't even ring to say I was sick, because if I were, courtesy would have demanded I call long before the very moment I was due for the interview.

In the end all I could do was ring the judge, tell the truth and throw myself on his mercy. However I could tell by his voice he was far from impressed. He said he would contact me soon to arrange another time. But he never did.

The only way I could explain to myself what had happened, was that I had experienced some sort of bizarre 'miracle'. I had not wanted to go back into the law, and I had not wanted it so badly my body just kept me sleeping till the very moment it was certain I would offend the judge and lose the chance at getting the position.

But the most miraculous part of that 'miracle' was that Agatha slept through the 13 hours as well, something she had never done in her life either. She wanted me to go back into the law. It was in her interests to wake up. But she didn't. She was angry with herself. She was angrier with me.

I did get a job not long after that, but not in the law. It was as a commissioning editor at Butterworths legal publishers. It was a fun job where I had to use my legal knowledge to dream up new books and other publications which law students and the legal profession might need, and then find people to write them. It meant visiting a lot of law faculties and barristers chambers, not only in Sydney but around the country.

Now that I had work, though poorly paid, we could afford to look for a house. In the end we bought a somewhat dilapidated two bedroom wooden/fibro 1860s workman's cottage in a charming street in East Balmain in the very early stages of Balmain's metamorphosis from the home of miners to the home of young corporate lawyers. When we bought, the street had a mixture of factory workers, unemployed, artists and television producers. The young corporate lawyers had not yet arrived.

The problem was that days after we signed the contract Australia plunged into a series of interest rate rises that more or less double the mortgage payments and made it impossible for us to afford to live in our own house. Mike told us not to worry. It would only be temporary, and in the meantime we could continue to stay at Aunt Eunice's flat. He was wrong. The interest rates kept going up and stayed up for two more years.

In fact we didn't have enough money to pay the mortgage even with a tenant giving us rent. So I took on some extra work. Butterworths published a number of series of Law Reports, the publications which record legal precedents and which barristers use in court. I worked outside of office hours as a reporter on several of these series.

I didn't mind this extra work because it was interesting and I found I had a real flair for it. I also wanted to be a writer and was keen to do any sort of writing. I was also writing restaurant reviews for the first edition of Cheap Eats in Sydney, articles on legal history for The Macquarie Book of Events and trying my hand at writing short stories, even winning the world's most obscure prize for best short story in the 'Eaglehawk Dahlia and Arts Festival'. And the skills I learned as a law reporter were to have unforseen benefits later on.

Nonetheless, for the moment, living in Balmain was out of the question. So we began what was to become a strange, cold existence at Aunt Eunice's. Agatha was not happy at the thought of living there, when a simple decision on my part to go back into the law could enable us to move into our own home. So what joy and what intimacy was left in our relationship continued to fade. Each night we would go to bed with Agatha up in the high frame single and me on the mat on the floor.

As I lay there night after night, I began to feel more and more repulsive, much as I had done when my mother rejected me at the age of 12. Of course I had no hope of consciously linking the two, which meant my adolescent rejection just fed my current one and with every lonely night my sadness grew deeper until I was close to despair. This made it difficult to sleep and my tiredness only worsened the situation.

Two years went by like this at Aunt Eunice's. Why didn't I just leave Agatha? Why didn't she just leave me? For all the same reasons it didn't happen in Alice Springs when it should have, or London when it should have. Only now we were more years down the track and the habit of my feeling disgusting and Agatha feeling whatever she felt, be it anger or frustration or just dead inside, were becoming more usual, and the possibility of separation was becoming more remote.

Towards the end of the two years I was at a legal conference in Hobart and was approached by Tony Lees who was the Managing Director of The Law Book Company. He offered me a job as Managing Editor with his company. It was a better job with better pay. The money wasn't anywhere near what I could earn in legal practice, but it would be enough for us to move in to our house, especially as the interest rates had finally started coming down.

When I had been working at The Law Book Company for only a month or so I got a call from my sister. She and her husband were at Teachers' College in their second or third year. They were both planning on becoming primary school teachers. The year before Steve had gone on a teacher training prac to New Guinea. It had been arranged by the Librarian at the College. Marilyn said it was going to be on again soon, but that they were short a couple of teachers and were willing to take people from outside the College. She asked if I would be interested.

The idea of going to New Guinea had always appealed to me, and here was a chance not only to go but to go to a remote area that most would never be able to penetrate. I probably also sensed it might give me time to think and perhaps put my life in perspective. However it would mean a month off work. I went to Tony Lees very tentatively. After all I had only been there a very short time, and a whole month off was a lot to ask.

But he was the sort of man who knew the value of a happy staff and he didn't hesitate to give me the leave. In fact he said he envied me. He had always wanted to walk the Kokoda Trail. Years later he did walk it, and hopefully my going had something to do with that. So on very short notice I got myself ready to teach primary school in the mountainous Huon Peninsula of New Guinea.

15. CHANTILLY LACE, GOT A PRETTY FACE

I was met in Port Moresby by Graham Stoker, the librarian at the teachers' college who had arranged the trip. He was more of a culture shock than the intense tropical heat and the shanty town feel of the capital. I had been ready to meet a slim bespectacled bookworm. Stoker's first appearance taught me the danger of dealing in stereotypes. For instead of the small timid intellectual I had been expecting, I got a very loudly spoken man of around 40, about 6'2" in height and wearing jungle greens.

'Ever been to the third world?' he demanded rather than asked.

I said I hadn't. When I look back now I think how wrong that was. The world of the Central Australian Aborigines is now acknowledged, sadly, as very third world. But back then we couldn't admit to it. So I told Stoker this was my first time.

'Watch your back. Don't make eye contact. Don't talk to strangers. Got it?'

'Got it,' I said, though as we walked the main street of Port Moresby the people we passed looked perfectly harmless.

'Stoker!' he barked at me, almost as an afterthought. 'Colonel Stoker!'

'I thought you were a librarian,' I said.

'Army reserve,' he blustered defensively. 'But don't think we don't do it tough! We do. Damn tough.'

I nodded, not quite knowing whether I should say anything.

But he didn't seem to notice my concern. Over time I would come to realise Colonel Stoker was really only aware of Colonel Stoker.

'I'm taking you to the Jasperson's for tonight,' he said, as he bundled me into a land rover.

The Jaspersons were a gently spoken elderly couple who lived on the outskirts of Port Moresby in a classic colonial stilted house. They had been missionaries for many years in the New Guinea Highlands and were now retired. As we sat in the lounge room of their house sipping cold lemonade Stoker held forth about the dangers of the country I had just arrived in.

'If the highlanders don't get you, the mosquitoes will,' he trumpeted.

'Did you find it dangerous in the highlands?" I asked the Jaspersons.

'Not so much,' Mr Jasperson said. 'If you learn the customs and treat the people with respect.'

'What rubbish,' said Stoker, 'those highlanders would spear you soon as look at you. They're the most violent people on earth.'

'They can be a tad warlike,' Mrs Jasperson admitted.

'A tad!' Stoker guffawed. 'It's a wonder there's any of them left.'

'But their battles are tightly controlled,' Mr Jasperson explained. 'You kill five, we'll kill five. It's all arranged in advance. And they never exceed their quota.'

'Well! said Stoker. 'That makes it all right.'

'I think Moresby's more dangerous these days,' said Mr Jasperson, sadly. 'All these different dislocated tribes, the young men with nothing to do.'

'Malaria's the real danger,' Mrs Jasperson said, tears welling in her eyes. 'Our Frankie died of malaria.'

'Didn't you have quinine for him?' I asked.

'He got cerebral malaria,' Mr Jasperson explained. 'There's no protecting against cerebral malaria.'

'No hope for you if you get that,' Stoker jumped in, oblivious of Mrs Jasperson's obvious grief. 'Sends you crazy, then it kills you.'

The Jaspersons then went off to fix dinner, leaving me with a brochure produced by some Government Department, which was designed to alert visitors to the dangers they might encounter.

'Have a read,' he said, 'but don't worry too much. Most of it is just common sense. Wear your mozzie repellent, take your quinine, you'll be fine.'

I can't remember what the brochure had to tell me, except for one stand out piece of information:

'There are 80 species of snake in PNG,' it advised. 'But don't worry, two of them are not deadly.'

While the Jaspersons were in the kitchen Colonel Stoker took the opportunity to explain our 'mission'. The next day we would fly by light aircraft to Lae, the coastal capital of Morobe Province and from there would take a much smaller light aircraft to the village of Pindui in the remote mountainous area of the Huon Peninsula inland from Finschhafen.

Pindui was a village of about 500 people and the centre of the region. It had its own airstrip. Being old (I was now just over thirty) I would stay and teach in Pindui. The rest of the student teachers, most of whom were already in Pindui, would be taken by Stoker on foot to the more remote villages. Then when our month's teaching was over he would lead us all on a forced march through the jungle to Finschhafen on the coast. I didn't like the use of the term 'forced march' nor the glint in Colonel Stoker's eyes as he used it. Nonetheless I was determined to keep an open mind.

So the next day, whilst Stoker stayed in Port Moresby to await the few remaining student teachers, I flew to Lae and then queued up on the tarmac with three Pindui men and their pigs and chickens for the flight on the six seater aircraft to Pindui.

When the plane took off I sat up next to the pilot. We flew low over the richest greenest jungle imaginable. The canopy of trees was so thick you couldn't see the ground. I started chatting to the pilot and at one point told him about Colonel Stoker's plan to walk the student teachers through the jungle from Pindui to Finschhafen. He turned and looked at me.

'Is the fucker mad?' he said.

'Maybe,' I replied.

'I'd say he was mad. Have you got any idea how tough that jungle is, how dense, confusing. I wouldn't put money on a troop of professional soldiers getting through, let alone a bunch of kids. Here take a look.'

And with that he dipped the plane sharply to one side and swooped down over the jungle only metres above the tree tops. It was a thrilling sensation even though I almost lost my stomach.

'See what I mean,' he said.

'To tell you the truth, I still couldn't see much for the trees.'

'Exactly! And you'd see even less if you were in amongst it. You tell the fucker, if he doesn't want a lot of deaths on his hands, he'll get rid of that mad idea.'

I promised I would tell Stoker what he said, and at the same time determined, come what may, I would not be going on that forced march.

A few minutes later we were on the approach to Pindui. I would not have known it if the pilot hadn't said, because to my eyes we just seemed to be heading straight at two mountain peaks. It was only as we got quite close I could see a small gap between them. At first it seemed impossible that anything, let alone a plane, could fit through. It was unnerving, but I reasoned to myself this wasn't the first time a plane had landed at Pindui.

As we entered the gap between the peaks I instinctively closed my eyes. It just seemed so inevitable we would hit one side or the other. As I opened them a second later I looked to see the wing tips apparently metres only from the rocky walls. And then we were through and immediately down on the other side on a short, slippery grass airstrip. The plane skidded to a halt. We had been flying at 4000 feet, but when we came through the gap in the mountains onto the plateau at Pindui we were suddenly at ground level.

Then hundreds of people, mainly children came running at the plane, making a lot of noise. They were gathering around in a very excited fashion. In the distance I could also see some young white people who were obviously the student teachers. As we stepped down from the plane everyone was suddenly silent. Then out of the crowd strode a very dignified man of about 40, well dressed in a collared shirt and permanent press trousers. He introduced himself as David Maluana, the Inspector of Schools for the Morobe Province.

He shook my hand warmly and then, as I stood on the landing strip, someone brought him a wooden box which he ascended and began making a welcoming speech. He exhorted the children to take advantage of this great opportunity to learn good English, and explained to them they shouldn't be deterred by the fact I was so old. I was still vigorous, he reassured them, and capable of doing anything a young person could do.

It didn't take me long to realise why I was seen as so old. Out of the 500 or so people, there would have been no more than a dozen over 40 and only three or four over 60. Malaria carried off most at a tragically young age. Not that they saw it as tragic. It was just how things were. They died at an age we would consider young, but they also lived a life, as I would come to understand, that was full but unhurried, and free of the frets of western civilisation.

During David's speech the plane had taken off again. I watched with a combination of horror, amazement and admiration as the pilot skidded down the ever wet runway trying to get airborne before he came to the end of that all too short landing strip. Finally he seemed to just fall off the end and momentarily disappear from sight before rising up again just in time to get between the twin peaks that guarded the village.

My admiration for our pilot was soon to be eclipsed by the man known only as 'the Chinese Pilot'. After I had been in the village for a couple of weeks, the weather set in very badly and we had constant drizzle and fog for several days. The villagers were self sufficient on food, but they depended on air traffic for the luxuries of life like tobacco and coca cola and the Sydney Morning Herald (which was not read but which sold by the sheet for a very expensive price as paper for rolling cigarettes).

All these items were available at the Trade Store run by an entrepreneurial family of red headed Melanesians from some other village. They had moved to Pindui to make their fortune. But they kept a limited stock and after about three days of the bad weather it was just about gone. The villagers were starting to miss their 'luxuries' but they didn't panic.

'The Chinese Pilot will get through,' they would say with total faith.

And they were right. One morning I could hear the roar of an aeroplane engine though I could see nothing. In fact the fog was so thick I could barely see five metres in front of me. The noise of the engine got louder and louder until suddenly his plane emerged out of the thick fog and bumped and skidded to a halt just before the end of the runway near the Trade Store. Less distance to carry the goods I guess. But how he got between the peaks, indeed how he even found the village in that fog, I can't begin to guess.

The villagers cheered and slapped him on the back. He was their hero. I never got to know him or even speak to him, but in my mind I imagined someone who, for lost love or other worldly disaster, had just decided he didn't care what risks he took. And then those risks became a way of life, indeed gave a meaning to his life. And what better meaning than to be adored by all those people in Pindui, and no doubt a range of other villages as well.

He kept up his daredevil deliveries for many years after I was there, but I did hear, about 15 years later, he was killed when his wing tip finally clipped one of the mountain peaks coming into Pindui. I guess it was inevitable. He was deeply mourned.

But for now David Maluana and the elders were leading me through the village and up the hill to my accommodation. It was 1983 and PNG had only had its independence from Australia for about 8 years. So the village still had its Kiap's House. Kiaps had been Australian government administrative officers who served a variety of functions at the village level. Whereas the villagers lived in small huts, the Kiap always had a western style house. As I was the honoured guest, and as the Kiap's house was vacant, that's where the villagers were going to put me.

However I was in for a few surprises. For a start the plumbing had not only ceased to work, but it clearly had ceased after someone had used the toilet to its full potential, or else someone had used it to its full potential even though the plumbing had ceased. Either way the bathroom was definitely a no go zone. So I learned to wash from the tap under the house and to use the communal pit toilets like everyone else.

The pit toilets were a fascinating masterpiece of construction. But you certainly didn't want to look down, because they were very deep and you might start to realise you could actually fall in, with consequences unimaginable. And that was not a relaxing way to use the amenities. One of the young girls did look in, and panicked. She didn't fall in herself but her glasses went in, and as she was very myopic and as no-one was about to try and retrieve them for her, she had to teach the whole prac semi blind.

In the bedroom of the Kiap's house was an old style single bed with a big wire spring base. There was no mattress. This meant I had a choice of sleeping on the wire base or on the floor. I would have opted for the floor but around dusk most of the floor would start to shift as hundreds of the world's largest cockroaches moved in for the night. They were a voracious breed. They ate anything and everything they could get their feelers on. They even ate the flowers the villagers had put in the lounge room. So despite being very uncomfortable at first, I slept on the springs.

The funny thing is when you work a hard day and you are tired but you're not subject to the stresses of commuting, shopping, bill paying, and all the mental struggles of western civilisation, the springs stop mattering and the cold tap under the house seems perfectly adequate. By the time I had been in Pindui for only three or four days, I already wondered why the hell we need mattresses and hot water. In fact after three or four days I was starting to feel incredibly relaxed and it was because I was starting to get in balance. This in turn was largely because the society I found myself surrounded by was in balance.

If you grow your own food and you have enough so you are never hungry, and the exertion of growing your food and walking everywhere keeps you fit and healthy and you sleep well at night because you are tired and it is dark and quiet, then you probably have a much greater chance of finding peace than someone in the west, even if you are 'poor' by western standards, especially as you are surrounded by people you know and whom you know care about you.

That's how it was for the people of Pindui. They didn't even have to worry about the safety of their children. There were no roads and no vehicles and no strangers who might hurt them. The children, when they were not in school, just roamed about in one big safe group, the older ones looking after the younger.

The peace I was finding came in a number of enforced ways. For example the first evening I was there I wanted to prepare for the class which I had to give the next day to the group of 10 and 11 years olds I had been assigned. But I had only just begun my preparation when the tropical dark suddenly fell. As there was no electricity I asked the locals how I could get enough light to read and write by. They told me I couldn't. It was dark and that was the time to stop.

So I literally couldn't prepare my class. Some of my neighbours came over with some beer and some amazing pancake like food they uninvitingly called 'lard cakes' (which were nonetheless delicious), and I did what everyone else did. I sat on the veranda of the Kiap's house with my neighbours and drank and smoked incredibly rough tobacco rolled in the Sydney Morning Herald and told stories.

In other words we did what people had been doing for 40,000 years before someone thought to invent civilisation. It was fun, it was incredibly relaxing and freeing and it felt in balance. The next day, though I was 'unprepared', I'm sure I taught a much better class than if I had worked all night for it, because I was fresh and well slept and keen, and my students were keen, and we just made it happen.

That first morning in the little wooden schoolhouse in Pindui will stay forever in my mind. I was greeted by total silence. There were maybe 20 children and they just sat there looking at me expectantly with their big eyes. They were shy and they were respectful, and once I got past those two 'impediments' I realised they were desperate to learn.

Our facilities were limited. I had half a blackboard in my class and one stick of chalk. David Maluana, who took me into the class and introduced me, explained we also only had half a piece of paper per student per day, and each had a tiny stump of a pencil they had to make last till their fingers could double over and hold it no more.

But these children had quick minds and they loved to learn and that makes up for a myriad of tools and facilities. My classes became a place of constant yearning and learning and laughter. The children absorbed everything and gave back so much more in their delight and their happiness than I could ever give them. How much we learned in the month I was there, I could never measure in educational terms, but in terms of the meeting of cultures, and the exchange of friendship and affection, it was immeasurable.

Perhaps my loveliest memory was when, for some crazy reason, I decided to teach them how to sing *Chantilly Lace*, the old fifties song from The Big Bopper. The first time I sang it for them I started slowly:

Chantilly lace, got a pretty face and a pony tail, hangin' down

Then faster:

A wiggalin', a walkin', a giggalin', a talkin
Makes the world go round round round!

Then getting very fast:

There aint nothin' in the world like a big eyed girl
Make me act so funny, make me spend my money,
Make me hang real loose like a long neck goose like a...

I paused, and their eyes were enormous with anticipation. Then I finished with a big production, copying as closely as I could the deep sonorous base voice of The Big Bopper, shaking my hands and rolling my eyes and singing at the top of my voice:

Woah baby that's what I LIKE!

And they all screamed with delight. After that every day, they demanded:

'Chantilly Lace! Chantilly Lace!' as I walked in the classroom. And no work would be done till I sang them the song. They were not interested in singing it themselves (though they sang lots of other songs I taught them). With *Chantilly Lace* it was always to be my solo, with the children moving closer and closer to the edge of their seats as I approached the climax, getting ready to let out their scream of delight at the end, which of course got bigger and more vocal every day, till David Maluana had to ask me what was happening each morning. They could hear the screams up in the village.

The day after I arrived, Colonel Stoker turned up ready to take his young charges deeper into the jungle. Most of them were already suffering severe culture shock. They didn't even have the luxury of the Kiap's house and had to sleep in village huts and lose their glasses down the pit toilet. But all this was nothing compared to the stories we later got of Stoker's adventures with them.

Each morning for several days he would take two or three of them with him to an outlying village, sometimes requiring them to scale sheer cliffs, pulling themselves up by jungle vines, sometimes swimming the turbulent Mongi River or trying to cross it by a string suspension bridge that hadn't been repaired since the War. When they got to the assigned village, they had facilities that made Pindui look like down town Manhattan.

Stoker would be regularly called away from Pindui to go and succour some poor young thing. A villager would have to make a half day trip down to Pindui and a half day back to tell him one of their young girls was sobbing and wouldn't stop. So Stoker would pick up his rucksack and would go crashing off into the jungle, with no regard for the fact he had just trampled through someone's pineapple patch. Then the next morning he would come trampling back through another pineapple patch, barking commands at some poor villager or another.

The people of Pindui didn't like him at all and, though they were always delightfully friendly and accommodating to me and the other teachers, they were quite cold to Stoker. He didn't seem to notice however, just kept bashing through their lives and their jungle on his way to solve the next disaster.

When he was in Pindui he took to hanging out on my veranda, where he would sit, sometimes for several hours telling stories about the army reserve and his adventures with previous groups in New Guinea. It was on one of the first of these visits I got an insight into why perhaps the man was the way he was. He told me how, at the age of ten, his father had taken him into the extremely rugged Jameson Valley in the Blue Mountains west of Sydney and left him there, telling him that a 'real man' would find his own way out.

This is a huge area of untamed country that claims the lives of experienced bushwalkers on a regular basis. I had been lost there once overnight myself when my sister's husband had taken us down to the bottom of the valley on the promise he knew what he was doing. We only got out by the greatest good luck and from that I learned just how thick and treacherous that country can be. So the actions of Stoker's father could only be seen as irresponsible, if not criminal. Stoker of course told it as a positive experience, as one of the key reasons why he was the tough self reliant man he had become.

After he had been to visit a few times, I decided to mention what our pilot had said about trying to take his young charges through the jungle to

Finschhafen. I told him I had spoken to several of the men in Pindui and not one of them, with all their knowledge of the country, said he would ever attempt such a trip. Stoker didn't even try to deny the dangers. He just looked at me and said:

'With a mission like this, there's bound to be some wastage.'

I know it seems impossible to believe, but those were his exacts words. I could never forget them. It was then I came to accept the real possibility that Graham Stoker was certifiably insane, and that any plea to logic would be wasted on him. I was very worried for the young students, and indeed later tried to talk some of them out of going. But they were very young and totally unable to defy Stoker. Nonetheless I told him I had decided not go.

'I am your commanding officer,' he told me coldly, 'and you will do as I command.'

'Listen Graham,' I said with equal *sang froid*, 'You're a teachers' college librarian and I'm a grownup. So I'm not going.'

'Oh ok,' he said casually. His change of tone was not re-assuring.

Graham Stoker aside, my time in Pindui, was one of the most joyous times of my life. Every day I would breakfast on lard cakes and wash from the tap under the house. Then I would walk down through the village and everyone I passed would smile and say:

'Morning true!'

And I would reply: 'Morning true!' and stride on my way to my enthusiastic and energetic students.

I came to know many of the villagers very well. In a place of that size, where everyone talks to everyone all the time, that is easy to do. I became friends with the young painter Seth Tamasese whose works had been hung in the new National Parliament Building. I got to know all the teachers of course, including the very gentle Koma Tofilau who was from the highlands, and who would go back to his village every school holidays, exchange his permanent press trousers for his tribal warrior's garb and do battle with the neighbouring tribes. During the holidays everyone in Pindui held their breath till he came back safely.

The villagers, who were very devout Catholics, would rehearse for the Sunday Mass, three or four times a week, practising their singing and their drumming well into the night. These were beautiful sounds I would sometimes listen to from the veranda and sometimes from close at hand when I was invited down.

Sometimes too we would sit on the veranda and look down at the neighbouring village hundreds of meters below, where the sound of their own drumming would drift up to me. It was amazing to think that those people spoke a language not just different from the people of Pindui, but of a different language group. But that was the situation in a country where the ruggedness of the terrain had, for millennia, cut people off so completely from one another that now New Guinea contained more than 40% of the world's languages.

I even got to meet the notorious mad Swede, whom everyone talked about, and who had been roaming naked around the Huon Peninsula for about ten years. One day he just burst out of the jungle near the Kiap's house, stark naked with his long tousled blonde hair flying in the wind behind him, carrying nothing but a black leather briefcase. I spoke with him a little, and he was very charming. There was no doubt he was mad, but not perhaps any more so than Colonel Stoker.

I think the most touching moment for me was when it was time for the Pindui Markets. Because Pindui was the biggest, and the central village for a whole area, they would host the markets once a month, and people would trek, sometimes two and three days, to sell their produce there or to buy the things they needed. The night before the markets some of the villagers came round and formally invited me to attend the next day.

I didn't think much of it, and being a Saturday, slept in till about 8.30, after which I wandered down to the main part of the village and the area where the markets were to be held. The villagers had assembled a square fenced area with a gate. The market stalls had been set up inside. What surprised me however was that no-one had entered the market compound as yet. They were all just standing around outside.

I said hello to Kona Tofilau and his gorgeous little three year old daughter, whom he had dressed up in her own little ceremonial warrior garb for the occasion, complete with war paint and tiny spear. I chatted to several other people but still no-one went in. I assumed it was part of the custom not to rush these things.

Then someone suggested to me I might want to have a look around. So I went in and started to browse the stalls, but still no-one else came in. A very old woman stopped me and tried to talk to me in German. I realised she may never have seen another white person since New Guinea was a German protectorate some fifty years before.

I was starting to feel a little self conscious and so decided to buy a couple of things and leave. The moment I went out through the gate, the entire population of Pindui and the surrounding villages rushed in on mass and bought everything in sight within about 5 minutes.

I came to understand that the people, many of whom had trekked for days to be there, were ready to buy what they needed by 6 am, but such was their sense of courtesy they were not about to make a move till I had had the first chance to choose what I wanted. They had stood in the sun for two and a half hours rather than breach the strict etiquette of hospitality.

By the time the month was up, I was very reluctant to leave. I felt I was at peace, perhaps truly at peace for the first time in my life. I often wonder what would have happened had I decided to stay. In that era it was a possibility still available to ex patriot Australians who were willing to teach in the remote areas, even if they had no formal teaching qualifications.

Perhaps the novelty of the experience would, after a time, have started to wear off. Perhaps I would have come to realise that for all its charm, the village of Pindui was 'in the world' as much as anywhere else, and so was subject to its own hostilities and jealousies and interpersonal strife. Maybe I had been shielded from all of that by the warmth and hospitality of the people, and once I became a local, the romance would tarnish. And then life would catch up with me.

I think the real answer is that PNG was the sort of world I did need to embrace as a first step to healing. But being there would never achieve the healing in itself. Nothing short of facing your demons can ever do that. Maybe Pindui would have provided the right sort of space and time, to start addressing my sadness honestly in the midst of a strong supportive community.

Or perhaps I still wouldn't have been ready to face the reality of my situation and would have just started to blame the people of Pindui or the climate or the PNG political situation or goodness knows what for my sadness, just as I had blamed Sydney and the Commonwealth Crown and Paul Everingham and any number of other scapegoats. And then the beautiful memory of the place would have been destroyed. Better in the end perhaps to go and work out my pain elsewhere, so that New Guinea remained forever a special memory.

On the day of my departure the whole village gathered around on the airstrip and David Maluana made a farewell speech that was truly touching. The villagers loaded me up with dozens of gifts, from woven billum bags to necklaces to lard cakes for the journey. Out of the window of the plane I looked back at the villagers still waving to me and wondered if I would see any of them again. It has been almost 30 years and I haven't been back. Those I knew would most likely not be alive any more.

I flew into Lae and then took the bus from there back to Port Moresby. On the trip I was reminded first hand of the virility of the disease that cuts a swathe through the youthful population of PNG. I had seen several people get the trembles whilst I was in Pindui, but on the bus was the first time I saw a full scale malaria attack. A man at the back was suddenly seized with the most violent shuddering, his body almost bouncing itself off the seat and against his wife who was sitting helplessly next to him.

Fortunately I still had some malaria tablets. I rushed to the back and gave them to him. He could not even hold the water bottle, so his wife held his mouth open for me to insert the tablets and then I held his head while she poured the water down his throat. It worked well and in a few minutes he was steady again. He was incredibly grateful. It really drove home the point about how good western medicine is and how easy it would be to save lives in the third world if only the money, perhaps not even a lot of money, could be made available.

When the bus arrived at his home he insisted the driver wait while he went into the village only to return soon afterwards with a very scrawny looking dead chicken which he proudly presented to me. It would have been the meal for his whole family that night and I really didn't want to take it. But I could see it meant a lot to him. So gratefully I took his offering and went on my way.

When the bus was only about five miles from Port Moresby the road crossed the main highway up to the highlands. There in the middle of the intersection stood 5 or 6 highlanders in full battle dress. The bus had to stop. Then the highlanders got on and told the driver to take them to Mount Hagen.

'But we have to go in to Moresby first,' I said to the driver.

'Try telling that to them,' he said. And he was right. They did look fierce. 'I suggest you get off here,' he told me. So I did and walked the last five miles in to Moresby in incredible heat.

I turned up at the house where I was supposed to meet Stoker and the others but they were not there. They had left Pindui several days ahead of me and should have arrived long ago. Another day went by and they still didn't turn up. So there was a pretty good chance they were lost in the jungle somewhere between Pindui and Finschhafen.

Miraculously they did arrive a day later, but in a pitiful state. As our pilot on the first day and the men of Pindui had predicted, the expedition got hopelessly lost and their food and water ran out. They would have died for sure except for having, very luckily, stumbled on a man with a bulldozer which had been dropped into the jungle by helicopter to start building a road. The driver abandoned his task for two days and used his bulldozer (with Stoker and a dozen student teachers hanging off it at all angles) to cut through the jungle and deliver the downcast young people into Finschhafen.

After taking my leave of the exhausted students and the unrepentant Colonel Stoker, I flew back to Sydney to our house and my new job.

Unfortunately I soon realised the joy of New Guinea had been about putting life on hold. In fact the bliss of that place now only served to highlight the pain of my 'real life' and to accelerate my downward slide, further and further into fear, anxiety and depression.

Yet the harder my unconscious knocked, the harder I denied, asserting how wonderful my parents had been, and sending them more money we could ill afford, in order to prove that it must be so. I also tried to escape by making myself very busy. Apart from my demanding regular job at the Law Book Company, I was still doing my law reporting work, and still trying to find time for my own writing. I had started the novel *Wesley In America* and was reasonably happy with what I had written.

But moments for Wesley were few and precious. The only way I could find time to write was to have no leisure time at all, to be working every waking moment. And thus I was back to where I was at 14 when I would get up at five in the morning and study to keep my mother happy. And just like then, I was totally exhausted. All too often, when driving home from work, I would toy with the idea of just turning the steering wheel to the side. Just to be done with it. Fortunately a stubborn numbness kept my hands straight on the wheel.

16. FUNCTIONAL CATATONIA

There comes a point at which denial will no longer work. The spirit just starts to sink, and I was sinking now. Yet still I wasn't ready for a life buoy. So I continued to work day and night and could hang the hat of my growing madness on the peg of workaholia. My life was without joy or without pleasure of any kind. I even came to believe laughter and smiling were things that young people did. This was not some metaphorical reflection on my own personal sadness. I actually developed the literal belief people over 30 were not supposed to smile, and certainly didn't laugh, ever. Almost as though I believed these wonderful natural human functions ceased working past a certain age. You might lose your hearing at 70 or your sight at 80, but you certainly lost your laughter at 30.

I also developed a morbid fear of speaking in public. If I had to make a presentation at work I was in a sweat the night before. Even a publishing meeting with half a dozen colleagues could be a source of terror. It got to the point where reading a poem to friends made me tremble. I would pick up the poem and try to read but my hands would shake and my voice quaver and I would have to stop.

Here too, like with the laughter, I was convinced my ability to speak was something I had lost forever. I would think nostalgically of the days I could stand before a Supreme Court and talk confidently, without my throat closing off so I could hardly breathe. I saw this as so much worse even than the loss of laughter. I felt great shame at my 'incapacity', like a runner who has lost his legs and can no longer bear to look at the twisted body that once served him so well.

This aspect of my madness would persist right through the latter part of the 1980s and well into the 1990s before one of my great angels, Angela Quinn, came to my rescue and helped me find my voice again. However for

150

the moment I was mute as well as cheerless and everything frightened me. I oscillated between bouts of severe depression and heightened anger. I once put my fist right through a wooden door, for reasons I could not have articulated at the time, just because I felt so overwhelmed with rage.

But apart from this one overt act, I kept my anger, my fear and my depression locked deep inside me. I was hollowed out, but amazingly, because I did such a good job at concealment, no-one knew what I was going through. I am sure friends had no idea. Clearly neither did anyone at The Law Book Company, because Tony Lees and other Board members always said they were happy with my work.

In fact when the long serving editor of The South Australian State Reports retired, and the judges of the Court were having trouble finding a suitable replacement, Tony Lees recommended me as a temporary editor. My long nights doing law reporting stood me in good stead. I got the job and ended up doing it for two years, at the end of which I received a very flattering letter of thanks from the Law Society of South Australia.

That in turn led to me later getting the Editorship of the Federal Court Reports (the authorised reports of the Federal Court of Australia), which is the largest series of law reports in Australia, and also the editorship of the companion Federal Law Reports. These are the sorts of jobs normally given to QCs in their fifties or sixties. They are not the sorts of jobs given to a madman. But I was not a QC, I was only 38 when I was first appointed, and I *was* a madman. It's just that no-one knew it.

I had ongoing insomnia and would wake at three in the morning, and drive down to Circular Quay where I would walk up and down amongst the debris and the drunks, punching my fist into my palm trying to quell the anger or the fear or the depression, whichever version of my madness had hold of me that night. But my nocturnal wanderings were not seen by the judges of the Federal Court nor the Board of The Law Book Company nor my friends.

I guess Agatha knew, but was occupied with her own demons. I guess my parents knew too, but so long as they got their weekly cheque, all was well with them.

I was a living breathing paradox. Nothing within me reflected what I achieved in my external life. The best way I can describe it, is to say I lived a life of 'functional catatonia'. I was devoid of happiness, unable to smile, unable to free myself from my prison. And yet I was a catatonic who functioned to the satisfaction of all except himself. Somehow, by the grace of God, I kept going. I think when I look back, that grace came in two forms, comedy writing and the world's cutest, smartest dog.

The dog was an oversized Sydney silky whom I called 'Doug'. My mother was furious because Doug was the name of the first husband she dumped just before he became a millionaire. Perhaps that's why I chose the name. Who knows? I hope so.

Anyway Doug was a stray who had been found in the middle of a major inner city intersection. He had been living off cheese sandwiches given him by the children at a local primary school. I'm not surprised he managed to extort the sandwiches, because he had a way of looking at people with his huge eyes that said: 'Please feed me. I've never been fed before'. And they just wouldn't be able to resist. I remember many years later in Perth when he did that to a girl in a cafe and she gave him some of her pastry snail. When he refused to eat it the girl was disappointed and confused.

'Why won't he take it,' she asked.

'He only likes the soft inner core,' I had to confess.

At which point she pulled out the core and gave him that.

The trade off was he truly loved people, had amazing empathy and an extraordinary desire to heal. I remember not long after we got him, Agatha's cousin was tragically killed in a car crash. We went over to her aunt's house to pay our respects. It was a house Doug had never been to. He had never met the aunt, and the room was full of maybe 100 people. Yet Doug had no doubt who the principal mourner was. In a room full of grieving people he sought out the worst grief. He wended his way through the crowd till he found the aunt, put his paw on her and then lay his head on her lap.

He was a healer for me too. He forced me to get out of the house and get out of myself. I would find time in the day to take him to Illoura Reserve by the harbour where I would throw a ball for him, sometimes for as long as an hour. That was an hour of clean air and happiness I would never have otherwise had. As a workaholic I couldn't justify pleasurable activities for myself. But I told myself this was for Doug.

And I think if you have some delight in your life, some love, you can avoid the padded room at Callan Park. Doug became one of my major angels. It is a role he loved and a role which grew over time. He kept me, if not sane, then functioning, he and the surprising act of writing comedy.

That all started when I was on a flight to Melbourne for work and saw an ad in the in-flight magazine. It was for a mystery story competition jointly sponsored by POL Magazine and the airline. I decided to enter even though I had never written a mystery story and really had no idea how to start.

The only thing I knew about mysteries was what I had heard about Agatha Christie. She would start by picking three unconnected items at random and then force herself to weave them together into a story. I quickly chose my three objects without giving myself too much time to think about it, as of course that would defeat the purpose.

I chose a lawyer, no doubt because I was a lawyer. I chose a double bass because I think the seat next to me was empty and it reminded me of when I was trying to get sponsorship for an Australian Symphony Orchestra for London friend Ray Holden to come out and conduct. I had learnt then that when symphonies travel the double bass can't go in the hold. Instead they have to buy it a child's fare, and strap it into a seat. Finally I chose a dwarf, for reasons I can't recall or imagine.

Then for some crazy reason, because I was about to try my hand at mystery writing, which I had never done before, I decided to add to the mix that the story would also be a comedy, something else I had never tried to write.

Hence was born *The Dwarf and the Double Bass Player*, a comedy mystery about Felicio Tagg, Australia's most incompetent barrister. Felicio is quite unique in the world of legal fiction. Most central characters in that genre are super clever. Even a series like *Rumpole of the Bailey* has a hero who, whilst eccentric, nonetheless always ends up winning the case. Felicio on the other hand was irremediably incompetent as a lawyer. He had never won a case and never would.

I found the writing of the story a liberating process, as though I were finding a way to release the comedy in myself. No, it was more than that. It was a way to release the humanity in myself. The man who thought he was not allowed to laugh, not able to smile, was finding a way to give others the chance to smile.

From out of 1200 or so entries, *The Dwarf and the Double Bass Player* made the final fifteen. The finalists were published by Hutchinson in book form as *The Golden Dagger Mysteries* and the winner was announced at a fancy dinner organised by the magazine and the airline. I didn't win, but the judge, Professor Stephen Knight, paid me the compliment of saying comedy/mysteries were almost impossible to pull off, but I had managed it.

Not long after that I got a call from the publisher at Allen & Unwin. He said they were looking for new and interesting works. He said he had read *The Dwarf and the Double Bass Player* and would I be interested in turning Felicio Tagg into a novel.

I was thrilled. I had not had much luck with *Wesley in America*, or rather I'd had plenty of luck but it had all gone awry. The novel had been accepted for publication three times. The first time the company went out of business after their premises burnt down. The second acceptance was by a company which was later taken over. The new owners decided they didn't want to publish fiction and so cancelled all contracts for novels. The third time it was accepted by the fiction publisher at a big international house, but later, just before the contract got to me, she changed her mind.

Anyway I wrote an outline for Allen & Unwin, they liked it and I was signed up to write *Rough Justice*. So there I was, still in pain, still sleeplessly wandering the Quay at three in the morning. Only now I was banging my fist into my hand not just to drive away the fear or depression. Half the time it was to jog the next comic line for my book. I was a nettle of paradoxes in those days. Not only was I a catatonic who functioned well enough to hold down a responsible job, I was also the man who never smiled whilst writing his comic novel.

But it was around the time I started writing *Rough Justice* I had my first breakthrough. I had been wandering the Quay one night when I started to get flashes, images no more than a millisecond in length, of a red tip. At first it wasn't even conscious. Then slowly I became aware of something, but I didn't know what. I saw something red, something hot. Then it passed and the image was forgotten. But the sense remained that I had a problem, and I needed to solve it.

Next night the idea I needed a solution to something was still there. I asked Agatha what she thought it could be. With barely a moment's hesitation she said:

'I think it's your mother.'

I'm not sure if Agatha's insight came from some last flicker of love for me, or from her ongoing dislike of my mother, but they say everyone is God's instrument, whether they mean to be or not. And Agatha was God's instrument that night. The moment she said 'I think it's your mother' the red tip returned and flared. I saw the cigarette tip that glowed in the dark in my little bedroom as a child. I saw it make a figure of eight. Then it was gone. But now it was far more than a millisecond. Now it was unmistakeable. Though I was a long way from a clear picture, though I was far from even naming what I saw, there was now no going back. The first nascent drops of healing had been splashed like holy water on my face.

'Yes it is,' I told Agatha. 'It is my mother.'

Meanwhile something else was about to happen which would change my life dramatically, something that would expose me to things I could never have imagined. It was something that would subject me to enormous pain, but which in the end would prove to be the greatest part of my healing.

Two or three years earlier Agatha had decided that as we couldn't have children we should adopt. It was, to say the least, an interesting use of the word 'couldn't'. I guess if you don't have sex you 'can't' have children. But that was not how Agatha meant it. Our 'couldn't' was because of my infertility. Of course I wasn't infertile, but being so detached from my own emotions, and in a way from reality itself, I had just accepted this.

So we registered for an overseas adoption. We put our names down for Thailand. Programmes were run by parent groups. These were parents who had already adopted from that country. The organisers of those groups and their members were by and large wonderful, knowledgeable and compassionate people. They arranged everything and recommended you for a particular child, but the decision as to whether you were suitable to adopt that child, was made in New South Wales by the Department of Community Services (DOCS).

As a prospective adoptive parent you were required by DOCS to go to several interviews. At many of these you were required to acknowledge you were 'grieving your womb'. You were not allowed to say you had come to terms with your barrenness, and you were positively prohibited from suggesting that part of your desire to adopt sprung from a wish to give an orphan child a home. These were 'delusions'. Any attempt to suggest otherwise might send you straight to the bottom of the list.

The worst part of all in the long bureaucratic tedium of forms and interviews were the 'gatherings'. At these they would bring together sometimes as many as 200 or 300 couples in a big room, and we would all sit like naughty children for hours listening to one DOCS officer after another explain to us how we needed to acknowledge the grieving of our wombs.

I found the whole process humiliating, not to mention illogical and confusing on a personal level. For a start we were supposed to be there because I didn't have enough sperm to get Agatha pregnant, which wasn't true. But even if it were true, why did Agatha have to grieve her womb when no doubt it was a perfectly adequate functioning womb? Indeed why didn't I have to grieve my sperm? Was it some sort of sexist assumption that all reproductive difficulties had to be the woman's fault? Or was it a sort of reverse sexism that said it was the woman who still grieved a womb which, whilst healthy, was not getting the chance to work. Either way the man didn't seem to matter much.

Also I found it difficult to explain to friends why we were doing this. They naturally assumed we couldn't fall pregnant, and subtly tried to work out why that was so. I wasn't about to tell them I had no sperm when that wasn't true. Nor could I bring myself to admit we 'couldn't' get pregnant because we never had sex. So I settled on telling them that, although we could have children, in an overpopulated world, we felt that to give a home to someone who was already here was a much better idea.

The funny thing was that I wasn't actually lying. My heart had always gone out to the orphans of the world. Perhaps I saw myself as one of them. So it was a truth that I was telling, but a sort of 'ex post facto' truth, because had I been married to anyone else I probably would have just gone ahead and had my own children without too much thought, just like anyone else would naturally do.

But of course what I told my friends was certainly very different from what I told DOCS. There I trod the party line and admitted to grieving my womb. Or was it Agatha's womb I was supposed to grieve? Well I was definitely grieving somebody's womb, oh yes sir!

Anyway we had been on the list to adopt from Thailand for several years and nothing had happened. Then I got a phone call. It was from the parent who headed up the Sri Lankan adoption programme. Even though you were registered with one programme that didn't stop another parent group recommending you for their programme if they thought it were appropriate. It just didn't happen very often. However the man from the Sri Lankan programme thought it should happen for us.

'I have siblings in Colombo who desperately need adopting,' he told me.' They're in a Mother Teresa Orphanage.'

'Siblings?' I had never thought of adopting two children.

'Yes,' he said, 'a 12 year old girl, her 10 year old brother and twin 6 year old sisters.'

I think I let out something like a long whistle and made some intelligent remarks like 'whoa!' and 'gosh' and 'like 4 children?'

'Yes,' he said. 'But they're a very tight sibling group. It would be impossible to separate them.' There was a long silence while I tried to take it in. 'Are you still there?' he asked tentatively.

'Why us?' I asked.

'I'll be honest with you,' he said after a long pause of his own. 'We've tried everyone on the Sri Lankan programme and no-one is willing to take on four children.

'I see.'

'In fact, to be totally honest, we've pretty much tried everyone on every programme.'

'So...we are your last choice.'

'Sort of.'

'I see.'

Then after another long silence, he finally said:

'You *are* our last chance, it's true. And if you don't take them, they'll die.'

'I see.'

I hung up the phone and explained to Agatha.

'I want to do it,' she said.

'His ultimatum is just a little unfair, don't you think? "If you don't take them they'll die."'

'Do you think it's true?'

'I don't think it's the sort of thing you say lightly.'

'Anyway who cares,' said Agatha. 'I want to do it. I want a family.'

I had only just started *Rough Justice,* after waiting a very long time for a break like Allen & Unwin had given me. I knew that if I were going to write it, with four orphan children in tow, it would be as hard as ever it could be. But a part of me really wanted a family too, maybe not one quite this big or quite this instant, but a family nonetheless, and this seemed to be the only way it was going to happen. On top of that, however real was the threat of death, and however unfair it was of the man to tell us, the fact was it had been told. For whatever reason this possible life and death decision had fallen to us to make, and I could only see one realistic choice.

So I rang the man back with our decision. He was ecstatic. Then he said:

'Listen, this is wonderful of you, but in all fairness there is something else you need to know. Sri Lanka is in the midst of a civil war.'

'I see.'

'And it's pretty bloody at that. The Sri Lankan Government is fighting the Tamil rebels. Your kids are Tamils. That's going to make it difficult to get them out.'

'I see.'

'And of course your own lives will be at risk most of the time.'

'I see.'

I told this latest to Agatha. She was not deterred. Nor was I. War is difficult to imagine if you haven't been in it. And having made the decision we weren't about to let a little civil war get in the way. So the head of the programme told DOCS about the situation and recommended us.

At first DOCS was very much against it and flatly refused their permission. They said it would be next to impossible to make an adoption work with 6 year olds, let alone a 10 and a 12 year old. No doubt they were talking sense. But now I had committed to this, and had totally accepted if we didn't do it the children would die. So I couldn't just let them die. As a result I harassed DOCS on a daily basis, threatening them with law suits and anything else I could think of. I knew Justice Michael Kirby at the time. He was always involved in humanitarian efforts. So I even threatened to get him involved. In the end they very reluctantly agreed. But I had undoubtedly made myself their most unpopular client.

We had planned to leave in a couple of month's time, but got a panicked call from someone else on the Sri Lankan programme telling us the Sri Lankan Government was about to introduce legislation banning foreign adoptions and if we didn't go straight away we would miss getting the children out.

I very much doubted that legislation currently being introduced was going to get through inside of several months. I knew the Sri Lankans worked under the same ponderous British parliamentary system we did. But the woman who rang was in a panic. So along the lines already drawn by 'If you don't take them, they'll die,' we couldn't afford the risk. So in under 48 hours I had us on a plane (at twice the price we should have paid if we had been able to book in advance), headed for Colombo.

17. WAR ZONE

The hotel we had booked, as recommended by the parent group, was the Mount Royal Beach Hotel at Mount Lavinia in the South of Colombo. We got there via taxi along the famous, or perhaps infamous, Galle Road. The noise of the traffic was like a cacophony of cries from Hell. And the heat and the dust might have come straight from the Ninth Circle too.

Despite the multiple use of the term 'Mount', the area was totally flat. The district of Mount Lavinia was reputed to be the most up market residential area in Colombo, and our hotel was reputed to be one of the most stylish in the city. But it badly needed a paint, had facilities that barely worked or didn't work at all, and was generally run down, as was the whole district of Mount Lavinia itself. To us this 'up market' area looked much like the rest of the suburbs we had passed along the Galle Road.

The tragedy was the smelly, noisy, run down city we encountered, didn't have to be that way. Back in the 1950s Sri Lanka had been singled out by the United Nations as the model developing nation. But from the 1960s onwards the Singhalese politicians of Sri Lanka found it all too easy to keep power through demonising the Tamil Independence Movement in the North. They took a prosperous country, and drove it down into the poverty and despair we were seeing. Thirty years of civil war will do that.

The one thing we couldn't help noticing straight away, even in Mount Lavinia, but certainly in and around central Colombo, was the massive military presence. Thirty years of civil war will give you that as well. There were soldiers on every corner and they would look at us suspiciously as we passed. Suspicion is also a product of a long, bloody and treacherous war.

There were of course beggars everywhere. But there was also a whole range of people who had learned to make their livings in creative ways. I remember one day in central Colombo a man in a suit stopped me in the street, smiled and said in beautiful English:

'I'm so sorry to disturb you Mr Kline, but you may remember I am the man who processed you through the airport on your arrival here in Colombo. For a small honorarium I am in a position to guarantee you a trouble free and expedited departure when it is your time to leave.'

How on earth he knew who I was, I can't imagine. It was unsettling to be called by name by a total stranger who 'appeared' to just encounter me at random in the street. It left me feeling 'watched'. I decided not to take him up on his offer. But at the same time I was worried. If indeed he were an airport official, maybe he could, and would, give us trouble when it was time to depart. His modus operandi was typical of how so many things were done in Colombo, in a country falling apart. Something was 'offered', but underneath, the offer was reinforced by an implicit threat.

At the hotel they told me about the possibility of hiring a 'limousine' to take us where we wanted to go. The limousines looked just as small and decrepit as the ordinary vehicles and taxis. But there was one key difference. The limousines had windows that rolled up and air conditioning. Over the next month of danger and endless bureaucratic frustrations, the ability to avoid the smell and the noise and the heat for a while in the comfort of the limousines, was one of the main things that got me through, that and Coca Cola.

On our second day in Colombo we hired a limousine and set off to meet the children at the Mother Teresa Missionaries of Charity orphanage, which was in the worst slum area of Colombo. The first thing that struck me was that the slum didn't look much worse than the upper class area in which we were staying. Sure the houses were smaller, but it was no more run down or smelly than Mount Lavinia. Whether the locals were prepared to admit it or not, perhaps the war was doing its democratic duty and having a levelling effect.

We were greeted by the Mother Superior who introduced us to the nuns, all in their blue and white head scarves. She then took us on a brief tour during which I came to realise the orphanage wasn't an orphanage at all. It was a Home for the Dying. The several hundred old and dying had somehow, in that desperate city, found themselves sharing their accommodation with about 50 orphan children who slept on the floor each night under their beds. I think the old people would have appreciated some quiet in their last days on earth. But they weren't going to get it, because the children just ran wild everywhere, including around, under and sometimes over the beds of the dying.

We went into a little room and sat down to wait for the children. It seemed to take quite a while. The nuns brought us warm Coca Cola which they took out of a sealed box. Soft drink was clearly for special guests. Still no children. Then we heard a child screaming outside, and the stern voice of a chastising nun. The Mother reassured us it was nothing to worry about.

Eventually a nun came in with the three girls following behind her, but not the boy. The twins, Babika and Babeta were small and malnourished. Later when we measured and weighed them we found they were 3'2" and weighed 9 kgs. In other words, at almost seven years old, they had the height of an average western three year old and the weight of a twelve month old baby. Their heads were shaven because of the lice and their faces were covered in pussy sores. They looked for all the world like sad sick little gremlins.

The twelve year old Rangani, by contrast, was healthy looking, almost plump. And whereas the twins had very black skin, she was a much lighter colour, almost a light brown. In fact she looked nothing like them.

The three girls sat on chairs on the opposite side of the room, looking at us. They didn't seem fearful or even suspicious. If anything their faces showed disinterest. So there we waited until eventually another nun brought the boy in, pulling him by the hand. Babuthan was dark skinned and resembled the twins. However he was much healthier looking, and a proper weight for his age. He was very suspicious of us. He looked angry.

When they were all seated we went over to them and shook the hands of the three girls. However when we got to Babuthan, he just started screaming and screaming and would not let us near him. Eventually the nuns escorted all the children out and we were left with the Mother Superior.

'It's nothing,' Mother reassured us. 'He'll be fine as soon as he gets used to you.'

But I was shaken by Babuthan's behaviour. It was not a good start.

Before we left, the nuns took us to see some of the local residents who wanted to meet the visitors from the other side of the world. We went into one house which was very simple, with no furniture at all except for two wooden chairs placed side by side in the middle of the one big room. It seemed to serve as lounge room, kitchen and dining area. The owner insisted we sit on the chairs whilst he and several of his neighbours crowded around. They were all men. The women stayed outside.

The first thing he wanted to know was whether I was the son of the great Australian spin bowler Lindsay Cline, and had I been there when he stonewalled with Slasher Mackay to save the Fourth Test against the West Indies in 1961?

His knowledge of cricket was encyclopaedic, and his love of the game all encompassing. This was before Sri Lanka was an international cricket nation. I had no idea how fanatical they were. But this man left us in no doubt he and his neighbours lived for the game. He brought us some tea and we continued to discuss more of the burning issues surrounding the Australian cricket scene including whether the rumours of Alan Border's retirement were true. It made me feel at home.

After we finished our tea the man's next door neighbour invited us to come and see his house. We felt it would only be polite. So he ushered us, rather slowly and extravagantly, out of the front door of the house we were in, stopping us from time to time, for reasons that escaped me. Eventually he took us in to his house, which looked exactly like the first house, including having no furniture other than two chairs in the middle of the room which were identical to the ones in the previous house.

So we had some more tea in his house at the end of which his neighbour on the other side also invited us to his place. And so we visited six houses that day and drank more tea than we would have thought possible, in each case sitting on two chairs that always looked the same as in the house before, and talked about cricket.

It was only some time later the nuns explained how we had been the recipients of a form of hospitality unique to their slum. The chairs in fact had been borrowed from the nuns, and placed in the first house we visited. Then as we were slowly ushered out the front door of that house, someone would grab the chairs, run out the back door with them, and bring them in the back door of the next house. We would thus always have somewhere to sit, and no one in the street would need to be ashamed of their lack of furniture.

We came back the next day and spent some time watching Babika and Babeta running around. For such sick children they seemed to have amazing energy. Later we learned the energy was always short lived because it came from eating sugar. In fact that's all they ate. Twice a day the nuns would put out a very limited amount of real food for the children and ring a bell for them to come and eat. But as the food was scarce, the children chaotic and the nuns busy, if any of the children didn't answer the bell and didn't eat their food, the nuns wouldn't know, or even if they did, certainly wouldn't chase them to eat.

So Babika and Babeta would never have a real meal. Rather they would wait, sometimes days at a time, for one of the patrons of the orphanage to come with chocolates or fairy floss, and then they would stampede the other children to get it. The sugar high would keep them buzzing for half an hour or so and then they would fall down till the next sugar hit. As a result they were sugar addicts, and that addiction was more than just a problem or an inconvenience. It was life threatening. But the nuns and the patrons didn't seem to notice, or if they did notice, they didn't have the time or the energy to care.

Babika was the leader of the two. She made all the decisions, and Babeta followed along behind her. One of the ways I could tell them apart in the early days was that Babika was the one with the darting eyes that needed to assess the changing environment, whilst Babeta had the glassy eyes that only needed to know where Babika was.

After watching the girls for a while we asked to see Rangani and Babuthan. We were told Rangani was at school. We asked how she could afford to go to school, why she was given that opportunity when none of the other children were. But the Mother Superior just smiled, shrugged her shoulders and gave us no answer.

So we were taken in to see Babuthan who was waiting in the meeting room with one of the nuns. This time he didn't even let us get near him, but started screaming as soon as we came through the door. We went away again.

The next day we came to the orphanage an hour earlier than we had said, and were surprised to see Babuthan in the courtyard happily throwing a tennis ball back and forth with a man. When the nuns saw us, they tried to hustle us away. But we knew something wasn't right.

We took Mother Superior into the meeting room and insisted she come clean. After some prevarication she admitted she had told a 'small untruth'. She would now tell us everything. Later we learned she still left out the most crucial details. But for the moment this is what she had to say:

The family were 'tea estate' Tamils, that is they were not part of the Tamils who had lived in and around Jaffna for nineteen hundred years, and who were waging the war against the Singhalese Government. Rather they were the descendants of Tamils from Tamil Nadu in southern India (also known as Indian Tamils) who had been brought across to Sri Lanka by the British in the nineteenth century to work the tea estates in and around Kandy.

These Indian Tamils were disenfranchised, that is even though they had been in Sri Lanka for over a hundred years and several generations had been born there, they had no political or social rights. So the parents of our children were from this very low caste. Nonetheless their father had managed to rise to a managerial position in the tea estates. He was a sort of impoverished middle class worker, who had enough money to father and support six children. Yes there were two more we had not been told about (another small untruth), and in fact the number of children later rose to a possible eight (another small untruth).

The mother died in childbirth, not with the twins, but with the one that came after the twins. The twins were then almost four. At the mother's death the father, who was also a kind of unofficial tea estate magistrate and in some way politically active (though for whom and for what was unclear), fearing for his own safety and the safety of the children decided to farm them out to relatives and neighbours to look after til all was safe.

He managed to find homes for all except the twins. They were girls, which makes it harder, and twins are considered unlucky in their society. So it was difficult to convince a friend or relative to look after them. Eventually he induced the nuns to take them 'temporarily'. He told the girls he would be back for them soon. A year later he still hadn't returned. The nuns tracked him down and asked if they could try to adopt the girls out. But the father refused, insisting he would soon be back to collect them.

'So Babuthan and Rangani found homes?' I asked, at which the Mother Superior blustered for a moment and then said:

'Oh no, sorry, Rangani didn't find a home either.'

'But you said he found homes for all but the twins.'

She blustered a little more but without any attempt to clarify, she pushed on with the story.

So three years after he put the girls in the orphanage, the father died. According to the nun his political opponents executed him in the delightful manner which had become quite common in that terrible war zone. They tied his hands, stood him upright, and then dropped old car tires over his head until he was encased in a stack of them. They then set fire to the tires so he burned to death, but slowly and in the most excruciating pain possible.

Whether the father really died this way or not, I will never know. It seems impossible to believe Mother Superior would want to make that up. But she did tell a lot of lies and maybe this was just one more designed to increase our pity and make sure we went through with the adoption.

What I came to understand was that the nuns of the Missionaries of Charity had no hesitation in telling any number of lies to westerners if they thought it would advance the cause of finding homes for their children. This was something I believe they had been taught to engage in. They had been taught that the Christian ethic of truthfulness had to give way to a greater good.

But it was more than being just about the ends justifying the means. They also displayed a naive and extremely materialistic innocence. They told themselves that however much misinformation they laid on the adoptive parents, and whatever problems that caused for those parents or the children they adopted or the wider community, it would all come good in the end when everyone got back to America or Sweden or Australia where western money would miraculously solve all the problems.

Be that as it may, it was clear the father of these children was dead but that Babuthan had a home with his uncle in Kandy. This was the man with whom he had been throwing the tennis ball. The nuns however, believing that no-one would want to adopt three girls, convinced the uncle to let Babuthan be adopted as well, so they would have a boy with whom to sweeten the pot.

But of course Babuthan didn't want to be thrown into the pot. He was happy with his uncle who clearly loved and cared for him. Even from the tennis ball throwing we could see that. So we told Mother Superior we were more than happy to adopt three girls. We didn't have to have a boy, and we certainly didn't need a boy who would be ripped away from his loving uncle. We hoped this would settle matters. But it didn't.

No-one, not the Mother Superior, not even the uncle to a degree, could accept what we were saying. First of all they doubted anyone could actually be satisfied with mere girls, especially three of them, if there weren't at least one boy to make it all worthwhile. And even if westerners were that crazy, they didn't want Babuthan to miss out on his chance of going to the West.

So the nuns and the local neighbours all pleaded with the boy not to miss out on his golden chance, and pleaded with us to, in effect, take him against his will, for his own good. But we of course saw that as absurd. So did Babuthan. We all held the line and eventually everyone was forced to give in. The uncle, even though he had been part of the push, was actually very pleased when the scheme fell apart, and told us so.

The real tragedy with the Babuthan lie was that it masked a much bigger lie. If I had not been so preoccupied with the boy, I may have been able to focus on what was a far more dangerous deception, and may have been able to halt it in time. Now, when we visited the orphanage, Rangani was beginning to show signs of not wanting to be adopted either. It was very unsettling, and had it not been for the trauma with Babuthan, I would have investigated closer. But the nuns assured us it was just nerves, and she would get over it. And as I was so unwilling to face another 'failure', I accepted what they said.

So we had our three girls who were the bottom of the Sri Lankan social barrel. First of all they were female and that was a bad start. Secondly they were orphans, and in that society, rather than being a trigger for pity it was a trigger for scorn. People without family were only to be looked down upon. Thirdly they were Indian Tamils and therefore disenfranchised and further despised. And finally, in the case of the twins, they were bad luck.

It was arranged that we would take the three girls back to stay with us at the Mount Royal Beach Hotel. They slept on camp beds in our room. The twins kept us awake with their snoring, because of course on top of the malnutrition and lice and sores, they also had adenoid and hearing problems.

Rangani was on the phone to the nuns several times a day. We couldn't tell what she was saying but by the tone it was clear she wasn't happy and didn't want to be with us. When she wasn't on the phone however she was very quiet and gave us no trouble.

We took the girls down to the pool. None could swim but we had bought them all water wings. When the twins went in however, with their puss and their sores, all the tourists and adoptive parents immediately cleared out. It was nice to have such a large swimming pool to ourselves.

There was a tiny push merry go round next to the pool which was really designed for very little children no more than two or three. But because the twins were so small we put them on the little horses and started pushing them around. They screamed in terror. It may be they were genuinely frightened. But my suspicion is it was all part of a syndrome we came to understand, a syndrome of feigned helplessness.

Because pressure on beds and space was so intense in the Home for the Dying/Orphanage, if the nuns felt a child was able to look after themselves, they would send them out onto the streets to make way for younger and more helpless children. So our girls learned early on that their best survival tactic was to play dumb. So long as the nuns thought they were helpless they would retain their precious space under the bed of the dying old lady.

Similarly with us they made the assumption that if they played helpless we would keep them, but if we thought they were bright or in any way self sufficient, we might cast them back onto the streets.

We noticed another tendency in the twins from early on, that perhaps hinted at a fearful war torn upbringing they couldn't articulate. It was the need to placate authority, particularly authority in uniform. If we were in the street and there was a policeman or soldier, they would rush up to them and try to cuddle them.

We had great difficulty, with no common language, trying to get them to understand they did not need to do that. Indeed it was a dangerous game to play with those men, because they seemed so trigger happy, and at 3'2" the twins were just at the right height for their heads to run straight into the soldiers' private parts. I knew it was a possibility because they had already done it to me more than once.

They also took every opportunity to cuddle and play up to other adults in the hotel. This was an insurance policy in case we abandoned them. After all they had been abandoned many times in their young lives, and had little faith in us or any other adult.

But these problems aside, we still had the major and more pressing problem of how to adopt them and get them back to Australia. We had only a one month visa and so we had to achieve all we needed to achieve in that time. We had to make a two pronged attack, bureaucratic and legal.

We had to get official permission from the relevant government departments and at the same time we had to tee up a court time on the assumption we would get that approval. If we waited till after we got it and then tried to go for the court order we would run out of time.

I started the adoption process with the Tamil solicitor the parent group had recommended. He didn't seem to have any idea about foreign adoptions, and kept saying less than reassuring things like:

'There shouldn't be any problems, old boy,' as though we were both civil servants in the British Raj.

He had an extremely young and attractive female 'assistant', who kept coming in and out during our interview, smiling at him and at me, but not appearing to do anything.

Our interview lasted for about three quarters of an hour during which he chatted about this and that but didn't write anything down. I came back twice more for similar interviews where nothing approaching legal substance was talked about and where he also didn't write anything down. On each occasion I paid him some more money. The interesting thing however was that each time he had a different young and attractive female assistant.

When he discovered I was a lawyer, he began to tell me about all his successes.

'And, did you know, old boy, we're about to notch up another big win in the Supreme Court tomorrow. Want to come along and have a look?'

I said I would like to come. I was very interested in how their system worked. I knew it was based on the English and therefore would be much like ours. But there were bound to be some interesting differences.

The next day as he drove us to the Supreme Court, he told me about the case, which they had lost in the court at first instance, but which he was very confident they were going to win on appeal.

'You see, old boy, we've got a bit of an ace in the hole. We've got some new evidence we didn't put up at the trial. Absolutely irrefutable.'

'Is this evidence that wasn't known at the time of trial?' I asked him, a little surprised.

'Oh no it was known. We just overlooked it. But we're fixing that now.'

'Ah,' I said, 'that is very different from Australia. In our system you can't introduce fresh evidence on appeal, except sometimes, rarely, where the availability of the evidence couldn't possibly have been known at the time of the trial.'

He took his eyes off the road for a moment and looked at me with some surprise. Then he blustered and laughed and assured me that wouldn't be a problem in this case. I assumed he knew what he was talking about and that their system had to be very different from ours.

When we got to the Court and cleared about an hour's worth of security checks, I took my place in the back and watched Mr Rajanathan talking with his barrister and the client. He looked very jolly and confident. The barrister looked a little less so.

The case was called and Mr Rajanathan's barrister rose to begin his argument. However before he could even open his mouth, the Chief Justice said:

'Mr Wikramanaya, from the documents you've lodged your case seems to hinge totally on this new evidence you expect us to admit.'

'Yes, Your Honour. This evidence changes the whole complexion...'

'But you knew about this before. You can't expect us to admit it now.

'Um, um, I would submit, with the greatest respect to the Court...'

'Did you or did you not have access to this evidence at the time of trial?'

'Yes Your Honour,' said Mr Wikramanaya, hanging his head.

'Well then stop wasting our time.'

He turned to his two fellow judges who nodded their approval. After a few more minutes where the barrister blustered away in vain, the appeal was dismissed. It must have been one of the shortest appeals in Sri Lankan jurisprudential history.

Now this didn't give me confidence in our solicitor. However I had neither the time nor the local knowledge to go elsewhere. I just had to hope Mr Rajanathan would come to grips with our adoption better than he had with an expensive Supreme Court appeal. But as I saw him smiling and leading his distressed (and no doubt now bankrupt) client from the court, I couldn't muster much confidence.

So now I had my legal representation 'in place', I could turn my attention to the bureaucracy. It seemed there were two departments we needed to deal with, the Department of Probation and Child Care Services and the Department of Immigration and Emigration. As the name of the former implies, it dealt with criminals and children (as you do) and so adoptions.

We needed to deal with the latter because the girls were Indian Tamils and therefore not citizens. As such they had no passports, and we had to get them some sort of identity documents on which they could travel. Strangely enough Rangani did have some travel documents, and that should have been another warning to me. But I was just grateful I only had to get two instead of three, and passed over the question I should have asked.

I began with Immigration and Emigration. The Department was housed in a square building with a large internal open air courtyard. All the clerks' windows faced inwards into the courtyard. This meant that the applicants all had to queue in the courtyard in the blazing equatorial sun. When I arrived at 10 in the morning the heat was already fierce and there were enormous queues, stretching back from each window, that tangled with one another and criss-crossed in the centre of the courtyard.

I joined the end of one queue and stood there for about an hour, during which time it didn't seem to move at all. I looked about at the other queues in case I should try a different one, but none of those seemed to have moved either. I asked the man ahead of me to mind my place and went up to the head of the queue to see what might be causing the delay.

The clerk at my window was sitting back a little with his feet up on the counter and was talking to the clerk at the next window who was similarly 'settled in'. I stood there for a while watching them chat, making no attempt to attend to the people queued at their windows. Then they went off together into the back and after a time returned with cups of tea. Now they moved further back into the building and sat at a little table to continue their conversation. They gave no explanation and made no apology to the people in their queues.

It was all rather strange but I couldn't see what I could do about it, so went back to my place in the queue. By 11 o'clock the queue still hadn't moved. I went back to the top and there were the two clerks, feet up as before, chatting as before, and the same man was at the head of the queue, just standing there silently waiting.

Then I walked around to look at all the other windows. At each it was much the same, clerks chatting, or reading a newspaper or just staring into space. But no-one was being attended to. I went back to my place in the queue and asked the man in front of me to explain what was going on.

'We are all Indian Tamils, you see.' But I didn't, so he explained further. 'And there is a religious festival in India, in Tamil Nadu, which is our homeland, don't you see.' Yes I did see that. 'Well we have no papers, because we are Indian Tamils.'

'That I understand very well,' I said and explained to him why I was there.

'Yes indeed, indeed,' he shook his head with that well known sub-continental waggle that looks like a 'no' to the uninitiated but really means 'yes I understand' or 'yes that is true'.

'So we have to come here for permission to travel,' he continued.

'Yes but why isn't anyone being attended to?' I asked.

'Ah,' he waggled his head again in the same way as before, but this time to mean something along the lines of 'yes life is strange, life is difficult'.

'It's because we are Indian Tamils, don't you see.'

'You mean because you are Tamils they might just never serve you?'

'It is a sad possibility,' he confessed, with another waggle of the head.

'But why doesn't someone complain to them?' I asked. 'Why don't people demand to be served?'

'Ah well, you see, then we certainly wouldn't get our travel papers.'

I was horrified, for him and for everyone queuing there, including myself.

'When is the festival?' I asked him.

'It starts in two more days,' he said sadly. 'If I don't get my papers today, I fear I will not be able to go. And then I will not see any of my relatives.' He had tears welling in his eyes. 'I haven't seen them for some years, don't you know.'

I felt very sad for the man.

'Have you been queuing since 8 am?' I asked him.

'Oh yes,' he said, 'since 8 am on Monday.'

This was Thursday.

I was experiencing Singhalese Government passive aggression at its finest. No-one could possibly blame the Government for persecuting Indian Tamils. They weren't passing any laws to curtail their freedom. They weren't saying these people couldn't travel. In fact the law guaranteed them their right to travel. All they had to do was come along to the Department of Immigration and Emigration and apply.

When the Singhalese Government tells the Australian Government that Tamil asylum seekers are not refugees because the law in Sri Lanka protects and cares for them, I think back to that day when I stood in 100 degree heat for hour after hour, my head pounding and my stomach churning with an anger I was advised by my fellow queuers not to express.

In the end I decided I would express it anyway. I could not afford to queue for three more days in that heat. For a start my body wasn't used to it and I would probably get very sick. But more crucially I had such a limited time on the visa. If I didn't get all paperwork done before it expired, we would certainly not get the girls out of Sri Lanka.

And that was starting to worry me a great deal. The parent group couldn't have been more wrong about the need to adopt Babuthan and Rangani. Babuthan had a home, and Rangani, for whatever reason, was well fed and being schooled. But the twins were very sick and malnourished, and there wasn't much doubt they would die, if someone didn't take charge of them.

So I felt driven now by the need to get Babika and Babeta out of Colombo and back to Australia where they could be fed and cared for and brought back to health. And the nuns stressed again and again that Rangani was their big sister whom they loved and depended on and therefore she had to go with them no matter what.

But now the question was how to overcome this first apparently insurmountable hurdle. As I stood there in the sun looking around at those immovable lines, history came to my aid. It occurred to me Sri Lanka's colonial days were not so far in the past, and most of the Singhalese clerks would remember them. So shamefully I decided to play the imperialist card.

I strode up to the head of the queue and banged on the counter so the man with his feet up nearly fell off his chair. Then in my best condescending tone and in my best British accent, I said:

'What is the meaning of this? I demand service now!' It was a very corny line, but the best I could come up with on the spur of the moment.

He hesitated for a moment. But I wasn't going to give him time to think. I was depending on a knee jerk reaction he might have learnt as a child:

'Well come on! It's time to get this done,' I barked at him.

At which he sat up in his chair, grabbed some paper and pencil and with head down said:

'What is the nature of your application, Sir?'

I explained everything to him in great detail and watched his head waggling constantly as he wrote. All the time he kept saying:

'Ah yes, I see, I see.'

After a few minutes he said: 'We will certainly expedite your application, Sir, but regulations require you to undergo a formal interview with my superior.'

'Oh very well,' I said, as though disgusted with his incompetence. 'Let's get that over with.'

'Regretfully,' he whimpered, his head now almost waggling off his shoulders, 'my superior won't be back till 4.00 pm tomorrow.'

'What?' I almost shouted.

'But, but, but, Sir,' he apologised, 'I will make an appointment with you for bang on 4.00, so you will be the first he deals with. If it is not too inconvenient, please arrange to return to this very window at 4.00 tomorrow and I will personally escort you to my superior.'

'Oh very well,' I snapped. 'And by the way,' I added, 'I should be most grateful if you would attend to my colleague as well.'

'Of course, Sir.'

At which I signalled for the man who had been ahead of me in the queue to come forward. I stood by long enough to be sure his processing was well underway and then went to leave. But as I started to go he took hold of my arm and looked at me. He said nothing but he didn't have to.

So I went back to the hotel, bought a cold bottle of Coca Cola, and went for a walk on the beach to try and clear my head. Late in the afternoon the locals of Mount Lavinia were out strolling on the sand. Some of the men and boys were swimming, but the women would only lift the very bottoms of their long saris to paddle near the edge. The Coca Cola stroll would become my daily ritual. After each long day of frustration I would return to wander and paddle, sugar hit in hand, trying to work out my next strategy.

I spent the next morning telephoning the Department of Probation and Child Care Services, trying to get an appointment. But the phone was never answered. I checked the number with the hotel staff. They assured me it was correct. I kept ringing, but still no answer.

At 4 pm I went back to the Department of Immigration and Emigration. The courtyard was deserted. There was a sign on the window.

'These offices close at 3.30 pm sharp'.

I was, to say the least, not happy. That simpering clerk had got the better of me after all. I hoped at least my friend from the line had got his papers and hadn't been sent away the moment I left.

I couldn't go back the following day because it was Poya Day. Every full moon is a Buddhist holiday in Sri Lanka. That's Poya Day. Everything was closed.

But I went back the day after that, bypassed the same long queues, stormed up to the same clerk, and continued my previous tactic. It may not have worked so well so far, but it was all I had.

'You deceived me! You told me to come at 4 pm knowing the offices would close at 3.30.'

'Oh no, Sir,' he insisted in his most innocent voice, though he could not quite keep the look of delight from his eyes. 'I said 3 pm. Unfortunately you did not keep your appointment.'

'Fix this now,' I shouted at him, and I was truly angry. Whether I managed to maintain my British accent I don't know. But he now looked genuinely frightened.

'You are at the wrong place,' he said without any waggle. 'Go upstairs to Room 403 where they deal with foreign adoptions.'

I went upstairs to room 403 and indeed that was the place I should have been all along. The woman there was truly nice and helpful. She explained in detail what I needed to do. It involved very many steps, and many more visits to her office. But every time I came she was always there and always progressed the application to the next step, until eventually we had our little red booklets that allowed Babika and Babeta to travel out of Sri Lanka on one occasion only.

Meanwhile I was still trying to get an appointment with the Department of Probation and Childcare Services. Finally someone answered the phone and they told me to come round the following day. But when I got there I couldn't get past the clerk on the front desk who denied any knowledge of any phone call or any appointment.

I went back to the hotel in despair. I had been driving up and down the Galle Road every day for two weeks now, and though we had travel documents, they were useless unless we got to adopt the children. I bought my coke and went for a walk along the beach. I was shuffling through the thick sand, furthest from the shore, near the stone wall that separated the beach from the grassed area above it. I was kicking the soft sand to try and get rid of my frustrations. It was lucky I had chosen that part of the beach for my walk. Often I would paddle down by the edge of the water.

If I had done so this day, I may not be here now. Suddenly I heard the strangest noise, which, because it was not a noise I was used to, took me a moment to identify as gun fire. I looked about and saw people scattering in all directions. But in my confusion I couldn't yet identify where the gun fire was coming from. Then a bullet pinged into the stone wall about five meters from where I was standing. That focussed me. I realised I needed to know who was firing and from where.

As the people scattered and dove into the sea or into the sand, I could see several men with rifles down by the edge of the water, some lying on their faces, some kneeling. They were all firing up at the grassed area, in a general direction no more than a few metres from me. I turned and saw a similar number of Singhalese soldiers up on the grass, firing down on the men near the water. I was pretty much in the cross fire of a gun fight between Government soldiers and Tamil rebels.

I remember feeling no fear whatsoever. I also remember thinking how strange it was that I didn't feel any fear. Then I saw one of the Tamil men stand up briefly. Half his face was missing. Then he fell backwards into the water. That brought my ruminations to a halt. I dove down and pressed myself against the stone wall. I didn't actually reason it through, but I guess in that split second I realised diving down behind the wall would protect me totally from the fire of the Government troops.

Unfortunately I was totally exposed to Tamil rebel fire. They had absolutely no reason to waste a bullet on a tourist, but I was still very much at risk from a stray or a badly aimed shot. So I knew I couldn't stay where I was. I had to move. Slowly I crawled along the sand, making sure I kept hard against the wall. Once I had made a few more metres I started to run, bent double so I was still shielded by the wall.

After about thirty seconds I judged I was far enough along to rise to my full height and sprint to the safety (or perhaps I now realised relative safety) of the hotel. I didn't look back and so do not know who won that particular skirmish. All I knew was that I was in one piece. When I got back to the room I realised that, even though I thought I hadn't been frightened, I had totally soiled myself. And the image of that Tamil rebel is with me to this day.

The next day, though I was still pretty shaken, I realised I had to hit the Galle Road again and make another try for the Department of Probation and Child Care Services. But now I was told by the desk clerk at the hotel not to bother. It was Ramadan. I couldn't see why that would matter. I knew there were virtually no Muslims in Colombo, most living over in the east of the country. Nonetheless the city celebrated the festival and shut down.

'What, for the whole month?' I asked.

'Oh no, just for a few days,' he smiled.

But a few days were precious, and I wasn't sure we could afford them, especially as I had made no progress with the adoption. I had the name of a Sri Lankan Supreme Court judge. Justice Michael Kirby had met him on one of his lecture tours, and given me the man's contact details, in case of emergency. I thought we were close to that now, so I contacted him and he graciously invited me to have afternoon tea with him.

He also lived in Mount Lavinia in a big house behind high security walls topped with broken glass. After I had cleared the security guards and the electronic surveillance, we had a pleasant couple of hours talking together. I couldn't help noticing that, like everywhere else, his house was run down. It seemed ironic that the Government had to pay for sophisticated electronic equipment and two armed guards but couldn't afford a coat of paint. The judge offered to help by contacting the Department and getting me an appointment as soon as the Ramadan holiday was over. He was as good as his word and the appointment was made.

Meanwhile I had a few days to spend some time with the girls. They seemed to be getting more comfortable with us, although Babika remained very nervous, always scratching her face, biting her nails and twisting at what little hair had grown back on her head. The thing that struck me most in those few days was how little the twins seemed to relate to Rangani. There was a formality between her and them, almost as though she were another stranger like us whom they were required to get to know. They played together, swam in the pool together, but Rangani never seemed to talk to them. I decided to pay a visit to the nuns. Something was starting to force its way into my conscious mind, something that wasn't quite right. I wanted to speak with the Mother Superior.

I asked her what was going on. She had to 'confess' Rangani had not been living in their orphanage as we had been told. Rather she had been in another Missionaries of Charity orphanage at the other end of the city.

'We thought it would be a good idea to bring them together again before you arrived.'

'How long has she been here?'

'She got here a week before you,' the nun said, looking decidedly uncomfortable.

'Then they haven't seen Rangani for three years?'

'Yes.'

'How can you say they are inseparable? If the twins haven't seen her since they were four, they would barely remember her.'

Mother Superior didn't answer. She just shrugged her shoulders.

'But why separate them in the first place?' I asked

'Oh, you know, these things happen in a war zone.'

This was far from satisfactory.

'So you told me another untruth,' I said, wanting to say 'lie' but trying to contain myself. It was hard. After all the bureaucratic nonsense I had had to endure, I was running on empty.

'A small untruth,' she said, 'a very unimportant one.'

But I didn't see it as unimportant. I saw it as quite important. Rangani had been portrayed as the inseparable sister of the twins, who in reality barely knew her.

'I don't think she wants to come with us,' I told the nun. 'She is on the phone to you all the time. I know you are trying to talk her into it. But what's the point if she doesn't want it?'

'No! No!' said the nun, almost panicky now. 'She wants to go. She is just a silly young girl and doesn't know it. She loves her sisters. She needs to be with them. It is the best for her. You must take her. Please! It would be a tragedy to leave her behind.'

I looked at the nun, and tried my hardest not to be angry with her. I realised too it would be unfair to Rangani to allow that anger to interfere with her future well being. If it were best for the girl to be with her sisters, I couldn't let the Mother Superior's lies and dissembling get in the way of that. No doubt her heart was in the right place. She just thought deceit was the best way to deal with westerners. I knew I needed to find the best outcome and not be influenced by all the unnecessary nonsense. So I re-assured Mother I would take Rangani with us.

After Ramadan we had less than a week left. In that time we had to get approval from the Department, get a court date and convince a magistrate to make the order for adoption. Then we had to buy air tickets (which of course there was no point buying in advance) and get on a plane before our visa ran out. The first step was my meeting with the head of the Department which my friend the Supreme Court judge had arranged.

I arrived at the Department, as arranged, and told the clerk on the desk I had an appointment with Mrs Weerasooriya. It was the same clerk who had sent me away at least twice before. He looked at me suspiciously, then down at his appointment book. Clearly what he saw disappointed him. But there was not much he could do other than take me in to see his boss.

Mrs Weerasooriya was a well dressed and well groomed woman in her early forties. She smiled broadly at me and indicated the chair on the other side of her very big desk. At the angle I was sitting I could see through the glass petition which separated her from the rest of the office. The first thing that struck me was how many people were wearing shoulder holsters. Clearly the parole part of the Department took precedence over the childcare services part. Either that or they had some tough kids to adopt out.

As Mrs Weerasooriya sat down on the other side of the desk, I heard a telephone start to ring. It was not in her office. Indeed she didn't seem to have a telephone in her office. I soon located the ring as coming from a telephone on a little table in the open central area of the Department. I glanced into the offices to the left and right of where I was. Neither one had a telephone. Quickly I realised the Department only had one telephone and it was centrally located for everyone's convenience.

It was also being ignored by everyone. Clearly no-one had responsibility for answering it. As Mrs Weerasooriya started to talk the telephone just kept ringing in the background. No-one came out of their office to answer it, and at the same time several people walked right past it, totally ignoring the ringing. I now understood why I'd had such trouble getting through.

'So are you enjoying your trip?' Mrs Weerasooriya was asking.

'To tell you the truth...', I began.

'I love to travel,' she cut in. 'I have such a jolly time. Particularly cruising. Nothing like a good cruise, don't you think?'

'Actually I've never had...'.

'All that salt sea air. Makes one feel alive. And so good for the complexion. I have a beautiful complexion, don't you think?'

As she hadn't let me answer her previous questions, I assumed she didn't need me to answer this one either.

'Don't you think?' she was repeating. 'My complexion. Rather nice, don't you think? Smooth and clear, isn't it?'

Obviously she did want a response.

'It's very nice,' I said, feeling extremely foolish.

'Yes indeed,' she beamed. 'I find that most men are very drawn to my complexion. Oh and of course my hair which is long and lustrous. Not that I can wear it out at the office, so of course you can't see. But if I did let it out, then of course you would see. But then I might start a stampede!' She laughed uproariously.

Then she stared intently at me. Clearly she needed a response to this as well.

'I'm sure it's very attractive,' I said. This was getting more uncomfortable by the minute.

'Oh indeed! Indeed it is. Not that physical attraction is the be all and end all. But it is important, don't you think. In a relationship between a man and a woman, isn't it important.'

'Oh yes,' I said.

What did this woman want of me? If it was what it looked like, it would be a bureaucratic hurdle I really had not anticipated.

'Mrs Weerasooriya, have you had a chance to look at our papers?' I blurted out, rather awkwardly

'Hmm?' she said, still leaning across the desk, her eyes now glistening.

'The papers? Um the children? You know the adoption?'

She looked a little disappointed. But then she shrugged and said:

'What do they call you?'

'I'm sorry?' I didn't understand what she was asking me. But I did know our 'moment' had passed, and I was grateful for that.

'The children,' she said. 'Do they call you Mummy and Daddy?'

I wanted to laugh and tell her they couldn't even say the words 'mummy' and 'daddy' in English, let alone conceive of us in those roles. But something told me not to. I hesitated for a moment and then said:

'Yes, that's what they call us.'

'Excellent!' She pulled out the papers and signed them there and then, after which she called out to one of the gun toting parole officers who looked a little like a Singhalese Al Pacino. 'This is Mr De Silva,' she told me. 'He'll take care of the finer details.'

Then she gave him the papers and I followed him out to the reception area. There we sat on two plastic chairs whilst he spread the papers out on a little table between us. He examined the papers for a moment, weighing them in his hands one by one, as though their avoirdupois was highly relevant. Finally he said:

'Do they call you Mummy and Daddy?'

'Oh yes,' I said.

'That is excellent!' Then he countersigned something and handed me the approval papers.

It seemed like the finer details were much like the courser details. But I wasn't going to complain. I took the papers and ran.

The next day I went back to our solicitor with the approval and asked him if it were possible to get a court date before the visa ran out. He wasn't sure but told me he would try. The day after that I was back in his office.

'We have a tentative court date for you,' he said. 'It is at 10 am on the morning of the 20th.'

'But that's the date our visa runs out,' I said.

'Yes, but not till 2pm,' said Mr Rajanathan, smiling.

'So let me get this straight,' I said. 'We have between 10 am and 2pm to have a court hearing, get a sealed court order and get on a plane out of Sri Lanka?'

'Precisely,' he smiled again, 'provided of course we can confirm the tentative court date.'

'And how do we do that?'

'We have to apply in person to the Clerk of Courts.'

'I see. So when will you do that?'

'Actually you need to do it.'

'Why is that?'

'Because I am far too busy.'

I wondered what I was paying this man for. But I wasn't about to argue the toss. There was too much else to worry about.

'What if there are other cases ahead of us, and we get delayed? Won't we risk missing our plane?'

'That is a risk,' he conceded. 'But there is a far greater problem.'

Of course there was.

'And that would be?' I asked wearily.

'The magistrate is Singhalese. Therefore he is very unlikely to grant adoptions for Tamil girls. In fact,' he waggled his head in some sort of mock disappointment, 'he may be quite hostile all round.'

'Is there any chance we could get a Tamil magistrate?' I asked.

'Oh yes,' he said, 'but not till next month.'

'Can we get our visa extended till then?'

'Absolutely not.'

I paid Mr Rajanathan some more money on account for his court appearance and left. I went to the court house at 9 am the next day. Tamil rebels had recently bombed it so that the whole front wall which faced the street was missing. It meant one could stand on the veranda and look in on all the court cases in progress.

I think too the bombed shell of the court house had become a sort of symbolic rallying point because there were hundreds of people on the veranda cheering as a seemingly endless convoy of military vehicles passed along the road.

'Is this a parade?' I asked the man next to me.

'They are bringing back the war dead, from the front.' His eyes looked crazed. 'The glorious war dead!'

As he spoke an open top truck went by piled with corpses, and then another, and then another. I watched as literally hundreds of war dead were driven past. With each vehicle the cheers from the crowd became louder and more frenetic.

I felt very sad as I walked round the back of the court to find the office of the Clerk of Courts. It wasn't hard to find, because the back wall was bombed out too. So I just stepped over the debris into what I assumed must be the Clerks' office. It was a large open plan office (now more open plan than the builders had intended) with dozens of desks. Only a couple were occupied.

The first man I came to was sitting with his feet up on the desk. He had a bottle of Johnnie Walker Red Label Whiskey in his hand. It was half empty.

'I am looking for the Clerk of Courts.' I said.

The man looked at me through bleary eyes. He didn't seem to register what I was saying. He was very drunk. I repeated myself but he continued to just stare through his drunken haze. Finally one of the other men said:

'He *is* the Clerk of Courts.'

Now here was another bureaucratic hurdle I hadn't anticipated. In a Buddhist country where nobody is supposed to drink, a key official was pissed out of his mind on whiskey at 9 o'clock in the morning.

'I need to confirm a court date,' I said, but it was clear he was not going to understand anything I said.

'Just leave the papers with him,' the other man said. 'It will be fine.'

What could I do? I had no choice. I tried to hand the papers to the

Clerk, but they just slipped through his grasp and lay on his chest where I left them.

I went back to the hotel, bought my coke and wandered about the hotel grounds. The beach had lost its allure for me. Things were not looking good. We had our approval. But did we have a confirmed court date? And even if we did, how were we going to get the adoption past the hostile Singhalese magistrate? In the meantime I had no choice but to buy all our air tickets on the vague chance things did work out. I couldn't possibly wait till after the court case.

The best I could do was a Singapore Airlines flight leaving at 1.20 pm. That cut our time frame down another 40 minutes. Of course we had to pay top dollar.

Two days later we were in a minivan heading to the court. We stopped at the orphanage on the way so the girls could say goodbye. There was a lot of crying and a lot of hugging and kissing from the nuns, and from Babika and Babeta, but not from Rangani. As usual she showed little emotion. And anyway, as I had discovered, she didn't really know any of them.

We took Mother Superior with us to the court in case we needed a referee, and arrived just before 10 am. I went up and looked at the door of all the courts, and there, by some miracle, in court no 2, we were listed. Somehow that drunken Clerk had sobered up long enough, sometime over the last couple of days, to actually confirm our court date.

Now all we had to worry about was the hostile Singhalese magistrate. Or so I thought. I looked about for Mr Rajanathan but he was nowhere to be seen. As the clock struck 10 am I was approached by an attractive young woman I had never seen before who told me she was Mr Rajanathan's assistant.

'Mt Rajanathan will not be attending,' she told me.

'Why not?' I blurted out. I think I was really close to losing it.

'He has run away.'

'What?'

'Because of the Singhalese magistrate. He is frightened of the Singhalese magistrate, so he has run away.'

I appreciated the woman's candour, but that was about all I appreciated.

'Then who is going to represent us?" I asked her.

'Mr Rajanathan has asked me to represent you.' She smiled a little nervously.

'Are you a lawyer?' I asked

'Oh no.' She gave a modest little laugh.

'But you know what to do with adoption cases?' I asked hopefully.

'Not so very much,' she confessed, looking at me with her bright eyes. 'Well not at all really.'

For all we had been through, this was the moment I most felt the need to leave the pages of this Kafka novel by diving into the custard of unconsciousness. But I knew that for all my desire to just fall apart, that was not going to be a useful option.

'Would it perhaps be better if I did it myself?' I asked. 'I don't know Sri Lankan law, but if it is like Australian law I might get by.'

'I think that would be a delightful idea,' she said, much relieved.

For some reason I thought back to my first morning teaching in New Guinea, where I went into the classroom completely unprepared, and just did it, and it all worked out perfectly. I felt I needed to replicate that right now as I heard our case being called.

I took a deep breath to try and still my pounding heart and entered the bombed out courtroom. Agatha and the girls and Mother Superior followed behind. The magistrate was sitting at a temporary 'bench' that looked like it might be a fold up bridge table. He had his head down writing but motioned me to sit on the other side of the table. Agatha, Mother and the children sat on a bench at the back.

It was one of the most surreal moments of my life. Here I was being a lawyer again but in a legal system I knew nothing about, far from home. And as I sat waiting for the magistrate to call on me, I looked out through the court house wall that was no longer there and watched the traffic going by.

Finally he raised his head and smiled at me. That was a shock, though obviously a pleasant one. He didn't seem surprised that I was representing myself. It was as though he had been expecting it.

'I have looked at the papers, Mr Kline', he said. 'Do you tender the authorisation from the Department of Parole and Childcare Services?'

'Yes Your Worship,' I said. 'I do.' I hoped magistrates were called 'Your Worship' in this country.

Apparently they were because he didn't flinch.

'And the certified copy of the travel papers provided by the Department of Immigration and Emigration?'

'Yes Your Worship.'

He was doing it all for me.

'Everything seems to be in order.' He took off his glasses and looked intently at me. 'Are you sure you want to do this?' he asked. 'Raising four, no three children...the boy is not coming?'

'No he is not.'

'Raising three children, who are not your own, three older children, will not be easy.'

'I know,' I said, though in retrospect I didn't know, not to anything like the degree I needed to.

'And you are ready for that?'

'Yes.' I said, though in retrospect I wasn't nearly ready.

'Then I congratulate you on a wonderful humanitarian act.' He signed the papers and sealed them and handed them across the desk to me.

'When do you plan to leave?'

I looked at my watch.

'In less than three hours I said.'

'Then you had better hurry,' he said smiling broadly at me. 'Colombo traffic can be a beast.'

As with almost everything else, Mr Rajanathan's assessment of the Singhalese magistrate could not have been more wrong, fortunately. We rushed to the minivan and bundled the children in. As I went to board Mother Superior grabbed my arm.

'Promise me something,' she said.

I felt her track record didn't entitle her to demand much, but nonetheless asked what she wanted.

'I know your wife is a Catholic but you are not. These are good Catholic girls. Promise me you will raise them as Catholics. Promise me you will take them to mass.'

'When I got married,' I told her, 'I swore to raise my children as Catholics. So I will.'

She smiled and let go of my arm.

We got to the airport just before the gate closed. Several of the immigration officers scrutinised our documents, very closely and with furrowed brows. But they let us through. We were the last passengers to board. The moment we were seated they closed the doors and the Singapore airlines jet started taxiing down the runway.

As I looked out the window at the receding terminal I felt like a character from one of those World War II movies, the guy who gets the last plane at the very last minute to escape the baddies. I half expected to see a crowd of Singhalese soldiers and bureaucrats running after the plane screaming for it to stop. But there was no-one there and the jet flew off for Sydney via Singapore and a whole new life.

18. A CROWDED HOUSE

The need to get the girls out of Sri Lanka had certainly taken my mind off my own problems. I had even forgotten, during my brief court appearance, that I couldn't speak in public. Now the girls' ongoing problems were going to keep my mind occupied for some time to come.

The first problem was one of communication. Rangani had a few words of English, the twins none. So we did a lot of pointing and acting out, and somehow got by. We were determined to get hold of a Tamil translator so we could ask some more detailed questions. But that had to wait. Health issues had to come first.

Rangani was well fed and fit, but the twins had almost everything wrong that could be wrong. For the first six weeks we were at the local doctor in East Balmain most days. I think Dr Graeme Romans had a permanent afternoon slot for us. He was very gentle, patient and caring with them. He was a doctor who liked being a doctor. So he welcomed a challenge. Often he would shake his head and say:

'I'm so proud to be your doctor.'

Of course he couldn't do it all and referred us to a number of specialists at the Children's Hospital and elsewhere. We saw dermatologists and ear, nose and throat specialists and eye doctors and gastroenterologists and probably a half dozen more I have forgotten. We also went to the dentist several times. The malnutrition of the twins had caused all their teeth to fracture and break, so they had a mouth full of half teeth and little spiky points. They were just baby teeth but were causing them a lot of pain and trouble. So we had one extraction after another, often with the chalky teeth just crumbling before the dentist could get them out properly.

They had arrived in late autumn of 1991 and though it was a mild enough by Australian standards, they were used to equatorial heat. They froze. What's more they had no resistance to local bugs, and over the winter between May and September they caught so many colds it was, in effect, one long cold. Of course, living in close quarters with them, we had one long cold too.

Then there were the head lice. Even though the twins had had their heads shaven, Rangani had not. So she brought half the lice population of Sri Lanka with her. But as we were taken up with more urgent matters we didn't notice till some months down the track when we were all infected and the lice were at a point where they just might uproot our little wooden house and carry it off.

We used anti lice lotion on the twins, but when we came to Rangani she refused. Her English was now good enough to say.

'No want oil.'

'Not oil,' I said, 'for the lice'. And I pointed out the offending creatures on the hair of the twins.

'No want oil,' she repeated.

I tried to explain to her that if she didn't have the treatment we would have to cut her hair. She understood me but said:

'No want cut hair.'

'That's all right,' I said, 'I understand. But then we will definitely have to give you some treatment.'

'No want oil,' she replied.

This was perhaps the first time we noticed what would become clearer over time. At first Rangani seemed perfectly well behaved. At any rate she was quiet and that was good because the twins were noisy in the extreme and extremely naughty.

But then we started to understand that Rangani was as angry with life and where it had taken her, as were the twins. The difference was she played out her anger as passive aggression. No oil/no cut/no solution for us.

She was even passive aggressive to her own disadvantage. For example she turned out to be a great distance runner, and at the first school cross country was at least 300 metres in front at the end. But when she got within ten metres of the finish line she just stopped and let all the other children run past her, despite the parents and teachers screaming encouragement for her to finish.

I tried to help her with her English, but it was soon clear she would have none of it. The first time I sat down with her I used a box of coloured pencils. Holding up a pink coloured pencil I said:

'What colour is this?' Then I answered myself: 'It's pink.' Then I asked again: 'What colour is this?' and indicated to Rangani to answer.

'Pink colour,' she said.

'Good,' I said holding up two thumbs. 'Now, what colour is this?' and I held up a red pencil. 'This is red. What colour is it?'

'Pink colour,' she replied.

Thereafter no matter what I did, no matter what colour I held up or how I tried to explain, I always got:

'Pink colour.'

Even the twins who were watching from the sidelines got it, and started chipping in with: 'Green' or 'Red'.

But as I say it took us a while to start to understand Rangani's anger, because we were too taken up with the twins' medical problems and with their equally problematic behavioural problems.

Babika and Babeta were mostly well behaved for us and, as far as we could tell, comfortable being with us and living in our house. The three girls shared quite cramped quarters in bunk beds in our second bedroom, but that was hardly a problem given the environment they had come from. DOCS were not happy, but I pointed out the same space in Colombo would probably have housed 5 dying people and about 10 children under their beds. So in their terms it was luxury.

At first each morning Agatha would have to dress them because they needed to wear a whole range of clothes they had never worn before, just to keep warm. But they soon got the hang of dressing themselves, and I would simply check them on their way out to school:

'Spencer? Skivvy? T-Shirt? Shirt? Jumper? Coat?'

And they would say 'Yes', 'Yes', as each item was checked off.

As they got healthier we would play in the park across the road after school, throwing a tennis ball, or later even using the tennis ball to try a little cricket. They all had a great eye and were clearly going to be good at sports, though in cricket they just had one big cross bat shot. Doug would join in too of course. He loved cricket and was very happy to play all the fielding positions.

We did have a problem teaching the twins how to use the toilet. They had never used anything but a pit toilet, and so when confronted with a western toilet they would climb up onto the seat and squat above it. As a result their accuracy was not the best. Nonetheless they got the hang of this too.

So whilst they had a lot of issues and a lot to learn, the twins were not such a problem for us at home. Their real naughtiness was reserved for others, and particularly for school teachers, principals and staff.

Though they were nearly seven, because they had no schooling and no English, we put them in kindergarten at the little local Nicholson Street Primary School. Rangani went into Grade 6. The twins got, as their kindergarten teacher, the very kind and long suffering Miss Parker. She was a relatively new teacher and had never taught twins before, let alone our sort of twins.

Babika and Babeta turned Miss Parker's hitherto civilised class of well behaved little Anglos Saxon children, into a riot. There was no way she was going to get them to sit on a chair. They had never sat on chairs before. Nor would they sit on the floor. In fact they would not sit at all. Being with other children was about running nonstop, preferably in the playground, but if needs be, round and round the classroom. Objects were to hurl and crayons were to eat. Paper was for tearing. Bottles were for breaking. Voices were for yelling and screaming.

They totally corrupted the other children who quickly and willingly sank to the lowest common denominator. All this would have been bad enough, but on top of everything else Babeta decided that in Australia she didn't need to follow Babika's orders. She decided to become her own person. Hence arose a fierce rivalry between the two of them for the friendship of other children, for access to toys and games, and for the affection of Miss Parker.

The rioting and the jealousy and competitiveness got so out of control the Principal had to call us up and suggest they separate the girls. But because it was such a small school with only one stream, there was no other kindergarten class. They couldn't put one of the girls in Grade 1 whilst the other stayed in Kindergarten, so the Principal suggested we move Babika up the road to the larger Balmain Primary School.

This we did, only to find they had no room in any kindergarten or even in first class. So they put Babika in second grade, which was right for her age, but way to hard for her given she had no previous schooling even in her own language, and virtually no English. Nonetheless it was all we could do to save the blighted Miss Parker from a nervous breakdown.

Babeta was put in Grade 2 at Nicholson St and so they both struggled at that level for the rest of the year, and both repeated it the following year. From there on in, though we were to move about a lot, they always had to be at separate schools. We tried them at the same school in different classes but that just meant rioting was reserved for recess and lunchtime. That was better than what poor Mrs Parker had to put up with, but far from satisfactory. And so getting them to two separate schools was to be the norm.

I ran into Miss Parker over the Christmas holidays. She seemed to have an eye twitch.

'Are you taking kindergarten again next year?' I asked her.

'Yes,' she said with a deep sigh. 'I got the enrolment list yesterday. I have five sets of twins.'

Of course the twins didn't reserve their naughtiness just for school. We had a number of friends who wanted to help out and offered to take the girls for outings or to their homes for the day. One friend who lived in an old Housing Commission terrace in The Rocks had the twins over and made the mistake of saying:

'Now girls, this house has nothing of value except for that tapestry on the wall. That was my grandmother's. Do your worst. Just be careful of the tapestry.'

Within 5 minutes the tapestry had been ripped from the wall and muddied to a state of near disrepair.

Another couple offered to have all three to their place for the weekend and to take them sailing. They wanted to give us a chance to rest. We didn't want to let them take the girls. We knew what the twins could get up to. However the couple had grown children of their own whom they had successfully raised to become responsible members of the community.

'Kids are kids,' they said. 'We can handle anything they throw at us.'

They weren't the last people to say that and they weren't the last people to regret having said it. Our friends were full of bright eyed optimism when they picked up the girls on Saturday morning. By Sunday evening those eyes were dull and shell shocked. In the interim the girls had combined to smash a hole in their back deck, sink their sail boat and complete the triple when Rangani vomited all over the back of our friend's head as he was driving them home.

They were very gallant about the whole thing and would accept no compensation from us. However, not surprisingly, they never offered to take the girls again.

I am ashamed to say one piece of twin naughtiness did please me. Early on in their time we took them up to Port Macquarie to see my parents who were by then living there. My father, as a shameless racist, had already said:

'You go ahead and do what you want, but I could never love them'.

'What about you, Mum?' I asked.

'Oh, well, I don't know. They are so different from us, aren't they?'

Nonetheless we were taking these new grandchildren to meet their reluctant grandparents. I had already had more flashes from my past, especially around the image of the glowing red tip of my mother's cigarette in my bedroom as a small child. I was still quite a way from synthesising the details of my abuse, but the knowledge I had a problem, and that the problem involved my mother, had found a permanent place in my conscious mind.

When we arrived Mum and Dad seemed quite relieved that Rangani wasn't as black as they had feared and they decided she was acceptable. However the twins were way too black. My mother would throw a few words at them but with a hard edged reluctant tone in her voice. My father said nothing at all. Their English was limited then, but that didn't stop them understanding the attitude of their new grandparents.

They did show a wonderful grasp of English on one occasion however, and this was what brought me my shameful pleasure. My mother had been suffering from some ailment which I can't remember but which I do remember required her to keep her back warm and dry. By some Machiavellian miracle the twins picked up on this, because when she was bent over doing some gardening, they found the garden hose, turned it on and trained the stream of water onto her back.

This pretty much sealed their fate as far as my parents were concerned, something they let us know in no uncertain terms. But of course the twins' fate had been sealed long before they arrived.

At home Babika and Babeta got on with life and, as I said, were a lot less naughty for us than for others. I think a lot of that was about our being the only people who took their individuality seriously. Teachers and others couldn't, or more often wouldn't, take the trouble to tell them apart. Even Rangani tended to just call them by the composite name the nuns had used in the orphanage, Sinaperia (big one/little one). But I knew how important their own clear identity had to be for each of them. In a sense, after being orphaned and uprooted, it was all they had to cling to.

So by the time we got back to Australia, even though physically they were very similar, I had studied their body language and the minutiae of their features and I literally couldn't confuse them. In fact they came to look totally different to me. I even got so cocky I would play a game with them where they would dress in identical red coats with hoods, walk up the street and stand facing away from the house. Then I would come out and they would adopt all sorts of unnatural poses. It was my job to then pick who was who. I got it right every single time.

It became a ritual for them. If ever one or both was feeling insecure or lost they would say to me: 'Red coat game!'

The only time the twins really got problematic for us was in Mass. I had kept my promise to the Mother Superior and was taking them every week. Rangani was over 12 so we gave her the option of going. She chose not to. But Babika and Babeta were only seven so faced an hour every week of what would have been excruciating tedium for them, especially early on when it was all in a foreign language.

So they would fidget and the fidgeting would turn to pushing one another which would turn to full on fighting which would end with them running up and down the aisles and diving under the seats, all the time screaming and yelling at one another. If we could catch one or both we would take them outside. But if not the congregation at Balmain Catholic Church was treated to a little 'side action', usually at some crucial moment like during the Elevation of the Host.

Their shenanigans reached crisis point one Sunday when Babeta got hold of a candle and set fire to a copy of the Parish Bulletin. Then I provided the 'side action' as I jumped up and down on the flaming pages, trying desperately to contain the fire. The priest was kind enough to pause in his Sermon till it was extinguished.

All this the churchgoers took in good grace. Most were the sort of people who had a strong understanding of the situation these girls had come from. Teachers and friends too understood and made allowance for behaviours which, whilst often not ideal, were explicable. No-one saw the naughtiness of the twins as any more than naughtiness. Most were convinced they had good hearts, and if they could be taught to trust, they would start to settle down, perhaps not immediately or even soon, but eventually. That is what I believed, and though perhaps all these years later learning to trust is still a great issue for them, I hope it is slowly coming to pass.

Rangani, on the other hand was starting to emerge as a serious problem. Her passive aggression was becoming far more pervasive, or rather people started to realise just how pervasive it was. She seemed to want nothing more from life than to thwart everyone's wishes. The knowledge that someone wanted her to do something would ensure she wouldn't do it, even if to her own benefit. The syndrome intruded into every aspect of her life.

We wanted to rid our house of lice. The school wanted to clean them out of the classrooms too. But that was not going to happen so long as Rangani could hold on to them and keep spreading them. She was so infested I would watch her tearing at her own scalp. But she would not allow us to bring her relief because that would mean giving others what they wanted.

People asked her to be clean so she would not wash. People reminded her to flush the toilet, so after that she was certain to never flush it again. Whatever teachers tried to teach her she would refuse to be taught. Innocent teachers would stay back after school to work with her, only to find the equivalent of 'pink colour'. Or else she would just refuse to speak altogether.

She loved cricket and was really good at it. But once she saw how happy we were and how much we all enjoyed playing with her, she refused to play. If we found her looking at a book and praised her for it, she would immediately put the book away and never look at it again. We even caught her playing with one of Babika's dolls and encouraged that because she looked happy and anything that was going to make her happy was good as far as we were concerned. But of course that was the end for the doll.

We got to a point where we realised the worst thing to do was show enthusiasm for anything. But then how do you effectively raise and love a child if you have to suppress your enthusiasm. It was a no win situation. And that was what, as a passive aggressive, it seemed Rangani wanted.

My parents, who had decided she was an acceptable grandchild, invited her up to stay with them for two weeks over the school holidays. It was an insult to the twins who were not invited, and it made me angry. Still they seemed keen and I was willing to give anything a try. But they sent her back after three days, confused and amazed that whatever they tried to do with her somehow just didn't seem to work out. I didn't know whether Rangani's 'defeat' of my parents made me angry or pleased. But whatever I felt didn't matter. What mattered was that, with Rangani, there seemed no way in.

I even attended a seminar run by a child psychologist who was a world expert on this sort of problem. He was very positive and upbeat, believing there was a solution for everyone. His advice to his audience boiled down to this:

'Every child has something they want, something they like. You have to find what that is, and when you do, that is your way in.'

I asked: 'What if there is nothing the child likes, nothing she wants, other than to frustrate you?'

He tried to dismiss my question by saying: 'That is very unlikely.'

'But it is possible,' I persisted.

'Well it is possible,' he conceded, and then because he saw how concerned I was, he diverted from his text to cross examine me about Rangani, suggesting lots of ideas and approaches. But we had tried them all. In the end I remember being quite saddened, not to say frightened, when he said:

'Look, I'll be honest with you. There are some kids who just don't want anything other than to make life difficult for everyone around them. They are rare, but they exist.'

It was around this time too that things took another sinister turn. The girls' English was coming on well, but it was still far from sophisticated enough to ask them any complex questions. So with all the health problems and the schooling problems at least now reasonably under control, we finally found the time to get in a Tamil translator so we could ask the girls all the things we had wanted to find out for so long, about their feelings and their needs.

We were recommended a lovely middle aged Tamil woman. Raisa had grown up in India and Fiji and spoke very good English. She sat down with the girls at the kitchen table and we retreated to the lounge room. We wanted to take the pressure off and just let Raisa take her time to get to know them. But after about five minutes she came into the lounge room looking confused.

'I can't talk to Rangani,' she said.

I thought she meant Rangani had refused to speak to her, and started to explain some of the problems we had had with the passive aggression.

'No, no,' she said, 'She speaks to me in English. But I *can't* speak to her in Tamil because she doesn't speak Tamil.'

'What do you mean?' I asked redundantly. I was finding this hard to absorb.

'She speaks Singhalese,' Raisa said. 'She is Singhalese.'

'But she is the twins' older sister,' Agatha said. "They are a Tamil family. She must speak Tamil.'

'I'm sorry,' said Raisa, somewhat embarrassed, as though we were accusing her of incompetence. 'But she can't be their sister. She doesn't speak Tamil.'

The thoughts came rushing in, of our surprise on the first day with how different Rangani looked from the other three. Then there was the fact that before they had English they never spoke, and when they had some English that's what they spoke. Yet still it was hard to take in.

But they call her Rangani, akka,' I said. 'Doesn't 'akka' mean older sister?'

'Yes', said Raisa. 'What do they call you?'

'Mummy and Daddy.'

'And why is that?'

'Because they were told to.'

'Well I think they have been told to call her 'akka'.'

So here was Mother Superior's final great 'untruth'. But why had she done it? Why had she gone to such lengths to pass off this girl as Babika and Babeta's older sister?

That night I lay awake trying to make some sense of it. Rangani's passive aggression was sad and frustrating, and would have been so for whoever had charge of her in Sri Lanka. But was that enough of a reason to go through such an elaborate charade, to rid some poor carers of the burden of an uncooperative girl?

Whoever those carers had been, whether the Mother Teresa nuns in the other orphanage (if the other orphanage existed), or someone else, they had been doing a good job with her. She was well fed and going to school. It didn't make sense. There had to be more to it.

Nonetheless we now had charge of Rangani, and for better or worse, we had to try and make it work. In a sense the fact that she was not the sister of the twins had been overtaken by events. De facto she was their sister now. It seemed to me there was no value in getting angry with the Mother Superior. What she had done was inexplicable, but it was done. And now Rangani was in Australia and needing a home.

It was already round three in the morning before I started to come to terms with the realities (or as much of them as I knew or could work out). I was finally starting to fall asleep. But my 'exciting' day was not yet over. Suddenly I heard a scream from the girls' room. I rushed in and found

Babika sitting up in bed, the tears rolling down her cheeks.

Nightmares. 'Every night,' she sniffled. 'Ugly. Ugly. Every night.'

'Why didn't you tell me?' I asked. But she just looked at me. The twins had just never known people they could confide in. It was something they still couldn't conceive of.

How I felt for her. My own nights had been much the same for most of my life. But I had no idea Babika was a victim too. I rocked her in my arms for some time. Then I found myself starting to say something. I didn't know where it came from let alone where it was going.

'Do you want to stop having these nightmares?' I asked.

'Yes I do,' she sniffled.

'Oh well that's easy. We'll just use the three fingers of love. You know all about the three fingers of love, don't you?'

'No.' She had stopped sniffling and her eyes were wide.

'Oh goodness,' I repeated, 'everyone knows about the three fingers of love. All you have to do is lay down and I'll put them on your forehead and then you'll never have bad dreams again.'

She snuggled down under the blanket. I took a moment to tuck her in. Then in an elaborate fashion I raised my three middle fingers high in the air and brought them slowly down till the finger tips brushed ever so lightly on her forehead.

'There,' I said. 'No more nightmares ever again.'

She smiled a little, rolled over to face the wall and went straight to sleep. And she never did have a nightmare again.

Mind you I had to give her the three fingers of love every night just to make sure. I also had to give them to Babeta. She didn't have nightmares but said she might. So she got them too. She wasn't going to miss out on something as good as the three fingers of love.

This became part of our nightly ritual for many years to come. I would come in to their room, tuck them in, maybe read a story or tell a story and kiss them goodnight. But the very last thing had to be the three fingers of love. If ever I would forget I couldn't get through the door without them both yelling out:

"Dad! Dad! You forgot the three fingers of love.'

And so we settled in to our life in our crowded little house. Rangani's attitude to life made things difficult for all of us, but there was not much we could do other than hope that if we just stayed calm, eventually whatever was driving her anger would dissipate enough for her to start feeling part of the family. Perhaps then she would let us find a way in.

My life was as busy as it had ever been. I still had a full time job at Law Book Company, and on top of that had all the usual parental things like homework and sports and parent meetings at three schools (as Rangani was now in a high school for speakers of English as a second language), not to mention regular calls to Balmain primary school to sort out Babika's latest scam.

My favourite, which epitomises Western innocence, involved the perennial lunch struggle. Each morning I would cut their lunch so they would have something healthy to eat. Mostly they would throw it away and then try to beg some chocolate from an older child. But this time Babika went to the headmaster's secretary and told her that her terrible father hadn't given her any lunch. Remarkably, without checking, the secretary just believed her and took her down to the canteen at lunch time to buy her the lunch of her choosing, which in this case was a pie and chips.

This went on for three weeks, Babika throwing away her lunch first thing when she got to school and then going straight to the secretary to once again complain about her cruel father. The secretary used her own money every day to buy Babika a lunch more suiting her desires. Then one day I was at the school for some other reason, and the secretary cornered me angrily:

'How can you do that?' she demanded.

'Do what?' I asked calmly, already experienced enough to guess Babika was behind this.

'Not give your child lunch.'

I looked at her, smiled and said:

'Do you think we would go all the way to Sri Lanka in the middle of a civil war and risk our lives to bring back malnourished orphan children only to starve them.'

She looked shamefaced. The moment I started to speak she knew what had happened.

'I've been conned, haven't I?'

I nodded. She went straight to Babika who confessed all. Then we had yet another round table conference in the headmaster's office.

I didn't write a word of *Rough Justice* for the first six months the girls were with us, not surprisingly. But then over the next six, slowly, miraculously I started to find time in amongst everything else, to do just a little. Allen & Unwin gave me an extension on the deadline. And I think they knew they might have to give me a few more. I was a workaholic again but at least I was a workaholic with a purpose. The book mattered to me. And though Rangani worried me terribly, the girls mattered to me too.

I decided that our crowded house was too crowded. I started to conceive the idea of moving to the country where the children would have more space and accommodation would be cheaper. I approached Tony Lees with a deal. I had two jobs at Law Book Company, one as Managing Editor for Practitioner Books and one as Editor of the Federal Court Reports. I suggested I leave the company and do my Managing Editor job as a consultant. That was a slightly radical idea in that industry.

Less radical was the suggestion I would also be an external Editor for the Federal Court Reports. This would be quite normal. All the other law report editors in the country were barristers in chambers or sometimes solicitors. But none worked inside publishing companies. I even asked for more money.

Fortunately Tony Lees agreed and Agatha and I began making plans to move to Kiama on the south coast of New South Wales. It was a beautiful seaside town of about 15,000 people in those days, and it offered clean air and space and a pace of life I hoped would suit the girls. At the same time it was only two hour's drive from Sydney so I could be available to Law Book Company in person whenever they needed me.

By this time the girls had been with us for nearly 15 months. The twins had started to speak very good English and Rangani's was more than passable. In fact her teachers all thought it was better than she was willing to let on. We gauged the twins had settled into life in Australia well enough that another move wouldn't be traumatic for them. They were healthy and at least as happy as could be expected at this stage in their Australian adventure. Rangani was still Rangani, but we hoped that too might change if we opened up some space for her. All in all it seemed like a perfect time for a move to the country.

So we all went down to Kiama one weekend and found a big four bedroom house to rent on the magnificent cliffs overlooking the pounding sea at Kiama Heights. The idea was we would settle things in Sydney and move down in a month. Then our house would be crowded no more. Each child would have a bedroom, and we would have an actual yard, in fact a huge yard. Balmain would be rented out and all would be well. Or so I thought.

19. MOTHER SUPERIOR'S FINEST HOUR

I came home early from work one day. Agatha had gone to the shops and left the twins with Rangani. They didn't hear me come in. As I got towards the back of the house I heard Babeta start to scream. I came into the dining room just as Rangani picked her up and threw her backwards across the room and into the french doors.

The force with which she crashed into the doors was horrifying. By some miracle the glass didn't shatter. But Babeta was shaken and was sobbing. I turned to Rangani.

'Why did you do that?' I demanded.

But Rangani just shrugged. She gave a sort of semi smile that sent a chill through me.

I picked Babeta up and carried her into the lounge room.

'Listen,' I said, putting her on the lounge and sitting next to her with my arm around her shoulder, 'I don't know what this is about, but I'm sure Rangani will never do anything like that again.'

'She does it all the time,' Babeta said, and then she looked about in fear. Seeing Rangani was in ear shot, she burst out sobbing.

'What do you mean?' I asked. But she wouldn't speak. 'Do you mean she has thrown you at the door before?' Still no answer. 'Tell me!' I raised my voice.

'Stuff like that,' she whispered.

I looked over at Rangani. Her face still wore that same half smile. I signalled for her to sit in the chair opposite and called Babika in as well. She sat on the other side of me. I looked at the twins and at Rangani, and decided the only way I was going to get any information was if Rangani wasn't there. So I told her to go across to the park till I called.

When I had the twins alone, I took some more time to calm Babeta, then said to Babika:

'Has Rangani been violent with you girls before?'

Babika refused to answer. I wasn't sure what to do. In the end I said:

'I promise you, I will protect you. But you must tell me what is going on.'

It was Babeta who finally spoke:

'She has a stick. She keeps it under the bed.' Her voice was wavering and she was fighting back the tears.

'She hits us with it,' Babika said. 'On the bottom. Sometimes other places.'

'When did she do this?'

'Every day,' Babeta said between sobs.

I was horrified. Could this be true? Could they be making it up? It certainly didn't feel like they were lying. But I had to find out more.

'Where is this stick?' I asked.

They took me in to their bedroom and Babika reached under Rangani's bed. She pulled out a thickish tree branch about two feet long. As I was turning it over in my hand, trying to come to grips with what I was hearing, Babika said:

'She makes us eat cockroaches too.'

'What?'

'Yes,' Babeta confirmed. She was starting to get braver now she could see I was determined to get to the bottom of this. 'She catches them and then she makes us eat them.'

I looked at these two terrified little creatures and really didn't know what to think, how to assimilate all this. If this were true we were not talking about passive aggression any more. This was very active aggression.

'How long has she been doing this?' I asked.

'Forever,' said Babeta.

'In Sri Lanka too?'

They looked at one another.

'I don't know,' Babeta said at last.

'We don't remember Rangani in Sri Lanka,' Babika said, almost ashamed.

'But for a long time here?' I asked.

'Forever here,' Babeta repeated.

'Why on earth didn't you tell me?'

They looked at one another again, and they both shrugged.

Afterwards when I thought about it, I could see why. Their lives had been a series of tortures, from the loss of their mother to their abandonment by their father to being told these strange people were now their parents and this strange girl was now their sister, to God knows what other forgotten nightmares. The fact that the new sister chose to beat them and make them eat cockroaches was just the next horrible thing in a life of horrible things.

Why *would* they think to report it, especially when the new sister forbade them to? How did they know in fact the new parents would even be against it? Why would the new parents protect them against the new sister? Better to just shut up and endure it. New parents, new sister, new horrors. It was all one to them.

It made me realise how hard it is to get inside the minds of people, especially little children, who have come from such a different background and who have experienced such different and terrible things. Be that as it may, I now had a big problem on my hands, and the first thing I had to do was make sure I had all the pieces in place, knew exactly what I was dealing with.

I waited till Agatha got home and briefed her on what I had discovered. Then we sent the twins to their room while we sat Rangani down in the lounge room. I was pretty sure everything the twins told me had been true, but how was I going to get Rangani to admit to it. In the end however, I felt this was not the place to try clever cross-examination. All I could do was put the allegations to her and see what she said. I was to get quite a shock.

'Rangani,' I said, 'the twins tell me you have been hitting them with a stick.'

'Oh yes,' she said, quite calmly.

That rocked me. This was about the last thing I expected her to say. Denial certainly, prevarication at least. But this? It was impossible to know where to go with it. But I kept going nonetheless:

'They say you do it every day.'

'Yes every day.'

'And you make them eat cockroaches?'

'Sometimes, when I can catch.' She smiled her half smile, as though she were thinking back to some lovely time in her life.

Agatha and I looked at one another in amazement. I felt that psychologically I was way out of my league. I had no idea what to do. In the end I just said.

'We know you are not their sister. But you are part of our family now, and we want you to stay with us. But you must promise never to hit the girls again or do anything else nasty like make them eat cockroaches.'

She looked straight at me and said:

'But I like hit them. I like make them eat cockroaches.'

It was at that moment (though we would not be able to verbalise it for some hours) we knew we were dealing with something much worse than passive aggression. We were dealing with something as close to psychopathological amorality as you can get. Rangani was doing terrible things, but she either didn't know they were terrible, or she totally didn't care. She liked to do them, therefore they would continue to be done. The well being of the twins was an irrelevancy.

We called in DOCS who seemed totally unsympathetic to the plight of the twins. They just took the opportunity to point out how foolish we had been to think we could adopt a twelve year old. They went to some lengths to remind us they had told us so. We tried to explain we couldn't keep Rangani with us, but they refused to see why.

So for a time we had the hellish experience of trying to watch Rangani 24 hours a day so she didn't inflict any more of her 'fun' on the twins. Then one day about a week later we went to pick up the twins from after school care, and the teacher told us their sister had already come to get them. Rangani had never picked them up before, but the teacher let her take them anyway.

We went into a panic and rushed home but they were not there. We drove all round Balmain and eventually, by some very good luck, found them in a park by the water over a mile from where we lived. Babika was screaming as Rangani was pushing Babeta towards the edge of a cliff with perhaps a 20 metre drop to the sea. I sprinted across the park like a teenager and miraculously got there in time to stop Babeta going over.

Then DOCS had to intervene and take Rangani into care. But they were not happy and acted as though her behaviour were all our fault. We had to go through some really gruelling interviews, which weren't interviews in any real sense, just accusation fests.

Nonetheless we had no choice but to endure it. We may have adopted the twins under Sri Lankan law, but the law of New South Wales didn't recognise that. If they were to be our children under New South Wales law they would have to be adopted all over again here. If we didn't 'cop' everything DOCS hurled at us, having 'failed' with Rangani, they might allege we were inappropriate parents and take the twins from us.

So we moved down to Kiama, just the four of us, and Rangani went into foster care. We were required to bring the twins up to Sydney every week so their 'sister' could have access to them. Despite all the evidence to the contrary, including the fact that they spoke different languages, DOCS refused to accept they were not sisters.

The couple with whom Rangani had been placed were, in effect, told we had just abandoned Rangani because she was too much trouble. The fact that she had abused the twins for fifteen months and was starting to put their lives at risk was not to be part of the 'official story'. DOCS refused to believe it, as of course then did the foster parents, even though Rangani herself readily admitted it.

At each access visit, after an excruciating period of coffee and cakes with the disapproving foster parents, the girls would be sent off to 'play' together. During these sessions Rangani would terrorise them with threats of what she was going to do with them when she got the chance. The girls would come away from the visits very scared. Because of their history together they saw Rangani as all powerful and therefore totally capable of carrying out her threats. One of the worst was when she told them:

'One day you'll be walking down the main street of Kiama and you'll look around and there I'll be, in a white car, and I'll get you.'

For weeks after that, whenever we were in town in Kiama, they would scream in fear at every white car that caught their eye. For all the condescension and the scorn they heaped on us, the foster parents of course couldn't control Rangani, and after a couple of months they returned her to DOCS. She then went through several other families in quick succession, from all of which we had to endure disapproval at the 'access' visits DOCS arranged, until they too realised what they were dealing with and gave her back.

Eventually she went into a Salvation Army Home where the head of the home told me Rangani was the most difficult child she had ever had to deal with, in twenty years working with children. We had access visits there too but at least with this woman we were not denigrated because she knew what she was dealing with, and wasn't foolish enough to take what DOCS told her at face value.

They had to move her to several different homes in their group until eventually, when she was fifteen, she disappeared. They saw her from time to time when she would turn up asking for money or a meal, but basically she was now living on the streets in Kings Cross.

We then struggled for over a year to secure the adoption of the twins. During this process DOCS made the Sri Lankan Department of Probation and Childcare Services look efficient and compassionate. They delayed and delayed, despite our having an array of reports from private social workers and psychologists to say we were doing a good job and strongly recommending us for adoption.

Eventually they couldn't hold out any longer and agreed to support the application for adoption. So now we were the legal parents of the twins both under the law of Sri Lanka and under the law of New South Wales. Rangani had had no further access to the twins, for the obvious reason that no-one knew where she was from one day to the next.

It's near impossible to explain my emotional state at the time. The logical part of me knew I had been seriously misled by Mother Superior. But a part of me still felt responsible that Rangani was on the streets. Could I somehow have done something to prevent it? However irrational, I still felt guilty. At the same time I was relieved that Babika and Babeta were now safe, and knew it was this latter I had to focus on. That and the need to find my own healing.

20. KIAMA BY THE SEA

When I went to Kiama I was still a little crazy. Let's be honest, I was still a lot crazy. Sri Lanka, and all the struggles that followed, had brought me out of myself and 'cured' my catatonia. Now I could speak again. Well sometimes, if the demands were not too great. But the underlying causes were still there and all the struggles surrounding the girls had only delayed what I needed to do. The difference was now I knew I needed to do *something*. I just didn't know what.

In other words I had emerged from my insane cocoon to a state of semi-greyness where I knew I was sad, I knew I was sadly lacking in self esteem, I knew my life in general was quite dysfunctional. And I wanted to fix all that. I didn't know where to start but somehow sensed that more space to breathe would mean more space to think would mean more space to heal. So though the move to Kiama was designed to give the girls room to grow, it was also designed to affect my 'cure'.

Of course no amount of moving around, per se, is going to fix anything. I ought to have learnt that by now. So the move to Kiama was never going to be the answer in and of itself. A lot more 'doing' would be required. Kiama wasn't going to heal the girls in and of itself either. They carried a long sad history with them too, ridiculously long in fact, given they were still only eight years old. And most of it was unknown to us.

I remember one night when we hadn't been in Kiama long and we hired the video 'Radio Flyer' to watch. Despite its up-beat cover it turned out to be about a step-father who physically abuses the younger of his two step-children. He does a Faustian deal with the older one where he promises to leave him alone if the boy doesn't tell the mother what is going on with the younger son. So the elder saves himself at the expense of his brother. It is understandable. He is only young himself and has no real choice.

But as the plot started to unravel, Babika became more and more agitated until half way through the film she was hysterical. Clearly it had touched off something in her own life. Perhaps Rangani had done a similar deal with her. Or maybe it went further back than that. We didn't know and nor did they on any conscious level.

So we were working without information and therefore dealing with a range of psychological problems where we could only guess at the origins. We were also still dealing with a vicious debilitating sugar addiction, not to mention the twins' sad, chronic belief that their survival depended on looking as dumb as possible.

I remember one afternoon after we had been in Kiama about a year, and Babeta had a friend over to play. The two girls were in the lounge room and didn't know I was in the kitchen where I could hear what they were saying. The friend asked Babeta how to spell 'hippopotamus', and Babeta spelled it for her, without a second's hesitation. I remember thinking how intelligent she must be to spell a word her Australian born friend couldn't spell, let alone her Australian born father. And yet had I later asked her to spell 'cat' I may very well have got 'kat'.

Nonetheless they were at the beginning of their track to healing. The open spaces, the clean air and the slow simple lifestyle were helping, not to mention being free of Rangani's tortures. Their physical health was good, they had friends, and a number of adults, especially from the Catholic Church, who cared about them and kept an eye out for them.

As for me, as I said, I was still on the wrong side of the border with crazy, but knowing I was, and knowing I had to do something about it, was a big start. Memories had started coming back, not the fundamental ones of my early abuse, but later memories of tortures like my mother's moustache bleaching, and her need to keep me chained to my desk from four in the morning.

A number of things came together early in my time in Kiama, which developed and pushed me towards at least the beginnings of my healing. When I look back over those couple of years two things strike me: first I doubt if any of it would have happened had I stayed in Sydney, and secondly it did seem to involve an inordinate number of miracles and special angels

Anyway my first angel was a woman whose name I don't even remember. I had started taking the girls to mass and I saw in the Parish Bulletin an ad for a self-esteem workshop run by a Catholic organisation in Wollongong. One thing I knew was that I had no self-esteem. So this seemed like a good place to start.

I went along to the first session fearful of even being able to speak. And in fact many of the group couldn't speak at all. They sat there most of the time with their heads bowed. But when the convenor asked me questions, I found I had answers. I discovered that on most things I had thoughts and beliefs and ideas, and what's more I could express them. Towards the end of the first session the convenor said to me:

'Victor I don't think you'll need to come back next time. You may not think you have any self-esteem. But you're wrong.'

It was said with the greatest kindness.

'I was sure I didn't have it or at least that I'd lost it,' I heard myself say, and felt quite foolish.

But she just smiled and said:

'Maybe you had lost it, but somewhere along the way, when you weren't looking, it has started to find you again.'

When someone tells you something good, something important about yourself, and they have absolutely no reason to lie, it can be a powerful boost. It was as though this woman had given me permission to start being my own person.

Then I met someone else who told me, in effect, that my 'own person' could be a happy one. A visiting priest from Sydney gave a series of talks on psychology. They were reasonably academic as the priest was not very interpersonal in his approach. I went along because I was interested, not because I expected any help on my journey.

Nonetheless, somewhere in one of the talks, he said something about 'developing towards happiness'. I was confused because I had come to believe that if you move towards sadness in your life, as I had done, it was a one way street. It was a crazy idea, much like my analogous idea that people over 30 didn't laugh. But here was this man talking about changing, and changing for the better. I found myself asking:

'Do you really believe people can change?'

He looked at me for a moment, obviously weighing how to respond. In the end he said:

'We're in the business of redemption. We have to believe in it. Otherwise we probably should go out of business.'

It was a clumsy way to answer me. He could have just said: 'Of course. There's no doubt'. But he was a self conscious man who had a tendency to speak awkwardly. Nonetheless it didn't matter. His answer hit me like a bomb. What I heard was that I was allowed to change.

Now most healthy people don't need to be told they are entitled to have self esteem and to seek and find happiness. For healthy people that is a given. But I was not healthy. For me none of this was obvious. So these pieces of information came to me like gifts of the purest gold. And maybe I was just about ready to accept them and start to store them away in the deep vault of my life.

Now here I was, early in my time in Kiama, and already I had been given back my right to reclaim happiness. That was a mighty fine start. But finer still was just around the corner. I was about to meet one of my truly great angels, and be given permission to reclaim my voice.

It began one Sunday when I had taken the girls to a special mass arranged to support AIDS victims. There had been a lot of very nice music and I had sung along with the rest of the congregation. After the mass was over, a young woman came up and introduced herself to me. She was Angela Quinn and she ran the music for the Parish.

'You have a great voice,' she said. 'Why don't you join our choir?'

Like the earlier pronouncements on self esteem and happiness, it had been said in a very straight forward low key way. But for me it was close to incomprehensible.

'I think you must have been listening to someone else,' I said.

'No,' she laughed, 'I was right next to you. Besides I'm a trained singer. I can tell who is singing on key and who isn't.'

Some things in life are unexpected and some things are *very* unexpected. This was one of the latter. The last time anyone had told me I had a good voice was when my Grade 1 teacher put me in the Infants School choir. But my singing career didn't last long then because my parents thought that sort of activity would interfere with my studies. And I guess they were right. At six or seven years old you can't afford to waste time on frivolous pursuits. But here in the Church of Sts Peter and Paul in the little town of Kiama on the south coast of New South Wales, at the ripe old age of 41, I was being told I could sing again. That's just a 35 year gap between gigs.

On the one hand the thought of singing in public, when not so long ago I had barely been able to speak, seemed unthinkable. But somehow I wasn't frightened. There was something very beautiful and comforting about Angela Quinn's spirit. And something that gave you confidence too. Though I had only just met her, I had a sense that if Angela Quinn thought I could sing, then I really could.

So I joined the choir, but only after making Angela promise she would put me up the back and never make me sing any part unless I had lots of people doing it with me. She promised, but had no intention of keeping her word. Even then she had plans for me which, whether she knew it or not, were going to change my life.

For a small town like Kiama the choir was amazing. Angela was a classically trained opera singer, and brought ideas, teaching techniques and standards to the singing that weren't going to be found in your average country choir. Her sister Marianne was also classically trained, and to hear the two of them sing together was spine chillingly beautiful. On top of that, if she needed a male voice she could call on one of the best there was, the resident priest at the nearby Jamberoo Abbey, Father Paul Gurr.

Paul was the 'rock star' of the Catholic world. Australian Catholics from Kalgoorlie to Kempsey, not to mention Catholics all over the World, know his crystal tenor voice and his million selling songs like 'Come As You Are'. When he sang with Angela and Marianne, the Catholic congregation or the public of Kiama were treated to world class singing. When I look back I wonder at the chances of so many amazing singers coming together in one small town. For me of course, to be even a tiny part of it, to hear my own voice going out into the ether in combination with those people, was a deep joy.

So here I was, a non Catholic, not only going to mass on a regular basis with my Catholic wife and Catholic children, but also singing in the Catholic choir. At the mass when everyone went up to take communion, I would just sit back and watch. I was quite comfortable with that. In fact I enjoyed watching the people file forward, so many different types, with so many different lives, but all of whom had one thing in common. It had a peace about it.

I came from a self isolating dysfunctional family, and so this was the first time I had really seen and been made to think about the bonds of family, and the bonds of community. As I watched Angela and Gary go forward to take the host with their little daughter Alicia between them, I was made to see that real families, who really loved one another, did exist. I imagine all of that was to play into a decision I was just about to make, though I had no conscious awareness of it at the time.

The Parish co-ordinator was a nun from the Sisters of St Joseph by the name of Sister Helen. One day after mass I was standing around with a group of people including Sister Helen. She was telling someone about the RCIA course she was about to start. RCIA stands for the 'Right of Catholic Initiation of Adults'. It is a course run by most parishes either on a regular basis or from time to time as required, which is designed to prepare non Catholic adults for reception into the Church. As she finished talking about it I heard myself say:

'I'll do that.'

Even as I said it, I wondered where my words came from, and why. Days after I still couldn't say what had possessed me to enrol. I had had some good experiences with Catholics. Mike and Margaret had always treated me well. Father Pacificus had shown true caring when I had come out of my operation. But I had always seen that as an encounter with a good man who happened to be a Catholic, not something central to Catholicism itself. And besides, it was a long time ago.

The Kiama Parish priest, Pat Kenna, was an intelligent and creative man, and gave some fine sermons. And then of course there was Angela and the choir. But none of it seemed to add up to anything dramatic enough to make me consider converting to a religion that could produce The Inquisition and the Mother Superior style of doing business.

I had always thought conversion had to be about flashy stuff like Paul on the road to Damascus. Yet my response was about as far from that as you could get. A casual chat with a nun in a group in the sunshine and I was volunteering to become a Catholic. It didn't make a lot of sense to me on a logical level. But it just felt right. I think it was a testament to my growing mental health that I could so trust my instincts.

Every Tuesday night after that I met with Sister Helen and three or four other candidates to discuss matters Catholic and biblical and generally prepare for the big Easter celebration where at the Vigil Mass on the Saturday night before Easter Sunday we would be received into the Church. Most nights Father Kenna would make an appearance to talk about some matter of doctrine Sister Helen had set for him. The idea was that we were free to say what we liked and challenge what we liked. Both Pat and Helen were enlightened modern Catholics. They knew we were adults and were not about to just feed us bible stories as though we were children in a scripture class.

Nonetheless I probably exercised my rights of critique more vigorously than most, in fact more vigorously than any previous RCIA candidate they had ever had. The other candidates were all laid back people who were married to Catholics and had agreed to become Catholics themselves. They weren't much interested in the finer details of apologetics or theological debate. They just wanted to find out what they had to do on Easter Saturday, so they could go ahead and do it.

I, on the other hand, wanted to challenge everything. After all, this was a big step I was taking, plummeting into religion. And this was a time when I was learning to speak all over again. Plus I had new found self esteem which I wanted to flex, didn't I? So I was not about to accept anything they told me without giving it a thorough testing.

Pat and Helen often referred to me as their 'star pupil'. I was however conscious of just the slightest tinge of irony in their voices. And I can't really blame them. In all honesty I think I spent a lot of my time being a big noisy child. I was indeed being born again. But not so much in the religious sense. I was more like the two year old who suddenly realises he has a voice and a perspective on the world, and who wants to make sure everyone knows about it.

Nonetheless I think Pat Kenna really enjoyed our tussles. He was a highly educated man who lived in a little fishing village. He didn't have much chance for high level theological argument. And whereas I might be a theological novice, I was remembering how to argue. The old cross-examiner was re-emerging in a new arena. In a way I think I was challenging Pat Kenna and Sister Helen to throw me out. I had lived so much of my life on other people's terms. I needed this to be a new step, a new love affair, and I needed to be loved unconditionally this time.

Pat and Helen must have sensed this because they let me rant and carry on with all sorts of blasphemous nonsense. Interestingly the only real sticking point between the Parish Priest and myself revolved around what was objectively quite a minor piece of procedure, or so it seemed to me. When children are confirmed into the Catholic faith at around the age of 12, they take a 'confirmation name', which is usually the name of a saint. So young Patrick O'Flaherty might feel a connection with St Francis of Assisi, and will choose Francis as his confirmation name. At the moment of confirmation the Bishop will make the sign of the cross on Patrick's forehead and call him by name into the flock. When he does this for young Patrick he doesn't call him Patrick, he calls him by his confirmation name, Francis.

Now Agatha had told me all about it and explained that as I was being received into the Church at Easter, I would get to choose a confirmation name too. I was very excited about that. Men don't usually get to take a new name in mid life. I thought about it long and hard and decided that as I loved the poetic St John's gospel, I would take the name John. Next time Pat Kenna turned up for an RCIA meeting, I told him enthusiastically:

'Pat, I've decided on my confirmation name. I'm going with John.'

'Oh it's OK,' he said dismissively, 'we don't have confirmation names for adults.'

All the other candidates breathed a sigh of relief. That was one less thing they had to worry about. But I was scandalised.

'That's terrible,' I declaimed, much to the surprise of everyone present. 'Aren't I going through exactly the same process, the same holy moment as any 12 year old?'

'Yes,' said the startled Pat Kenna. He was always ready for me to be argumentative. But this one took him by surprise.

'Well if I am going through the exact same process as the 12 year olds,' I said, 'I expect the same privileges as the 12 year olds.'

'It's not a pri...,' Pat began, but I cut him off.

'Yes it is! The right to take a special name is as precious to me as any adolescent. More so! I want to be linked to the saints too, you know!'

This brought a smile to everyone's lips.

'I've chosen John,' I said, a little more calmly, feeling I had exceeded the dramatic potential of the moment. 'You'll be the one receiving me into the Church, not the Bishop. And when you do, I want you to call me John.'

'Well I can't,' Pat said.

'Yes you can,' I told him, 'if you want to.'

'No I can't,' he repeated.'

'All right,' I said, 'if you can give me one reason, logical or doctrinal, why you can't, I'll re-think my position.'

He thought for a long moment and finally said:

'It's just not the way it's done.'

'Not the way it's done?! That's not good enough,' I insisted. 'Would Jesus have taken that attitude?'

This brought deep groans from the other candidates who could see me causing them yet again to miss *Walker, Texas Ranger.*

But they were safe. Pat was not prepared to discuss it further. And that's how we left it - unresolved. I insisted he call me John. He insisted he couldn't. I realised I had taken things as far as I could. It was now up to Pat to decide what was more important: 'how things were done' or the 'passionate' desire of his candidate.

I know that if the same issue arose today I wouldn't dream of making the fuss I made then. Strictly speaking I was right, but so what. It just didn't matter what I was called. The important thing was what I was about to do, the step I was about to take. But I think at the time it was just another test I was throwing up to them, saying: 'love me, and love me unconditionally on my terms'.

The RCIA course ran for about three or four months leading up to Easter 1993. During that period I experienced an ongoing miracle via the person of Paul Gurr. Apart from my contact with him through the choir, he would also come down from Jamberoo to conduct the mass in Kiama when Pat Kenna was away. It was always a special time for me because he brought the most gentle loving presence imaginable, and his sermons always started from a place of compassion, exhorting people to be kind to others but most importantly to be kind to themselves.

Perhaps because he was so demanding of himself as a priest, he knew the dark side of perfectionism, and was always stressing the value of 'being easy on yourself'. Also I think he was just wise enough to know that you can't love others properly till you learn to love yourself.

So his masses were beautiful and his sermons uplifting. But the miracle was found in the text or story he chose for his sermons. Let's say on the day he was due to preach I was particularly worried about whether I was doing a good job as a parent. Amazingly his sermon wouldn't just be about the need to be kind to yourself, but specifically about not beating up on yourself for your parenting misdemeanours.

It felt to me like no matter what my concerns on the day, amazingly Paul would be preaching on that very subject, talking directly to me, as it were. Now that would have been miracle enough. But it went further. One day I was talking to some people after the mass and I happened to mention how once again Paul's homily had been exactly about my personal concerns.

'I'm worried about my kids, so he talks about kids,' I say.

'No he didn't,' the man next to me says, 'he spoke about the problems of finding work, which is what worries me right now.'

'You're both crazy,' says a third, 'his homily was all about the agonies of divorce.'

'Are you getting divorced?' I ask him, and of course he tells me he is.

In other words the miracle of the Paul Gurr sermon was that somehow it managed to address everyone's concerns, no matter what they were, all at the same time. The sad thing was that Paul had no idea of the power and the love he brought to the masses he conducted. When I got to know him better, he would talk about how insecure he was with his homilies. He felt he just made no sense and bored everyone to tears.

Perhaps the only way someone can perform such miracles is if he has no idea of his own power. That way he will never be tempted to take pride in his own performance. In other words his was a 'gift' in the true sense of the word. The gift was not for him, but for him to give.

My gratitude and respect for Paul also extended to far less esoteric matters. I loved the fact that he took such a warm personal interest in Babika and Babeta. And, my goodness, did he put up with a lot from them. In the early days in Kiama they were still pretty wild and during the mass when he was saying some prayer or another and would have his arms stretched out to the horizontal, they would run up to him in unison, one on either side, leap up and catch hold of his hanging sleeves, where they would swing. And despite the sacredness of the moment, he would let them, till we came and took them down. It was not a miracle in the traditional sense, but it was certainly a miracle of tolerance.

And so Easter was approaching and, unbeknown to me, I was to be offered two extraordinary opportunities. First of all Pat Kenna, who had a strong theatrical bent, was planning on staging the Passion of Christ as part of the Good Friday Celebration in the Church. He suggested I play the part of Jesus.

He had two reasons why he wanted to cast me: first of all his encounters with me in the RCIA classes convinced him I could hold my own in public and would have no trouble with nerves. How funny was that? But he knew nothing of my history. Secondly he thought it would be delightful to have a real Jew play the part of Jesus.

As a child I had been baptised an Anglican, and even if I hadn't, I literally couldn't be a Jew because my mother was not Jewish and Jewishness is passed through the female line. Nonetheless my father was Jewish and the members of the congregation preferred to see me that way. Whereas they had had any number of Anglican converts, they had never had a real Jew before. That was way more glamorous for them. And the idea that Jesus could be portrayed by a real Jew was very exciting.

Besides, they saw it as their last chance. The day after, at the Saturday Vigil mass, I would become a Catholic, and then their only Jewish Jesus would be converted. So they felt they had to grab me for the part whilst they could.

The thought of standing up in front of 300 people on Good Friday and trying to effectively render the best role in the world, had me a little tense, to say the least. It wasn't a full production where I would have to learn lines. We were to carry script. Still I was mighty frightened. But when someone offers you the chance to play Jesus, you can't very well say no.

If this first 'gig' had me worried, my next theatrical offer took worry off the scale. On the Saturday night the ceremony in Kiama is always full of music. The high point is the singing of the responsorial psalms. The way this works is that someone reads a piece from the bible and then someone else responds to this with the solo singing of a psalm.

Angela explained to me that on the Saturday night there would be four readings and hence four responsorial psalms. She and Marianne and another man would sing the first three. And her idea was I would sing the fourth. Well, I just freaked. The 300 people from Friday would be back on Saturday night plus a couple of hundred more. That's around 500 people to watch me croak like a frog.

'You'll be fine,' she said, her eyes twinkling.

'I'm not a singer,' I insisted. 'I've been up the back of the choir for a few months. That's all. The last time I sang was a rendition of *I Think That I Shall Never See a Poem as Lovely as a Tree* in Grade 1.'

'I wouldn't let you do it unless I was sure you could.'

'Well I'm sure I can't.'

'Nonsense,' she said, and handed me the psalm I was to learn. 'Besides we'll have a rehearsal.'

'*A* rehearsal! I'd need a hundred rehearsals.'

'Stop panicking,' she laughed, 'there's only one or two notes at the top of your range. The rest is a piece of cake.'

Of course I didn't even know what the top of my range was, but I could read music enough to see there were some notes I would have thought were best left for tenors. And I was definitely a baritone, if not a bass.

This could not be happening to me. Sure I'd learnt to speak again, was even about to speak to 300 people 'as Jesus', but this was an altogether different thing. This was terror on a stick. I toyed with just flatly refusing, but there was something about the way Angela was putting this to me, that told me she was doing it for me, not for herself or the congregation or the quality of the performance, but just for me. After all she had any number of singers she could have chosen instead, people who were calmer, more experienced, and, in my opinion, a great deal more talented.

It just looked like she knew about my voiceless past, and that she also knew if I could do something this big, I would never have to return to that past again. It was as though she were offering me a chance to find my voice definitively and forever.

But how could she know about my past? Or was her spirit so pure and her instincts so good, she just knew she had to do this, even if she didn't quite appreciate why. Somehow she just understood I needed this 'tough love' and she was determined to give it to me.

So I accepted my second big gig in as many days, and looked down the barrel of an Easter to remember. First I had to somehow find enough acting ability to convince a Church full of people I wasn't just any ordinary Jew, but the Big Guy himself. Then on Saturday night, whilst still a Jew, I had to do a solo performance of a Christian psalm. Only then would I be allowed to progress with the other candidates to become a member of the Church. And at that third and final 'encounter' I just had to hope Pat Kenna would call me John.

Fortunately it was a mild autumn that year, and so I could do a lot of swimming in the sea leading up to my scheduled performances. It was the only way I could find to keep my jangled nerves at least partially under control. Surprisingly on Good Friday I wasn't as nervous as I feared. I was just nervous enough, as actors say, to buoy the performance without being so nervous as to sink it.

I found within moments of the opening of The Passion I had relaxed into the role and felt like I actually understood what Jesus needed to be in this, his last week on earth. I understood little of the craft of acting then, but I knew a silent attentive audience when I saw it. It was a very empowering and a very fine feeling.

Although I didn't even dream of it at the time, later in life I would actually become an actor. And this was as good a debut as any actor could ever hope for. It was also a wonderful debut as a Catholic, even though in the eyes of the Church I was still an Anglican, and in the eyes of the congregation still a Jew.

But my success in The Passion did nothing to allay my fears for Saturday night. As the mass got underway, I sat with the other readers and singers in the front row. I felt physically sick. And once the readings began my heart started to beat so hard I couldn't even hear the words that were being read. I'm sure Angela and Marianne sang beautifully, but I couldn't hear that either. I just sat there with my heart trying to bash its way out of my chest.

When the man before me finished his psalm I knew I was next. My reader went up to the pulpit and began to read. I needed to listen to what was being spoken. But my crashing, thumping heart obliterated all sound. All I could hear was some sort of vague hum. It was an impossible situation. If I couldn't even hear, how would I be able to sing?

Then I saw my reader lift her head. She was finishing. And now for the first time that night, miraculously, I heard the words that were being spoken. They were the concluding words of her reading.

'Fear not,' they said, 'for I am with you.'

The moment I heard them my heart stopped pounding. I was, quite literally, more relaxed than I had ever been in my life. Slowly but willingly and gratefully I walked to the pulpit and began to sing. My voice was clear and tuneful. It soared through the rafters of the church, tenor notes and all. Then I sat down, and though I didn't know it at the time, it didn't take me long to realise the magnitude of the gift I had been given.

Later in the mass the RCIA candidates lined up to receive Pat Kenna's blessing. As he came to each he made the sign of the cross on their forehead and received them into the Church. When he got to me, he also touched me with the sign of the cross. His fingers were warm and I felt his gentle love. He said:

'Welcome to the Catholic Church, Victor.' Then he gave me a big smile and added: 'John'.

It was the perfect solution.

I had one more significant encounter not long after that with someone who, though not a priest, had been one. It seemed I couldn't avoid them. Sid Raper was a social worker employed by the Kiama Council. He had been a Jesuit Priest, but had left the Order to marry.

Sid ran a men's group which I started to attend. Going along each week was valuable to me in several ways. First of all it made me realise I wasn't the only man who had been abused as a child, and indeed not even the only one to be abused by a woman. It's always valuable to be taken out of yourself in that way. It forces you to focus on the needs of others and at the same time gives you a feeling of community, of solidarity.

Sid taught us the very simple idea that there is a point of balance between repression and blame. Most people think they have only two choices when trying to deal with their abusers and the memories they throw up. Either they try to repress all memory, which never works, or they fall into the blame game.

'Blame doesn't help,' Sid would say, 'because as long as you are blaming, you're still saying "I am a child who needs these people to fix what they've done ". But you are not a child, you are an adult, and you can fix it yourself.'

For Sid the balance between repression and blame is 'acknowledgement'. Just acknowledge who your abusers are and what they did. But don't waste time blaming them. And don't try to pretend they didn't do it.

This, for me, was like the opening of a big wide door that let the sun come flooding in. It separated me from my abusers and diminished them. They stopped being 'my parents' with all the connotations of dependence that entails. They became just bad people, whom I could acknowledge as bad, but who no longer were entitled to exercise their power over me. It even provided me with the first glimmerings of forgiveness, because I started to see just what suffering they must have caused to themselves.

But perhaps his greatest gift to me was Sid's idea that the best way to heal yourself and separate yourself from your abusers is to write them a letter explaining what they have done and why it was wrong.

By now he knew a lot about my mother, not all of course, because I hadn't recalled it all myself.

'You need to write her a letter,' he said. 'It's essential.'

When he said that it set up a real panic inside me.

'I really don't think I could send her a letter,' I said.

'I didn't say you have to send it,' Sid explained. 'You have to write it. Whether you send it or not is up to you.'

So I wrote my mother a letter. But I put it in a drawer and didn't send it. That's what my instincts told me to do. And I'm glad I trusted them, because of course there was more I needed to remember and therefore more I needed to put in the letter, the core of my abuse in fact. Later when I retrieved that core I would write again, and then I would send the letter. But that was a little way off.

After the powerhouse year of 1993 with all its angels and miracles, life in Kiama in 1994 was peaceful and settled. My book *Rough Justice* came out and was well received. It even sold some copies. In the middle of 1994 Angela Quinn was commissioned to produce a big concert for the Illawarra Musical Society to celebrate the Year of the Family. I got a role and experienced the thrill of my first time on a real stage.

The girls were starting to grow up, and to find a place for themselves in the world. They had joined a hockey team and were absolute naturals. With their hockey and their running they would go on to represent at State level.

From my own point of view, though my marriage to Agatha was still far from ideal, the rest of my life started to feel like a real life. I had regained so much confidence, found my voice, found a spiritual dimension I never dreamed I could possess, and was stumbling into joyous experience all over the place. In a real sense I was healing. But there was more I needed to remember, more I needed to do. And my next 'lesson' was about to be as tough as they get.

It started one morning when we were woken early by a knock on the door. Babeta answered and ran upstairs to tell us a strange man wanted to see me. When I went down I discovered it was a process server. He handed me court documents and said:

'Sorry about that, mate.'

I thought that was a very civilised approach for a process server to take.

I took the documents upstairs and sat on the edge of the bed reading them. I was sort of conscious of Agatha continuing to ask me what they were about, but I was too stunned to bring her questions into my conscious mind. I just kept staring at them trying to make some sense of what I was reading.

It was an application by DOCS on behalf of Rangani. They were seeking an order for Rangani to have regular access to the twins. The stinger was that the access was to be for two full days at a time, and it was to be unsupervised. In other words an extremely dangerous 15 year old, who lived on the streets in Kings Cross, was to have the twins all to herself for 48 hours without any supervision from their parents or from anyone else.

21. A TERRIBLE BEAUTY

On the surface this seemed like a legal action with nowhere to go. Yet the people running DOCS were not idiots, nor presumably were their legal advisors. They wouldn't make this apparently insane claim unless they had reason to believe they could succeed. And if they did succeed, by whatever means, then the lives of Babika and Babeta would be in serious danger. I felt sick.

I felt a lot sicker as the litigation burgeoned, over the next twelve months, into a massive battle, running simultaneously in three court systems. DOCS of course had limitless funds, so they could afford any legal representation they felt they needed. I, on the other hand, could only afford me. I was driving up from Kiama every other day, running from one court to the next. In the times in between I was also my own solicitor, preparing an endless array of documents.

Every time I appeared in court I was confronted not only by the DOCS barrister, and instructing solicitors, but by no less than three, sometimes four DOCS officers. These latter were always young, fit and male, wearing always black suits. Their job was to spend the whole day in court glowering at me with fixed and threatening stares. It must have been very hard work for them. From my perspective it would have been funny if it weren't so sinister. It was also interesting that DOCS, who regularly complained of being understaffed and underfunded, could afford four of their youngest and finest to deploy in this way.

About six months into this conflagration I was on the point of exhaustion. The terrifying thought that Rangani could get her hands on the girls drove me on, but it also ensured my sleep patterns were a lot less than satisfactory. I knew I couldn't give up, but I also wondered how I would be able to continue, especially as, incredible as it may seem, DOCS looked like they might actually be able to win, at least in one of the conflicting court systems.

I was being helped outside court by the amazing Dr Michael Gliksman. Apart from running a very successful practice, Michael was himself a foster parent, was Patron of the Foster Care Association and had had a lot of experience with DOCS. He spent all his spare time helping people like me. His counsel kept me sane. He also worked hard on the media end of the struggle, including when one courageous and supportive journalist received anonymous death threats against her four year old son. Through Michael I met a number of other people who were also struggling with DOCS. One of these, Mary, was to be the trigger for taking me into the darkest moment of my life, and also out again into the bright of the light.

As a child Mary had been subjected to satanic ritual sexual abuse, on a weekly basis, by groups of devil worshippers in their 'temple'. She was now a middle aged woman with severe health problems. Nonetheless she still did what she could to prevent similar fates befalling other children, and through her struggles she kept in contact with a network of people who were fighting paedophilia in all its incarnations.

I told her what DOCS were trying to do, and how frightened I was for the safety of the twins.

'Rangani will never even see them,' she said.

'How can you be so sure?' I asked, amazed at the confidence with which she spoke. But somehow her words were not reassuring.

She looked at me for a long time. Clearly she was trying to decide what, and how much to tell me. In the end she sighed deeply and continued:

'The classic case is where a child has a drug addled mother. First of all the child goes into care because its life is at risk. Then when a buyer is found...'

'A buyer?'

'When a paedophile is found who is interested in the child,' she explained. 'Then suddenly DOCS are back in court arguing that a child must always be, where possible, reunited with its natural parent. And now they assure the court this parent has reformed. If necessary they will ply the mother with money and clothes and sober her up long enough so she can make a tearful plea for her child in court. So the magistrate makes an order for the child to be restored to its mother. After the case is over they just hand the mother a stash of heroine, she goes off into lala land, forgets about the child, and DOCS deliver it to the paedophile.'

'And no-one ever does anything about it, does anything to protect this child?' I asked, astonished.

'Who is going to protect it,' she said. The magistrate thinks he's doing the right thing. The mother is in lala land, and DOCS and the paedophile have what they want.' I had felt sick to my stomach for much of the past six months. But this took my nausea to another level. 'The system is all sown up,' she said. 'If anything goes wrong and the paedophile goes too far and the child dies, DOCS can always blame the mother.'

'But when a child dies,' I said, 'we all hear about it. The media is in an uproar. It happens all the time.'

'That's the point,' she said, sadly, 'it happens all the time. But does anything change? No.'

'Why?' I demanded.

'Because when the media accuse DOCS of doing nothing to prevent the child's death, they just counter they are desperately underfunded, and so can't watch out for all the children they need to. Then the media's outcry becomes an outcry for more funding. Under that pressure the Government usually obliges, and so DOCS gets more money to run their paedophile business.'

'But DOCS are supposed to be in the business of protecting children,' I almost yelled.

'Yes, and so are priests and scout masters. The fact is the best place to take advantage of children is where they are most vulnerable. DOCS have the time and the money and the profit motive and the best product.' She almost spat these last words.

'Are you telling me DOCS is just one big paedophile business? I can't believe that.'

'Most DOCS officers are caring, hard working people,' she said. 'But there are cells, certain officers that run this business. It's the same in every State, probably in every country in the world. Unfortunately for your children, you may have come to the notice of the wrong people.'

'But Agatha and I are not drug addicts,' I said.

'Yours is a slightly different case, but in the end it's just a variation on the theme,' she said. 'They have no interest in Rangani getting access to your girls. She's just the equivalent of the drug addict mother. They'll bribe her in some way, probably with something as simple as clothes or shoes or the promise of some dope, and she'll make a court appearance schooled up to say how much she loves and misses her sisters, and DOCS will strongly support her application, and then when they get the court order Rangani will never even see them. But like the addicted mother, she won't care.'

'But two days unsupervised access with a violent street girl? How can they get that past any judge?'

'That's the bit I can't quite work out,' said Mary. 'Maybe it's just a bargaining chip. You'll battle the whole thing out and they'll 'lose' because the judge will just give Rangani limited access supervised by DOCS. But of course that's all they'll need.'

'This is still different,' I insisted. 'The twins do have parents, two parents, who are not drug addicts, who care about them and who will fight to prevent this happening.' I was talking tough, but mainly to stiffen my own resolve. 'I'm a lawyer,' I said. 'I know a bit about how the system works.'

'You don't know,' she said very seriously. Then she hesitated for a long moment. 'Besides', she said at last, almost in a whisper, 'any struggle they may have with you would be well worth it from their point of view.'

I insisted she explain.

'In paedophile circles,' she said, looking me straight in the eye, 'twins are highly sought after, and black twins are the most sought after of all. They can sell them many times over, and then they will film it all, and sell the film rights around the world. Your girls are worth millions to them.'

Of all Mary's horrors, the words 'film rights' cut most deeply into my gut. This was 1994 and so the internet was only in its infancy. But paedophiles, like everyone else, will use whatever technology is available to them. Babika and Babeta's abuse would be cut, printed, put in the can, and distributed around the world.

When I look back on that time, with the benefit of hindsight and endless reflection, I think that, at least in our case, Mary was wrong. In our case I think the driving force was simply pride. DOCS were used to getting their own way and did not take kindly to being thwarted. They had tried to prevent us going to Sri Lanka. They had said the adoption wouldn't work. In the end they had not been happy when I had 'beaten' them in that struggle. Then, as they saw it, they had been proven right, when Rangani had to go into care.

My guess is they launched the access proceedings as a way to seize the high moral ground, and perhaps to even the score. But they did so without proper investigation of Rangani's situation, and without thinking it through. When the litigation got out of control, they just threw more and more money at it, driven by the same pride that had launched them in the first place.

But of course at the time, I had no way of knowing where the truth lay. All I knew was that Mary was someone with enormous experience in the area, and if she were right, the consequences for the girls would be unimaginable. I couldn't afford to take the risk of just ignoring what she said. The only sensible course was to work on the assumption she was right. This meant the terror of Rangani getting unsupervised access to the twins for two days at a time, was superseded by an even greater terror, if that were possible. Now I was looking down the barrel of the twins suffering open ended sexual abuse.

So here is the very centre of my story. A major part of my unconscious need to have children was driven by a desire to love and protect them, and make sure they didn't suffer what I had suffered. Yet if Mary were right, that is just what was going to happen to them, and in a far more terrible way than anything I had experienced. Under those circumstances my unconscious mind couldn't afford to lock away my past any more. If I were to save the twins from a fate like mine, only far worse, I had to recall the full horror of what my past had been.

So, under the pressure of necessity, the cork couldn't stay in the bottle any longer. In a rush and a torrent it all came out, all the details of my mother's sexual, physical and emotional abuse of me. It all came out, and there I stood, looking at it, covered in shame, facing the prospect it was all going to happen again, to my own children.

Unfortunately that much information, all at once, was more than my psyche could deal with. I went down in a crash. Waves of depression and fear rolled over me. I could barely move, could hardly speak. I knew I had to pull myself together, or DOCS would just walk away with their 'prize'. Yet I couldn't get out of my chair, let alone get into court to fight what now looked like an army ranged against me, an army ready to perpetrate the most horrible of war crimes.

Two things stopped DOCS from winning by default. First of all Michael Gliksman's dedicated medical and personal care got me back on my feet in a few weeks. In the meantime Agatha's parents Mike and Margaret generously paid for lawyers to hold all the forts till I was ready to start slugging again.

When I did venture back into court I was far from my best. But fortunately, soon after, the litigation started to run our way. The Full Bench of the Family Court of Australia agreed to hear our case. Everyone's best guess was they were not going to let DOCS continue with their madness. In an attempt to counter that, DOCS sacked their current legal team and briefed the Solicitor-General of New South Wales, who is of course not a solicitor at all but the State's most senior QC.

He told them they should drop the case. Initially they ignored him but then, a few weeks later, without any warning or explanation, DOCS did withdraw. Two days after that I received, in an unmarked envelope, the Minutes of the most recent meeting of the Cabinet of the Government of New South Wales. Whoever had leaked them had blacked out all the resolutions, except Resolution 3 which read:

'Resolved to abandon legal action against Klines'.

We had reached the highest level of Government and that's what it took to ensure my children would be safe.

As for myself, the secret I had so carefully kept locked away, was now out. The threat to my children, which was the most terrible moment of my life, was also to be my greatest gift. Now I understood fully who I was, where I had come from and what my battle was to be. Now there would be no going back for me. I knew where all the anger and the pain came from. I knew my enemy and I felt I could beat it. The struggle wasn't complete but the outcome was assured.

22. AFTER THE DELUGE

After the case we moved to Perth, permanently or temporarily we didn't know at the time. All we knew was we needed to get as far away from the Department of Community Services as possible.

The light was so bright in Perth, a beautiful clear clean light. The air was fresh, a clean breathable air. I now held in my hand, the pieces of my life's puzzle. Under that light, and breathing that air, I was ready to start putting them together.

I had worked on my madness from the inside out, with the help of DOCS and my girls. I had found the ugly woman that dwelt quietly and insidiously there. I had ripped her out like the extraterrestrial in 'Alien', and was holding up the squirming body to the fierce light of the Perth sun.

Now I wrote to my mother, and this time I actually sent the letter. I did not want to accuse. Nor did I want to blame. It was just an 'acknowledgment' of what had happened, as Sid Raper would have termed it. I said I was sure terrible things must have happened to her too, otherwise she would not have done what she did.

I guessed what her response would be. But the intensity of it was surprising.

My mother's reply spat poison from the page. The language she used and the verbal abuse she piled up would have made the Alien proud. For all its horrors however, I remember reading it quite calmly. Then I put it in a little ashtray and burned it.

That was almost the last encounter with my mother. I now understood that, whether the letter results in reconciliation or just closure, it doesn't matter. Either way you find peace. It's better for your abuser to reconcile. But if they don't want to, that's their choice. It is not your concern.

I was also starting to peel away the layers of addiction that had 'protected' me from looking in at the Alien. About a year before the case with DOCS I had given up smoking. It was incredibly hard and at one point I was quite literally eating carpet, that is I found myself down on all fours chewing on the corner of a rug. But the difference to my physical well being was astounding. I was breathing young again, had lungs ready for the clean West Australian air.

I was also freeing myself from workaholia. I had bought a book on the subject. It was a terrifying read. The story I remember most (though it wasn't the worst) was the district nurse who developed a serious bladder infection because, during the whole of her 12 hours shift, she would not go to the toilet. She saw that as time wasting, as 'invalid'.

I recognised myself in the stories in the book. At the same time I realised I didn't need it anymore. With my work as a law reports editor, I decided I would trust my reporters more, delegate more, and not agonise over their work. As a result I cut my work time to less than half.

I was terrified the judges of the Federal Court would fire me. But I knew I couldn't continue to work sometimes 70+ hours per week. I wanted to have a life now, to make up for lost time. And so I decided to take the risk.

I was astonished to find the judges were in fact happier with my work. I realised the insidiousness of workaholia is that you finds ways to do things badly to make sure you spend more time fixing them up.

So now I had hours to spare, and I put it to good use. First of all I had so much more time to spend with the girls, taking them to hockey, or just going to the beach or hanging out in the park throwing a ball for Dougy to chase.

I began my training as an actor at the Hole in the Wall Theatre. It was a joy for me. I sang in the Fremantle Choir and at the Catholic Cathedral in North Perth. All these of course were strengthening the voice I had lost for so long, and whose most recent gig had been some pretty stressful advocacy.

Now that life had settled I felt it was worth trying to make things work again with Agatha. There was a lot of muddy water under the bridge, but rivers have been cleaned up before. So we sat down and talked, and especially about the fact that a marriage without any physical dimension, is barely a marriage. She agreed. Unfortunately nothing changed. After not so very long, I knew the murky waters would stay that way, and the best thing I could do for myself was to go.

But now there was another reason to stay, and this time a real one. Babeta and Babika were still only 12 years old. They had just come out of a year of litigation which had, of course, impacted badly on them. On top of that they were still carrying most of their original baggage. What with the horrors concerning Rangani and the case, no-one had had time to do any unpacking. So I knew for their sake I could not leave Agatha, not yet. We spent the next 18 months in Perth, and then returned to our house in Kiama, where my wife and I settled into an 'existence'.

Apart from the marriage I was having a wonderful time back in Kiama, singing in church and for Angela's choir, and on one occasion, doing a duet with Paul Gurr in front of 500 people, where I got to sing my favourite of all his hits. I had even been cast in my first few roles as a semi-professional actor. But these were just the externals. What mattered was my growing internal peace. I regretted the state of my marriage. That was right and natural. But I didn't fear shadows and I no longer suffered the deep sadness that comes from far away.

Babika and Babeta were going from strength to strength. They played State hockey, and I had the joy of watching them take up two lanes in the State 100 metre sprint final at the new Homebush Olympic Stadium. This was a triumph almost as important for them as when they entered Doug in 'the waggliest tail' competition at the Kiama Show, and he won.

Not long after our return to Kiama my father died. My parents were then living outside Brisbane on Moreton Bay, and he had been hospitalised with an array of problems. Fundamentally he had just so abused his body with smoking and eating exclusively fried food and a rugged determination never to exercise (he would drive the 100 metres to the corner store to buy his cigarettes), that his body just packed in.

I decided to go and see him before he died. But I wanted to make sure I didn't run into my mother. So I rang the nurses and asked when she visited. They said she always came late in the afternoon. So I got an early plane and went to see Dad at around 10.30 am. We spoke a little about his life. He was attempting to be reflective. Yet there was not an ounce of self-insight in anything he said.

He was terrified of dying and complained a lot about life's unfairness. My sister said that when he got near the end he just made a tragic spectacle of himself railing against the injustice and begging for life. The idea haunts me. I don't want to go like that. A few years later when Dougy died, he passed with such calm, love and dignity. Occasionally I have the rather strange thought that I want to die like my dog not like my father.

Anyway I was sitting there by his bed listening to the same sort of nonsense he always talked, when in walked my mother. I stood up. As she stared at me, a burning hatred in her eyes, I realised I had had a residual fear of her. That's why I had gone to the trouble of trying to avoid her. But destiny can be kind, as it was to me that day. It made sure I did see her because I really needed to, just one more time. Now, as I looked at her, all I could think was:

'This is an old woman, and she can't hurt me anymore.'

She turned and walked out of the room. And that was the end of my mother, forever. She was no longer someone to fear, not even someone to think about. I felt no anger, no distress. Forgiveness was easy now because it wasn't even necessary. In a real sense you have no trouble forgiving those who have become meaningless to you.

So my father died in 1997. I heard from my sister that Mum died last year, during the writing of this book. Marilyn was there when she went. Apparently Joy woke, saw my sister, made a kind of spitting snarling sound at her, and then was gone.

Neither death had much impact on me. There was a moment, a few months back, when it did occur to me that lots of people have loving parents, and why couldn't that have happened to me? It was the first time I had ever had that obvious thought and it made me sad for a couple of hours. But then Katharine came home from University and I forgot about it.

By the end of 1998 the girls were almost 15 and I was beginning to think of leaving Agatha again. I felt they were going to be old enough to handle it. In fact it was Babika's maturity which perhaps gave me the final push. She said to me one day:

'Dad, sometimes I see you just sitting there, never being able to say anything, and I know how sad you are.'

I had a strange feeling when she said that, because it seemed she was talking about something that used to be. I felt that, although Agatha and I had no relationship to speak of, and I was sad about that, the rest of my life was filled with happiness. But then I realised my daughters, by and large, didn't see the rest of my life. They saw me when I was with Agatha. Therefore they saw sadness. And that couldn't be a good thing. Be that as it may, this was Babika's tacit approval. Babeta, in her own way, gave me her approval too. I was very grateful to them.

About a week later Agatha and I were in the bedroom and were disagreeing about something so trivial I can't even remember. I heard myself say:

'I think it's time I left.'

And so, somewhere in the early spring of 1998, just over 24 years after it had started, our marriage ended with a whimper. I moved out and rented half of the old magistrate's house on the Collins St hill.

I spent a lot of time in my new place just marvelling at the silence and having a heightened awareness of the most mundane things, like opening a screw top jar or spreading peanut butter on a piece of bread. It was as though every piece of the world, however banal, was totally new.

I washed around in this demi-monde for a week or so until one night, very late, I started to get all the symptoms of a heart attack, the pain in the chest that feels like you've swallowed a dead bird, the tingling arm, the breathlessness, all the things I had heard about.

I remember thinking to myself:

'I'm 47 years old and have finally left my sham of a marriage, and two weeks later I am just going to die.'

But at the same time a part of me suspected this was some weird psychological reaction, that my anxiety was causing me to create bogus symptoms mimicking a heart attack.

Anyway for some reason I decided on a rather unique way of determining whether or not I was actually suffering a heart attack. This was an early spring night. It was cold. The ocean water on the South Coast would be very cold. I decided I would dive in. I reasoned if it weren't a heart attack, the shock of the freezing water would get rid of the bogus symptoms, and if it were a heart attack that would finish me off. Both options seemed acceptable.

So I ran out of my front door, bare footed, wearing nothing but my shorts, sprinted down the hill and across the park in front of surf beach, and dove into the dark icy water. It was even colder than I had guessed. I rose up from the water like a high diver coming up for air and screamed:

'Fuck! Fuck!'

It was so cold. But the symptoms were gone.

I was free!

I moved up to Sydney during the Olympics of 2000. Babeta came to live with me for 12 months whilst Babika stayed with Agatha. Then Babeta went back down the coast. Both girls now have families of their own. Babika works as a teacher and Babeta as a nurse. I gave Agatha all our common property. She inherited some money as well. I believe she is living comfortably in Kiama.

Once I moved to Sydney I worked a lot in theatre and television as an actor, director and playwright, even working briefly on a few occasions off Broadway in New York. I also dove into a ridiculous round of dating and short term relationships. With the advent of internet dating sites, it was all too easy. I told myself I was making up for lost time, but really I was re-playing the sexual hunting addiction my mother had instilled in me all those years ago.

I started to realise it was not what I wanted. In fact on most occasions, when the hunting was over, I would go to great lengths to prevent the sex from happening. That was because I didn't like sex. And given my background, was that such a surprise? Well it was to me, at first, but not for long. Having made that leap of understanding, all that was left was to ask myself what it was I did want.

The answer wasn't far away. All I had to do was think about everything I had written, my novel *Rough Justice*, the two full length plays produced by Factory Space Theatre, *The Rehabilitation of God* and *Love.Com*, and any number of other short plays and short stories. Whatever else they were, they were all romances. They were always about two people finding great love, despite whatever impediments lay in their way. A great healthy love. I had been writing about something I had never personally known. But I was so confident of its existence, I was willing to sign my name to printed versions of that confidence again and again.

My prayers told me if I wanted to find in my own life what I had played out in my art, I would have to let go and see what God had in store for me. So henceforth I would hunt no more. I would trust that if I were destined for real love it would come and find me. And if not, I would remain satisfied with having peeled back my last addictive layer of madness. Aloneness and blessed sanity would be my lot, unless or until someone equally blessed and sane came my way.

23. THE LOVE OF ALL MY LIVES

By the time I met Katharine I had been alone for eight years. It was a valuable and necessary time. Healing, even when you have expelled your demons, is a slow process. You still have a lot of thinking and understanding to do. You have to wait whilst the see-saw of your life finds its point of balance.

When Katharine did appear we were so comfortable with each other and so happy so quickly, we would joke this couldn't be our first time round. For some reason we settled on 43 previous lives. Hence the dedication to this book: 'To Katharine Kline, the love of all my lives'.

Now the man who never laughed, was laughing all the time. He's still laughing seven years after that first meeting. Life has had a spice and a sparkle ever since. Seeing us so happy together some people said it was God making up for what I had been through. I know what they mean, and of course Katharine is a gift so wonderful that even now I'm finding it hard to describe.

But maybe it's closer to the mark to say God gives you an opportunity, and if you'll let Him, he gives it to you just at the right time. If Katharine had come any earlier in my life, there is every chance I would have pushed her away. She would not have fitted the image I had of myself as someone unworthy of giving or receiving love. But He brought her after He had brought me to the point when I was ready for her.

So things were wonderful and in any objective sense I had healed. But healing is not something that finishes. It gets better. This incredibly beautiful creature brought with her an intelligence that went way beyond what is usually meant by 'smart', to a deep and true understanding of people and a profound compassion for them. Of course she understood me too, where I had come from, and what my demons had been.

For the first time in my life I could talk about all I had known and felt, including that terrible irrational shame which all abused people feel, and which I realised was still with me. But Katharine took charge of that. And because there was no limit to her time and her love, under her warm, firm hand, that shame melted away like the snows of a distantly remembered winter.

Then too I was to learn that if you love someone, and you both have a spirit of adventure, and you know how to laugh, sex can be wonderful. I used to say to Katharine that before I met her I was a virgin, and of course she would laugh. But in a real sense it was true. I had not had sex, as sex should be, before I met her. It was a mighty big gift for her to give me.

And finally there was that unconscious part of me who still wanted to create a child of my own, to love and protect, and so redress the balance of what had been done to me. In fact I asked Katharine to have a child with me even before I asked her to marry me. She said yes to both, the first in a little Italian restaurant, and the second, about six months later on the deuxième étage of the Eiffel Tower. Six months after that we were married on a beautiful spring day at Orso's on The Spit, and mid way through the next year Katharine was pregnant.

We were so excited we told everyone after only eight weeks. I was middle aged but I was naive. I didn't know you were supposed to wait before telling, because I had no idea that one in four pregnancies end in miscarriage. Anyway, it was a very bad day. It started in the afternoon, and was not over till the early hours of the next morning. Our gynaecologist was away, his replacement refused to see us, our GP was unobtainable, and in the end it happened, with Katharine in terrible pain, me holding her in my arms, on the cold bathroom floor that winter's night. I wrapped it up and took it away.

I now know she would have lost it anyway, and no medical intervention would have made a difference. But I didn't know that at the time, and it could have been made a lot less lonely and frightening.

I took her to the San Hospital, and they put her in a room for observation. But by then it was all over, and I just sat by her while she lay resting. After some time she said to me:

'I know how much you love me now.'

'Didn't you know before?'

'I thought I did,' she said, 'but when I saw the concern in your eyes, there on the bathroom floor, concern for *me...*' her voice trailed away.

'I was terrified I might lose you,' I heard myself say. And at that moment I realised fully for the first time the incredible depth of the love I had for her.

We told everyone the next day, and of course they were all very sad. The one who surprised me the most was Babika. She wept so bitterly, you would think it was her own child she had lost. I don't really understand it, but at that time she was yet to have a child of her own. Perhaps she too felt the need for a little brother or sister to love, to make amends for her own childhood abuse.

But Babika didn't need that. Nor did I. What I learned from that night was that, if you want to get the Universe in balance, you don't need to replicate or replace. All you need to do is learn to love, and learn to accept love in return.

Though the doctors told us the chances of our falling pregnant again were slim, we were surprised to find that didn't bother us too much. The night of the miscarriage had taught us how much we loved one another. In fact we learned that our love was as close to perfect as human love can be. That was more than enough to balance the evil. That was gift enough for both of us. That was, in my 44th life with Katharine, the way it was meant to be. The universe unfolding as it should.

APPENDIX

That Red Light

A dark bird hovered over my crib,
Dark wings that spanned the ceiling,
Beating slowly a sombre, shadowed
Ripple of fear, to cloud and cover
And smother my innocence.

A dark room lit only by
The drawback glowing,
The small hot red light
Of a cigarette tip.
Hot ash to blind mine eyes,
Cold ash to mark my forehead.
Scored in ash, the mark of Satan
On a young brow.

Without defence, without explanation
Of why careless evil filled my tiny bedroom
With wings and glowering red tips.
Why not kill me then?
Too much trouble, perhaps,
To bury the little body.
Easier, perhaps, to mark and scar
And scorch and break its tiny frame,
And leave it for a lifetime
To rot in that same crib.

Easier, perhaps, to take away its manhood,
Before even it knew what its manhood was.
Much, much easier to turn a beautiful boy
Into a toy-thing, a thing to toy with,
And forget about.

A mere body to sear
With the glowing red tip of abuse,
Whilst always the wings of the bird
Cast their shadow, beat the rhythm
Of non-escape.
Always there, forever watching, reminding,
Sending waves of despair, on and on
Into a long sad future.

How many lifetimes did I need to fit into one life,
To give me enough time to slay the bird,
And stub out the cigarette of abuse on my abuser?
No wonder there never seemed days long enough,
No wonder Sundays always threatened
To be not just the end of the week,
But the end of life itself.

But God is the great expander of time,
The Gift Giver!
He gave me back my years,
Made me young again,
Young for the first time really.

Presented me with the bow,
And with the arrow
With which to draw back
And let fly, to slay the bird,
The bird of darkness, which is no more.
To fell the smoker,
And put out that red light.

Blessed be the real light
Blessed be the light of God,
Blessed be the Name of the Lord.

ABOUT THE AUTHOR

Victor Kline started his working life as Sydney's youngest barrister. He worked as a Federal prosecutor in Sydney before going on to become a defence barrister in the Northern Territory in its wild west days. Victor has also worked as a playwright, theatre director and actor off Broadway and in various parts of Australia. As well as New York and Central Australia, he has lived and worked in London, Paris, the South of France and New Guinea. He has returned home to Sydney to become Editor of the Federal Court Reports and Federal Law Reports, and lives with his wife Katharine and a little grey cat called Spud.

www.victorkline.com

www.ingramcontent.com/pod-product-compliance
Lightning Source LLC
Chambersburg PA
CBHW060019100426
42740CB00010B/1533